THE BRITISH CAMPAIGN
IN FRANCE AND FLANDERS
1917

BOOKS BY A. CONAN DOYLE

THE FIRM OF GIRDLESTONE.
THE WHITE COMPANY.
THE MYSTERY OF CLOOMBER.
MICAH CLARKE.
THE REFUGEES.
THE CAPTAIN OF THE "POLESTAR."
THE DOINGS OF RAFFLES HAW.
THE GREAT SHADOW.
THE PARASITE.
A STUDY IN SCARLET.
THE SIGN OF FOUR.
THE ADVENTURES OF SHERLOCK HOLMES.
THE MEMOIRS OF SHERLOCK HOLMES.
THE RETURN OF SHERLOCK HOLMES.
ROUND THE RED LAMP.
THE EXPLOITS OF BRIGADIER GERARD.
THE STARK-MUNRO LETTERS.
RODNEY STONE.
THE TRAGEDY OF THE KOROSKO.
UNCLE BERNAC.
THE GREEN FLAG.
SONGS OF ACTION.
SONGS OF THE ROAD.
THE GREAT BOER WAR.
A DUET, WITH AN OCCASIONAL CHORUS.
THE HOUND OF THE BASKERVILLES.
THE ADVENTURES OF GERARD.
SIR NIGEL.
THE VALLEY OF FEAR.
THE LAST GALLEY.
THE NEW REVELATION.
THE VITAL MESSAGE.

THE BRITISH CAMPAIGN

IN FRANCE AND FLANDERS

1917

BY

ARTHUR CONAN DOYLE
AUTHOR OF
'THE GREAT BOER WAR,' ETC.

The Naval & Military Press Ltd

Published by

The Naval & Military Press Ltd
Unit 10 Ridgewood Industrial Park,
Uckfield, East Sussex,
TN22 5QE England

Tel: +44 (0) 1825 749494
Fax: +44 (0) 1825 765701

www.naval-military-press.com
www.military-genealogy.com
www.militarymaproom.com

In reprinting in facsimile from the original, any imperfections are inevitably reproduced and the quality may fall short of modern type and cartographic standards.

PREFACE

THIS, the fourth volume of *The British Campaign in France and Flanders*, carries the story through the long and arduous fighting of 1917, which culminated in the dramatic twofold battle of Cambrai. These events are cut deep into the permanent history of the world, and we are still too near it to read the whole of that massive and tremendous inscription. It is certain, however, that this year marked the period in which the Allies gained a definite military ascendancy over the German forces, in spite of the one great subsequent rally which had its source in events which were beyond the control of the Western powers. So long as ink darkens and paper holds, our descendants, whose freedom has been won by these exertions, will dwell earnestly and with reverence upon the stories of Arras, Messines, Ypres, Cambrai, and other phases of this epic period.

I may be permitted to record with some thankfulness and relief, that in the course of three thick volumes, in which for the first time the detailed battle-line of these great encounters has been set out, it has not yet been shown that a brigade has ever been out of its place, and even a battalion has seldom gone amiss. Such good fortune cannot last for ever. *Absit omen!* But the fact is worth recording, as it may reassure the reader who has natural doubts whether history which is so recent can also lay claim to be of any permanent value.

The Censorship has left me untrammelled in the matter of units, for which I am sufficiently grateful. The ruling, however, upon the question of names must be explained, lest it should seem that their appearance or suppression is due to lack of knowledge or to individual favour or caprice. I would explain, then, that I am permitted to use the names of Army and Corps Commanders, but only of such divisional Generals as are mentioned in the Headquarters narrative. All other ranks below divisional Generals are still suppressed, save only casualties, in connection with the action where they received the injury, and those who won honours, with the same limitation. This regulation has little effect upon the accuracy of the narrative, but it appears in many cases to involve some personal injustice. To record the heroic deeds of a division and yet be compelled to leave out the name of the man who made it so efficient, is painful to the feelings of the writer, for if any one fact is clearer than another in this war it is that the good leader makes the good unit.

The tremendous epic of 1918 will call for two volumes in its treatment. One of these, bringing the story up to June 30, 1918, is already completed, and should appear by the summer. The other may be ready at the end of the year.

ARTHUR CONAN DOYLE.

CROWBOROUGH,
January 20, 1919.

CONTENTS

CHAPTER I

THE GERMAN RETREAT UPON THE ARRAS-SOISSONS FRONT

PAGE

Hindenburg's retreat—The advance of the Fifth and Fourth Armies—Capture of Bapaume and Peronne—Atrocious devastation by the Germans—Capture of guns at Selency—Definition of the Hindenburg Line—General survey 1

CHAPTER II

THE BATTLE OF ARRAS

April 9 to April 23, 1917

Vast preparations—Attack of Snow's Seventh Corps—The Ibex Trench—Attack of Haldane's Sixth Corps—Attack of Fergusson's Seventeenth Corps—A Scottish Front—The splendid Canadians—Capture of Monchy—Essex and Newfoundland—A glorious episode—The Chemical Works—Extension of the battle to the north—Desperate fight of the Australians at Bullecourt 20

CHAPTER III

OPERATIONS IN THE ARRAS SECTOR FROM APRIL 23 ONWARDS

Advance of April 23—Middlesex and Argyll—Grand fighting of the Fifteenth Division—H.A.C. at Gavrelle—Operations of May 3—The Gavrelle Windmill—Loss of Fresnoy—Capture of Rœux—The long fight at Bullecourt 64

CHAPTER IV

THE BATTLE OF MESSINES

Plumer's long vigil—The great mines—Advance of Australians—Of New Zealanders—Of the Twenty-fifth Division—Of the Irish Divisions—

viii THE BRITISH CAMPAIGN, 1917

PAGE

Death of Major Redmond—Advance of Nineteenth Division—Of the Forty-first Division—Of the Forty-seventh Division—Of the Twenty-fourth Division—General results 94

CHAPTER V

OPERATIONS FROM JUNE 10 TO JULY 31

Fighting round Lens—Good work of Canadians and Forty-sixth Division—Action on the Yser canal—Great fight and eventual annihilation of 2nd K.R.R. and 1st Northamptons—An awful ordeal—Exit Russia 113

CHAPTER VI

THE THIRD BATTLE OF YPRES

July 31, 1917

Attack of July 31—Advance of the Guards—Of the Welsh—Capture of Pilkem—Capture of St. Julien by Thirty-ninth Division—Advance of Fifty-fifth Division—Advance of Jacob's Second Corps—General results 133

CHAPTER VII

THE THIRD BATTLE OF YPRES

August 1 to September 6

Dreadful weather—German reaction—Attack of August 16—Advance of Cavan's Corps—Capture of Langemarck—Dreadful losses of the two Irish Divisions—Failure in the south—Splendid field-gunners—The Forty-second Division upon September 6 . . 158

CHAPTER VIII

THIRD BATTLE OF YPRES

September 6 to October 3, 1917

Engagement of Plumer's Second Army—Attack of September 20—Fine advance of Fifty-fifth Division—Advance of the Ninth Division—

CONTENTS

Of the Australians—Strong counter-attack upon the Thirty-third Division—Renewed advance on September 26—Continued rain—Desperate fighting 179

CHAPTER IX

THE THIRD BATTLE OF YPRES

October 4 to November 10, 1917

Attack of October 4—Further advance of the British line—Splendid advance of second-line Territorials—Good work of H.A.C. at Reutel—Abortive action of October 12—Action of October 26—Heavy losses at the south end of the line—Fine fighting by the Canadian Corps—Capture of Paschendaale—General results of third battle of Ypres 202

CHAPTER X

THE BATTLE OF CAMBRAI

First phase, November 20—Tanks *en masse*—Attack on the Tunnel Trench—Byng's great advance—Fine work of the Sixty-second Division—Hard fighting of Pulteney's Third Corps—Exploit of Fort Garry Horse—Second day of battle—Rally of Germans—Capture of Bourlon Wood by Fortieth Division—Attack by the Guards on La Fontaine 235

CHAPTER XI

THE BATTLE OF CAMBRAI

Second phase of battle on November 30—Great German attack—Disaster to three divisions—Desperate fight of Twenty-ninth Division—Fine advance by the Guards—Capture and recapture of Gouzeaucourt—Hard battle in the Bourlon Sector—Heavy losses of the Germans—Retraction of the British line 269

INDEX 301

MAPS AND PLANS

	PAGE
Fighting Line, February 24, 1917, and Fighting Line, March 1, 1917	*Face page* 8
The Arras Front	39
Chart of Order of Battle, Arras, April 9, 1917	63
Order of Battle, Messines, June 7, 1917	111
Line of Battle, August 16, 1917	165
The Ypres Front	178
Third Ypres Battle, September 26	201
Order of Battle, October 4, 1917	207
Fighting Line, November 20, 1917	239
Battle Line of Third Army, November 20, 1917	259
Fighting Line, November 30, 1917	269
Battle Order of Third Army, November 30, 1917	281
Map to illustrate the British Campaign in France and Flanders	*At end*

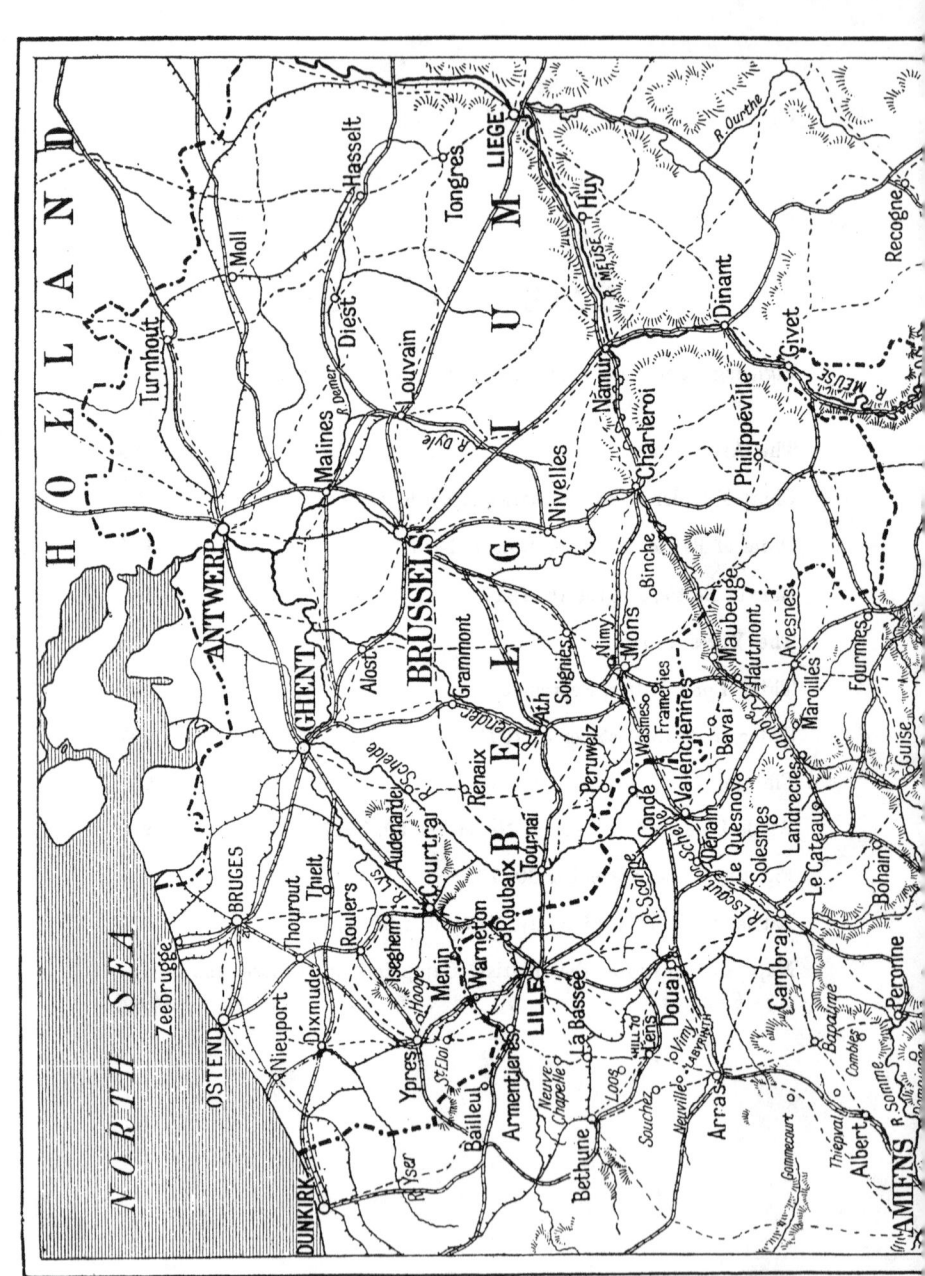

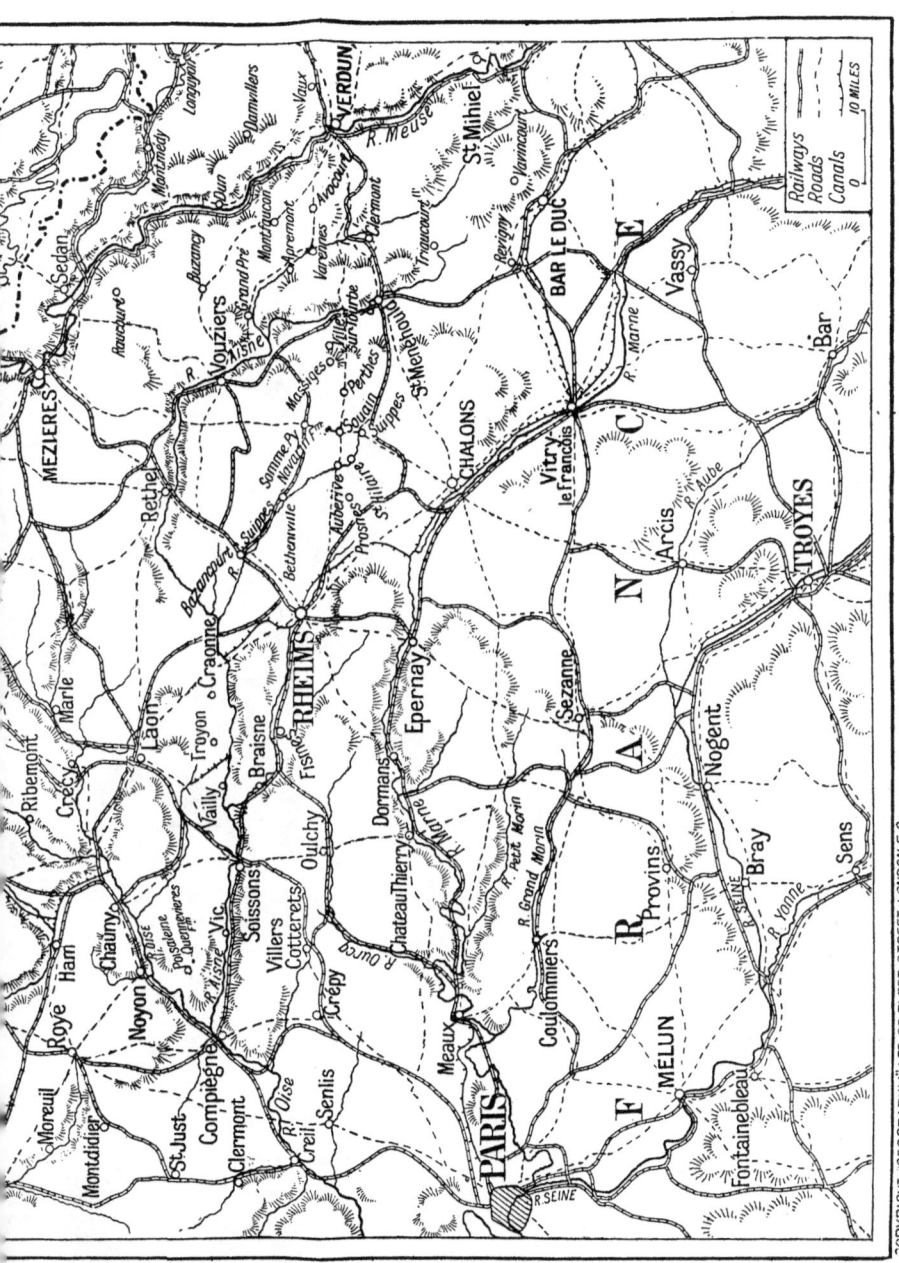

CHAPTER I

THE GERMAN RETREAT UPON THE ARRAS–SOISSONS FRONT

Hindenburg's retreat—The advance of the Fifth and Fourth Armies—Capture of Bapaume and Peronne—Atrocious devastation by the Germans—Capture of guns at Selency—Definition of the Hindenburg Line—General survey.

IN the latter days of 1916 and the beginning of 1917, the British Army, which had in little more than two years expanded from seven divisions to over fifty, took over an increased line. The movement began about Christmas time, and early in the New Year Rawlinson's Fourth Army, side-stepping always to the south, had covered the whole of the French position occupied during the Somme fighting, had crossed the Somme, and had established its right flank at a point near Roye. The total front was increased to 120 miles, which may seem a small proportion as compared to the whole. In making such a comparison, however, one must bear in mind the difference in the effort of sustaining an army in one's own country and in a foreign land with all communications by water. The task of the British was continually made more difficult by the precarious nature of their connection with their base. Dulness of vision may be as dangerous to a nation as treason,

CHAPTER I.

The German Retreat upon the Arras-Soissons Front.

and no enemies could have harmed the country more than those perfectly sincere and patriotic individuals who had for so long opposed the construction of a Channel Tunnel.

The general disposition of the British forces after this prolongation to the south was as follows. Plumer's Second Army still held that post of danger and of honour which centred round the Ypres salient. South of Plumer, in the Armentières district, was the First Army, now commanded by General Horne, whose long service with the Fifteenth Corps during the Somme Battle had earned him this high promotion. Allenby's Third Army carried the line onwards to the south of Arras. From the point upon which the British line had hinged during the Somme operations Gough's Fifth Army took over the front, and this joined on to Rawlinson's Fourth Army near the old French position. From the north then the order of the armies was two, one, three, five, and four.

The winter was spent by both sides in licking their wounds after the recent severe fighting and in preparing for the greater fighting to come. These preparations upon the part of the British consisted in the addition to the army of a number of fresh divisions, and the rebuilding of those divisions, fifty-two in number, which had taken part in the Somme fighting, most of them more than once. As the average loss in these divisions was very heavy indeed, the task of reconstructing them was no light one. None the less before the campaign re-opened, though the interval was a short three months, the greater part of the battalions were once again at full strength, while the guns and munitions were very greatly in-

THE GERMAN RETREAT 3

creased. A considerable addition to the strength of the army was effected by the civilian railway advisers, under Sir Eric Geddes, who by the simple expedient of pulling up their own lines at home, and relaying them in France, enormously improved the communications of the army.

CHAPTER I.

The German Retreat upon the Arras-Soissons Front.

In the case of the Germans their army changes took the form of a considerable new levy from those classes which had been previously judged to be unfit, and a general comb-out of every source from which men could be extracted. A new law rendered every citizen liable to national service in a civilian capacity, and so released a number of men from the mines and the factories. They also increased the numbers of their divisions by the doubtful expedient of reducing the brigades, so that the divisions were shorn of a third of their strength. The battalions thus obtained were formed into new divisions. In this way it was calculated that a reserve force had been created which would be suddenly thrown in on one or the other front with dramatic effect. Some such plan may have been in contemplation, but as a matter of fact the course of events was such that the German generals required every man and more for their own immediate needs during the whole of the year.

It has been shown in the narrative of 1916 how the British had ended the campaign of that year by the brilliant little victory of Beaumont Hamel, which gave them not merely 7000 prisoners, but command of both sides of the Valley of the Ancre. This victory had been the sequel to the capture of the Thiepval Ridge, and this again had depended upon the general success of the Somme operations, so that the turn of

CHAPTER I.

The German Retreat upon the Arras-Soissons Front.

events which led to such considerable results always traces back to the tragic and glorious 1st of July. It was clear that whenever the weather permitted the resumption of hostilities, Sir Douglas Haig was in so commanding a position at this point that he was perfectly certain to drive the enemy out of the salient which they held to the north of Beaumont. Hamel. The result showed that this expectation was well founded, but no one could have foreseen how considerable was the retreat which would be forced upon the enemy—a retreat which gave away for nothing the ground which cost Hindenburg so much to regain in the following year.

Although the whole line from the sea to the Somme was a scene of activity during the winter, and though hardly a day, or rather a night, went by that some stealthy party did not cross No-Man's-Land to capture and to destroy, still for the purposes of this narrative the three northern armies may be entirely ignored in the succeeding operations since they had no occasion to alter their lines. We shall fix our attention in the first instance upon Gough's Army in the district of the Ancre, and afterwards upon Rawlinson's which was drawn into the operations.

Gough's Army consisted, at the beginning of the year, of three corps, the Fifth (E. A. Fanshawe) to the left covering the ground to the north of the Ancre, the Second Corps (Jacob) immediately south of the river, and the First Australian Corps (Birdwood) extending to the junction with Rawlinson's Army, and covering the greater part of the old British line upon the Somme. It was upon the Fifth and the Second Corps that the immediate operations which opened the campaign were to devolve.

THE GERMAN RETREAT

The Fifth Corps was formed at this period of three divisions, the Eleventh, Thirty-first, and Seventh. Each of these divisions by constant pressure and minor operations, backed by a powerful artillery fire, played a part in the wearing process of constant attrition which ended in making the position of the Germans impossible. On January 10, the 32nd Yorkshire Brigade of the Eleventh Division carried an important trench due east of Beaumont Hamel, taking 140 prisoners. On the next day the movement extended farther north, where three-quarters of a mile of trench with 200 prisoners was the prize. On January 17, another 600 yards north of Beaumont fell into British hands. Of the 1228 prisoners who were taken in January a considerable proportion came from this small section of the line, though the largest single haul consisted of 350 men who were captured by a brilliant advance of the Australians in the Le Transloy sector upon January 29.

The movement along the valley of the Ancre was continued in February, but at an accelerated pace, the Second Corps, which consisted of the Sixty-third, Eighteenth, and Second Divisions, moving in conformity with Fanshawe's men upon the northern bank. The chief initiative still rested with the latter, and upon February 3 another push forward of 500 yards upon a mile front yielded a hundred more prisoners, while two sharp counter attacks by the Germans only served to increase their losses. A number of small spurs run down to the river upon the northern bank, and each of these successive advances represented some fresh ridge surmounted. Upon February 6 the Second Corps was moving upon Beaucourt, which is to the immediate

CHAPTER I.

The German Retreat upon the Arras-Soissons Front.

Jan.

south of the river, and upon the 7th the village was evacuated—the first of that goodly list which was to adorn the official communiqués during the next two months. On the 9th the advance crept onwards upon both banks, gathering up a hundred prisoners, while eighty more were taken in Baillescourt Farm upon the north bank. These men were Hamburgers of the 85th Regiment. Upon February 10 the left of the Fifth Corps began to feel out towards Serre, that village of sinister memories, and 215 prisoners were taken from the trenches to the south of the hamlet. This provoked a new counter from the enemy which was beaten back upon February 12. A period of impossible weather suspended the advance, but again upon February 17 the British tide swelled suddenly into a wave which swept forward on either bank, engulfing some crowded trenches north of Baillescourt Farm, which yielded 12 officers and 761 men of the 65th, 75th, and 395th Prussians. The main success was gained by the Sixty-third Division upon the left of the Second Corps, but it was aided by the work of the Eighteenth and Second Divisions to the south of the Ancre. The latter met with strong resistance and had considerable losses. The burden of this work fell chiefly upon the 99th and 54th Brigades, both of which reached their objectives in the face of mist, darkness, uncut wire, heavy fire, and vigorous resistance. This blow stung the enemy into a sharp reaction, and three waves of infantry stormed up to the lost position, which for a time they entered, but were again beaten out of. During their temporary success they claim to have taken 130 prisoners.

All these advances, with their accompanying and

ever-extending bombardments, had been like those multiplied causes, each small in itself, which eventually loosen and start a great landslide. The effect must undoubtedly have been begun some weeks before when the Germans perceived that they could no longer hold on, and favoured by wind, rain, and fog, started their rearward movement to the great permanent second line, the exact position of which was still vague to the Allies. Upon February 25 the whole German front caved in for a depth of three miles both north and south of the Ancre. Wading through seas of mud Gough's infantry occupied Serre, Pys, Miraumont, Eaucourt, Warlencourt, and all the ground for eleven miles from Gomiecourt in the north to Gueudecourt in the south. On February 28 Gomiecourt itself had been occupied by the North Country troops of the Thirty-first Division, while Puisieux and Thilloy had also been added to the British line. The advance was not unopposed. The battle-patrols continually extended to attack some trench of snipers or nest of machine-guns. Mined roads and all manner of obstructions impeded the onward flow of the army. The retreat was orderly and skilful, and the pursuit was necessarily slow and wary. By a pleasing coincidence the Thirty-first Division, which occupied Serre, was the same brave North Country Division which had lost so heavily upon July 1 and November 13 on the same front. On entering the village they actually found the bodies of some of their own brave comrades who had got as far forward seven months before.

On March 4 the advance which had steadily continued in the north spread suddenly southwards to Bouchavesnes north of Peronne, the sector held

CHAPTER
I.

The German Retreat upon the Arras-Soissons Front.
Feb.

by the Twentieth and Forty-eighth Divisions of Rawlinson's Army, which from this time onward was more and more engaged in the forward movement. Three machine-guns and 172 prisoners were taken. There was some interruption of the operations at this stage owing to severe snowstorms, but upon March 10 Irles, west of Bapaume, was taken by assault by the Eighteenth Division. This was a formidable point, well wired and trenched, so that the artillery in full force was needed for preparation. The infantry went forward before sunrise, and within an hour the village with 15 machine-guns and 290 prisoners was in British hands. The losses were light and the gain substantial. Grevillers also fell next day. This advance in front of Bapaume was of importance as it turned Loupart Wood, forming part of a strong defensive line which might have marked the limit of the German retreat. It was clear from that day onwards that the movement was not local but far reaching. The enemy was still too strong to be hustled, however, especially upon the northern sector of the operations, where Jacob's Second Corps was feeling the German line along its whole front. An attempt at an advance at Bucquoy upon the night of March 13, carried out by the 137th Brigade of the Forty-sixth North Midland Division, met with a check, though most bravely attempted. The two battalions concerned, the 5th South Staffords and 5th North Staffords, found themselves entangled in the darkness amid uncut wire and suffered considerable loss before they could extricate themselves from an impossible position.

On March 19 and 20 the whole movement had become much more pronounced, and the French as

To face page 8

well as the British were moving over a seventy-mile front, extending from Arras in the north to Soissons in the south. Each day now was a day of joy in France as some new strip of the fatherland was for a time recovered, but the joy was tempered by sorrow and anger as it was learned with what barbarity the Germans had conducted their retreat. To lay a country waste is no new thing in warfare. It has always been held to be an occasional military necessity though the best commander was he who used it least. In all Napoleon's career it is difficult to recall an instance when he devastated a district. At the same time it must be admitted that it comes within the recognised chances of war, and that when Sherman's army, for example, left a black weal across the South the pity of mankind was stirred but not its conscience. It was very different here. These devils —or to be more just—these devil-driven slaves, with a malignity for which it would be hard to find a parallel, endeavoured by every means at their command to ruin the country for the future as well as for the present. Buildings were universally destroyed, including in many cases the parish churches. Historical monuments, such as the venerable Castle of Coucy, were blown to pieces. Family vaults were violated and the graves profaned. The furniture of the most humble peasants was systematically broken. The wells were poisoned and polluted. Worst of all, the young fruit-trees were ringed so as to destroy them for future seasons. It was considered the last possibility of savagery when the Mahdi's men cut down the slow-growing palm-trees in the district of Dongola, but every record upon earth has been swept away by the barbarians of Europe. As usual these outrages

Chapter I.

The German Retreat upon the Arras-Soissons Front. March.

CHAPTER I.

The German Retreat upon the Arras-Soissons Front.
March.

reacted upon the criminals, for they confirmed those grim resolutions of the Allies which made that peace by compromise for which the Germans were eternally working an absolute impossibility. Their Clausewitz had taught them that it is of supreme importance to make peace before there comes a turn of the tide, but he had not reckoned upon his descendants being so brutalised that a peace with them was a self-evident impossibility.

Turning from the deeds of savages to those of soldiers, we have now to trace the progress and scope of the great German retreat, the first pronounced movement upon either side on the Western Front since September 1914. From Arras to Roye the British Army was advancing while the movement was carried on to Soissons by the French. On the curve of the trenches the front measured more than a hundred miles. So close was the touch between the two Allied armies that the patrols of French and British cavalry rode together into Nesle. On March 18 the Australians had occupied Bapaume, with the Seventh Division moving upon their left and the Twentieth upon their right, the cavalry fringe being formed of the Indian Lucknow Cavalry Brigade of the Fourth Division. To the south the Warwick Brigade of the Forty-eighth South Midland Division passed through Peronne. At each end of the long curve the Germans held fast, Arras in the north and Soissons in the south being the two fixed points, but the country between, to a depth of ten miles in the British sector and of thirty miles in the French, was rapidly overrun by the Allies, the cavalry patrols feeling their way everywhere while the infantry followed hard upon the heels of the horses. Guns and

THE GERMAN RETREAT

munitions had been successfully removed by the Germans but incredible quantities of barbed wire and other defensive material had been abandoned in their positions. Towards the end of March the left of the French and the right of the British were in touch in the immediate front of St. Quentin. There had been scattered fighting all along the line, and the resistance thickened each day, so that it was evident that the final German position had been nearly reached. On March 24 the Australians had a sharp fight at Beaumetz between Bapaume and Cambrai. The village was taken, lost, and retaken with considerable loss upon both sides. It was clear that in this quarter a definite German line had been approached. Similar reports soon came in from Croisilles, from Lagnicourt, from Ronssoy, from Jeancourt, and all along from Arras to St. Quentin. So gradually the famous Hindenburg line defined itself, and the Allied Generals became more clearly aware of the exact nature and extent of this new German position. Early in April, by pushing up to it and brushing aside the advanced forces which screened it, its outlines were more clearly mapped. This process of definition led to more serious fighting, the worst of which, as will presently be shown, fell upon the Australians at Bullecourt, some ten miles from the Arras end of the new line. Some foretaste, however, of the considerable resistance which they were about to meet with in their section was encountered by the Australians at Noreuil on April 2. The brunt of the attack upon the village was borne by the South Australians, who behaved with great gallantry, having to rush a difficult position intersected by sunken roads. A small body of the stormers, some sixty in number, were cut off

CHAPTER I.

The German Retreat upon the Arras-Soissons Front. March.

CHAPTER I.

The German Retreat upon the Arras-Soissons Front.

April.

and overwhelmed, but the main body captured the village, taking 137 German prisoners. Among other brisk skirmishes occurring at the beginning of April was one at Epehy, fifteen miles north of St. Quentin, where the 144th Brigade of the Forty-eighth South Midland Division cleared the hamlet and sugar factory of St. Emilie. In this operation, which was carried out chiefly by the 4th Gloucesters, 5 officers and 80 men fell, but the German loss was considerable. A few days later the 145th Brigade of the same division distinguished itself by the capture after sharp fighting of Ronssoy and of Lempire, the first village being carried by the 4th Berks and the latter by the 5th Gloucesters. This brought the British line in that quarter up to the final German position.

Some sharp fighting had also taken place at Savy and Selency to the immediate west and north-west of St. Quentin, upon the front of the Thirty-second Division, which, together with the Thirty-fifth and Sixty-first, had been pressing the German line. On the morning of April 2 the 14th Brigade of this division was ordered to attack Selency. On the two previous days the village of Savy had been taken, and a strong attack made upon the Bois de Savy by the 96th and 97th Brigades. The advance of April 2 was at early dawn and the veteran 2nd Manchester Battalion was in the lead. The whole operation was conducted under heavy machine-gun fire, but by swift movement and a judicious use of the ground the losses were minimised. Whilst the Lancashire men made direct for the village the 15th Highland Light Infantry kept pace with them upon their right flank. A

THE GERMAN RETREAT 13

battery of six German field-guns opened fire in
the very faces of the stormers, but C Company
of the Manchesters, with admirable steadiness and
presence of mind, swerved to each side and rushed the
guns from the flank, capturing them all. The attack
was at 5 A.M., and by 6.30 the whole objective had been
captured. No further advance was possible as the
front line was already close to St. Quentin, which was
a German stronghold. The position at the end of the
action was that the village was in the hands of the
British but that the six guns with their caissons were
in the open where the Germans could cover them with
their fire. The victors were determined to have their
trophies, and their enemy was no less eager to make it
impossible. The moment that darkness had fallen
a party of Manchesters, under the lead of Lieut.
Thomas, the adjutant, and Lieut. Ward of the 161st
R.F.A., endeavoured to man-handle the guns into
the British lines, but directly they began to haul so
sharp a fire of shrapnel was opened at a range of
800 yards that they were compelled to desist. A
covering party of the 15th Highland Light Infantry
lay round the guns till dawn, and during the day they
remained safe under the rifles of the infantry. At
eight o'clock on April 3 a further attempt to bring
them in was made by Major Lumsden of the Staff, with
Lieutenants Ward and Lomax of the gunners. Horse
teams were brought down, and amid a terrific barrage
the gun wheels began at last to revolve. Maddened
by the sight seen under the glare of their star shells,
the German infantry surged forward and for a time
were all round the Highlanders who still guarded the
guns. One small party of Germans dashed in upon
the guns with a charge of dynamite and managed to

CHAPTER
I.

The
German
Retreat
upon the
Arras-
Soissons
Front.
April.

14   THE BRITISH CAMPAIGN, 1917

CHAPTER I.

The German Retreat upon the Arras-Soissons Front.
April.

blow in the breech of one of them. They were driven off, however, and the six guns were all brought in, while upon April 4 the six artillery caissons were also salved. So ended a most satisfactory little operation for which Major Lumsden received a Victoria Cross and later the command of a brigade, while the other officers were decorated.

On April 2 in the north of the new line, near the spot where very great things were pending, Snow's Seventh Corps had taken Henin and Croisilles, with the aid of the Fifth Army upon their right. It was a small operation in itself, but it was preparing the jumping-off place for the great battle of April 9. There was continued bickering along the line where the British were pushing in the German outliers. In this work the Thirty-fifth Division in the Epehy district distinguished itself greatly during the early summer. One attack upon a hill held by the Germans and carried by the 15th Chesters and 15th Sherwoods of the 105th Brigade was particularly brilliant. In addition, upon April 4, the village of Metz with the adjoining position was taken after a sharp fight by the 59th Brigade of the Twentieth Division. The 10th and 11th K.R.R. were the battalions chiefly engaged in this fight, which at one time had an ugly aspect, as the Germans slipped into a gap between the Twentieth on the left and the Eighth Division on the right. They were cleared out, however, and the line was advanced beyond the village to the right of the Australians.

A more serious action was that which began upon April 13, when the Thirty-second Division was ordered to support the left of the French in their unsuccessful attack upon St. Quentin. The task

THE GERMAN RETREAT   15

assigned to the British division, with the Thirty-fifth Division co-operating upon its left, was to attack the village of Fayet. This was carried out very gallantly by the 97th Brigade, with the 2nd York Light Infantry and the 16th Highland Light Infantry in the lead. The village with 100 prisoners was taken at the first rush, but it was found to be more difficult to get possession of a wood called the Twin Copses, beyond the village. So severe was the fighting that the General of the 97th Brigade had seven battalions under his command before it was finished. Finally, the Twin Copses were splendidly carried by the 11th Borders. The total of prisoners came to 5 officers and 334 men in this very spirited operation.

CHAPTER I.

The German Retreat upon the Arras-Soissons Front. April.

With the conclusion of the German retreat and the solidification of the new line, some more general view may be taken of the whole operation. It cannot be denied that it was cleverly planned and deftly carried out, though it can hardly be said to have deserved the ecstasies of admiration which were bestowed upon it by the German Press. It was not, for example, as formidable an operation as the British withdrawal from Gallipoli, an extraordinarily clever manœuvre which received less than its fair share of recognition at home, because it was associated with the sad ending of high hopes. It was also universally taken for granted in Germany that Hindenburg was going to "reculer pour mieux sauter" as he had done once before at Tannenberg, and that some extraordinary burst of energy at some other point would soon change the exultation of the Allies into despair. Nothing of the sort occurred during that year, and it speedily became evident that the old

Marshal had simply moved because his lines were untenable, and because by shortening them he could make some compensation for the terrific losses of men at the Somme. That he ever regained the ground was due only to the subsequent Russian debacle.

We have it upon the authority of Sir Douglas Haig that the great local retreat of the Germans had no very great effect in modifying the Allied plans. Those plans, so far as the British were concerned, were to make a combined assault from the north and from the south upon the Ancre salient, Gough attacking from the south and Allenby from the north. As the salient had now ceased to exist, the rôle of Gough was confined to following up the German retreat until he came to the new Hindenburg line, which was an obstacle of so formidable a character that it checked anything short of a very powerful attack. Allenby's part of the programme was still feasible, however, and resolved itself into an attack upon the high ground held by the Germans and their whole line down to the point where the new positions began. How Allenby carried out this task, and the great success which attended his efforts, will be described in the coming chapters.

Before passing to this and the other great battles which will make the year 1917 for ever memorable in our history, it would be well to briefly enumerate those world events which occurred during these three months and which directly or indirectly influenced the operations in France. The French line had remained stationary save for the forward movement already described. In Russia the lines had also remained firm, and there was no outward indication of the convulsions into which that unhappy country was about to be thrown by the revolution which broke out on March 12 of this year. From Italy also there was nothing momentous to report. The most cheering news which reached the Allies was from the British Eastern lines of battle, where both in the Sinai Peninsula to the east of Egypt, and in Mesopotamia, good progress was being made. The Sinai desert had been practically cleared of that enemy who had advanced so boastfully to the capture of Egypt, and the British lines were now upon the green terrain which faces Gaza upon the frontier of Palestine. The chief success, however, lay in Mesopotamia. A great soldier had apparently appeared in the person of General Maude, whose name may be recalled by the reader as the Commander of the 14th Brigade upon the Western front. Leaving his limited activities in the prosaic trenches of Flanders, he had suddenly reappeared, moving swiftly along the track of so many of the old conquerors, and leading his picturesque force of Britons and Indians against the ancient capital of Haroun-el-Raschid. In February he had avenged Townshend by recapturing Kut with more than 2000 prisoners. Following up his victory with great speed, he entered Bagdad upon March 11 at the heels of the defeated Turks, and chased them north along the line of the German railway, the constructors of which had never dreamed what strange stationmaster might instal himself at their terminus. The approach of a Russian force seemed to hold out hopes for further combined operations, but meanwhile the whole of southern Mesopotamia remained in the hands of the British, and no Turk was left within forty miles of the ancient capital.

The chief event in Great Britain was the successful

CHAPTER I.

The German Retreat upon the Arras-Soissons Front.

flotation of the great war loan, which attained proportions never heard of before, and ended by bringing in the huge total of one thousand million pounds.

Beyond the usual skirmishes of light craft and isolated sinkings of warships by mine or submarine, there was nothing of importance in naval warfare, but an immense influence was brought to bear upon the course of the war by the German decision in February to declare a war zone round the allied countries, and to torpedo every merchant ship, whether neutral or hostile, which entered it. The measure was a counsel either of ignorance or of despair, for no one who knows the high spirit of the American people could imagine for a moment that they would permit their vessels to be destroyed and their fellow-citizens to be killed in such a manner. Within two days of the declaration of unlimited submarine warfare the President of the United States broke off diplomatic relations with Germany, an act which was the precursor of war, though this was not formally declared until April 5. Great as were the loss, discomfort, and privation caused to Great Britain, and in a less degree to the other Allies, the accession of the United States with its enormous reserves of men and money to the cause of Democracy was far more than a sufficient make-weight. As events progressed, and as it became evident that Russia, swinging from the extreme of autocracy to the extreme of individualism, had ceased for a long time to come to be a useful ally, it grew more and more clear that the help of America was likely to save the Western Powers, not indeed from defeat, but from that pernicious stalemate and inconclusive peace which could only be the precursor of other wars to follow. Apart from the vast material help, the mere thought that the great race which has inherited our speech and so many of our traditions was lined up with us upon the day of Armageddon was a joy and an inspiration to every Briton.

CHAPTER I.

The German Retreat upon the Arras-Soissons Front.

CHAPTER II

THE BATTLE OF ARRAS

April 9 to April 23, 1917

Vast preparations—Attack of Snow's Seventh Corps—The Ibex Trench—Attack of Haldane's Sixth Corps—Attack of Fergusson's Seventeenth Corps—A Scottish Front—The splendid Canadians—Capture of Monchy—Essex and Newfoundland—A glorious episode—The Chemical Works—Extension of the battle to the north—Desperate fight of the Australians at Bullecourt.

<small>Chapter II.</small>
<small>The Battle of Arras.</small>

WHILST the German line was falling back to its new positions, and the Allies were eagerly following it across the ravished countryside until the increased resistance and the familiar lines of barbed wire warned them that the immediate retreat had come to an end, Sir Douglas Haig had managed, without relaxing his pursuit, to collect a strong striking force at the point of junction between the new German line and the old. The blow which he contemplated was no small local advance, but was a wide movement extending from the neighbourhood of Lens in the north to Arras in the south, a front of more than twelve miles. Upon this sector a tremendous concentration of artillery had been effected, and four corps were waiting the signal for the assault, the three southern ones forming Allenby's Third Army, while the fourth or northern one was the right-hand corps of Horne's

First Army. The southern corps were the Seventh (Snow), which operated to the south of Arras, having Croisilles for its southern boundary; the Sixth (Haldane), which advanced due east from Arras with the Scarpe for its northern boundary; the Seventeenth (Fergusson), which had its right on the Scarpe and its left on Thelus, with its front facing the three spurs which form this end of the Vimy Ridge; and finally the Canadian Corps (Byng), which faced this long and sinister slope, the scene of so much bloodshed in the past. Each corps was marshalled with three divisions in front and one in reserve, so that there were roughly 120,000 men in the storming line with 40,000 advancing behind them. Maxse's Eighteenth Corps was in reserve in the rear of the Third Army, while M'Cracken's Thirteenth Corps was behind the First Army. The Germans had six divisions, the Eleventh Prussian, Fourteenth Bavarian, First Bavarian Reserve, and the Seventeenth, Eighteenth, and Seventy-ninth reserve in the line. Their guns also were numerous, as subsequent captures were to prove, but it is probable that an extension of the Hindenburg retreat was in contemplation, and that some of the heavy artillery was already on the move. A second strong line from Drocourt to Quéant was known to exist, and its occupation would form a natural sequel to the retirement in the south.

The German strategists had imagined that by withdrawing their troops over a long front they would throw out of gear all the preparations of the Allies for the spring offensive. What they actually did was to save their force in the Gommecourt peninsula from being cut off, which would surely have been their fate had they waited. But in the larger issue they proved to be singularly ill-informed, for they had stayed their retreat at the very points of the line on which the offensive had been prepared, so that the plans of attack were neither modified nor delayed. That this is true is evident, since such tremendous blows as Arras in the north and Rheims in the south could not possibly have been delivered had the preparations only begun after the Hindenburg retreat.

One of the most difficult problems of this attack was how to arrange it upon that section which was covered by the town of Arras. It is true that the German line was 1700 yards east of the market-place, but the suburbs extended right up to it, and it was fringed with houses. The town itself, in which the storming troops must assemble and through which all supports and supplies must pass, was full of narrow streets within easy range of the German guns, and previous French experience had proved that each exit was so carefully and accurately barraged by the German fire that it was most difficult for the troops to debouch from it. This problem was solved by a fine piece of military engineering. The large cellars and other subterranean excavations with which the place abounded were connected up and fresh tunnels constructed, so that it was eventually found to be possible to put three whole divisions underground, with permanent headquarters and every necessary detail, including water, electric light, and a three-foot tramway. This fine work was carried out by the New Zealand, the 179th, and the 184th Tunnelling Companies. A huge dressing-station with 700 beds was also constructed. In this great underground place of assembly the greater part of the Sixth

Corps was assembled, while many of the tunnels on the south side of the town were allotted to the use of the Seventh Corps. All this had been carried out during the winter in the anticipation of a big attack being made at this point. For purposes of communication, over 1000 miles of twin cable was buried in six-foot trenches or secured to the sides of tunnels. Besides these special preparations, the usual immense labour of preparing for a modern attack had been thoroughly carried out along the whole line, including the construction of very many gun positions, trench mortar emplacements, dressing-stations, and innumerable dumps of munitions and engineering stores. Some dislocation had been caused in the plans by a partial withdrawal in the enemies' front trenches upon March 18, opposite the right end of the British lines. The abandoned works were occupied and linked up with the old system, so that upon April 9 all was in order for the assault. The extreme difficulties caused by the formidable defensive preparations of the enemy were fully realised, but everything which human forethought could suggest had been done to meet them. Above all, two great lessons taught by the Somme experience had been thoroughly assimilated; the one that the broader the attack the more successful it is likely to be, as it prevents a concentration of the German guns upon a single area; the other that it is wiser, even in the heat of battle and the glow of victory, to limit your objective to an area which is well within the range of your guns. That last blue line so far forward upon the map has been the cause of many a rebuff.

The British bombardment, which came in gusts during the days preceding the attack, did enormous damage to the German defences. The evidence of prisoners showed that for several days they had been reduced to their emergency rations. The wire, which in places was a hundred yards thick, was mostly destroyed in the first line, and greatly damaged in the second, though in the third it was found to be largely intact, save upon the left of the line. The space between the first and second German lines was roughly 500 yards. Between the second and third it was about 3000. The usual forms of bombardment were varied upon April 4 by the use of a large number of Liven's gas projectors, throwing drums of compressed gas, which were seen to burst in the second German line. Fifteen hundred of these were discharged upon the front of a single corps, and they were said to have considerable effect, the reports of prisoners stating that in the suburb of Blangy alone there were 460 casualties from this cause. On April 8 there was a severe gas bombardment from 4-inch trench mortars. Finally, in the early morning of April 9, came the fearful whirlwind of fire which was the prelude to the attack. Some idea of its intensity may be gathered from the fact that the number of guns was so great that they could have rubbed wheels from end to end of the line had they been so placed. At 5.30 the word was given, and in the first dim grey of a rainy, windy, and sleety morning, the infantry dashed forward to the attack—"wave after wave of grimy, mud-covered, determined men, with hearts as hard as steel and as light as feathers," to use the words of one of them. The events may best be described from the south of the line as being the nearest to Arras from which the battle derives its name.

THE BATTLE OF ARRAS

Snow's Seventh Corps had the Twenty-first North Country Division upon the extreme right, the Thirtieth Lancashire Division in the centre, the Fifty-sixth London on their left, and the Fourteenth Light Division upon the extreme northern wing. The soldiers, soaked to the skin, with the rain beating upon their backs, and their feet ankle-deep in the mud, set about their task in a calm, businesslike fashion which would take no denial. No village or notable fixed points lay in their path, but they plodded without a check or halt over the first two lines of entrenchments, finding no very strong resistance, save at one point upon the left of their line, and suffering little loss from the German artillery. Considerable numbers of the enemy were found scattered in their shattered trenches or cowering in the dug-outs. Over a thousand of these were sent to the rear. The advance was at the point where the new German line branched away from the old one, the Twenty-first Division on the right joining the left of Gough's Army in the neighbourhood of the Cojeul River, while the Fourteenth Division was in touch with the Third Division on the north.

The immediate objectives of the various divisions of this Seventh Corps were Telegraph Hill in the north opposite to the Fourteenth Division, Neuville Vitasse opposite to the Fifty-sixth Division, St. Martin-sur-Cojeul opposite the Thirtieth Division, and the Hindenburg line opposite the Twenty-first Division. Taking them in turn from the south, we shall first follow the fortunes of the north countrymen of Campbell's Division. This division upon the first day was not expected to do more than make a strong demonstration, because both it, and to a less extent the division upon its left, had in front of it sheets of uncut wire and all the devilries of the fixed German line. The object, therefore, was that they should make a holding attack in the hope that the northern divisions of the corps should get well forward to the east, and then swing to the south in such a way as to make the German position untenable. This was eventually done, and a way was cleared so that the two divisions in the south should be able to advance with the remainder of the line. The whole operation of the Seventh Corps has to be continually judged by the fact that they were on the edge of the abandoned area, and that therefore their southern front bulged out to the east in a way which brought the successive divisions almost into an echelon formation.

On the left of the Twenty-first Division were the Lancashire pals of the Thirtieth Division. Upon April 8 they had made a good start, as the 2nd Bedfords carried the village of St. Martin, an outlier of the Hindenburg line, but on the same date the 21st Brigade was held up in an attempt to advance upon the left. They advanced on April 9 with the 21st Brigade upon the left and the 90th upon the right. The first dash behind a splendid barrage was most successful, but the 21st Brigade, after passing the front German lines, ran into uncut wire and was held, the 18th Liverpools suffering severely. The brigade upon the right managed, however, to get forward for some distance, but it also was faced by uncut wire, and was compelled to dig in as best it could. The attack was renewed two days later with the aid of four tanks, but the wire still held, though the devoted infantry tried again and again. Finally, however, the Fifty-

THE BATTLE OF ARRAS

sixth Division having cleared its own front sent the Victoria Rifles bombing down the front of the Thirtieth Division, who in turn cleared the front of the Twenty-first Division on their right, and so by the evening of April 11 the line was finally advanced. The clearing of the front of the Twenty-first was done by the 18th Manchesters, who, unsupported, bombed their way down 1700 yards of Hindenburg line, a very notable achievement.

To Hull's Fifty-sixth Division, the next upon the north, was assigned the capture of Neuville Vitasse and the strong works which surrounded it. The advance was carried out at 7.45—the zero time was earlier as it travelled up the line—and was led by the 167th Brigade upon the right and by the 168th Brigade upon the left, while the 169th were in support. "The bombardment and the covering fire were magnificent," says one who marched in the ranks; "I almost felt sorry for the poor old Hun, only, after all, he is such a Hun." The chief fighting was on the right, where the 3rd London and 8th Middlesex stormed the main portion of the village. At 10.30 all the eastern edge had been secured, and the 1st London moved forward to take the Cojeul Switch line. Unfortunately, they struck up against uncut wire and a very heavy belt of fire. Colonel Smith, the commanding officer, and the great majority of the other officers were killed or wounded, and the advance was brought to a stand. The 18th Liverpools of the 21st Brigade upon the right had also been halted by the uncut wire. The colonel of the 7th Middlesex took command of this difficult situation so far as it affected the advance of his brigade, and threw his battalion in to strengthen the 1st Londons, so that

CHAPTER II.

The Battle of Arras.

together they captured the Cojeul Switch Trench. The Londoners were then well ahead of the Liverpool men upon their right, so the 1st London threw back a defensive flank while the 7th Middlesex stormed forward against the powerful Ibex Trench. Three separate attempts were made, much impeded by the deep mud, and all ending in failure, so that darkness fell before the task had been accomplished, but with true British tenacity, at 3 A.M., in the darkest hour before dawn, the Middlesex men tried once more and carried Ibex, taking a number of prisoners. The 168th Brigade had with varying fortunes kept pace upon the left, and in the early morning the London Scottish on its right were in touch with Ibex Trench. The position of the 167th was still dangerous upon the flank, as it was always ahead of its southern neighbours, so that instead of advancing eastwards, the colonel of the Middlesex now turned south, his depleted ranks being strengthened by the 9th London (Victorias) from the reserve brigade. The enemy were only forty yards off upon the flank, with a perfect warren of trenches, and the mud was so dreadful that some men who got in could hardly be dragged out again alive. In spite of every difficulty the Londoners, after an initial check, swept triumphantly down Ibex and Zoo trenches, clearing in one wild, glorious rush the whole position, capturing 197 more prisoners of the 31st Prussian Regiment with several machine-guns. Captain Cousens, who led this charge, after being badly wounded, was unhappily killed by a sniper in the moment of victory. The Victorias were too late to join in the victorious charge which stands to the credit of the 7th Middlesex, but they helped to hold and to extend what had been won.

THE BATTLE OF ARRAS

The general effect of the advance of this division was to turn the flank of the southern German defences and to open up a road for the Thirtieth and Twenty-first Divisions upon the right.

The Fourteenth Light Division to the north of the Londoners was faced by the slight slope and formidable defences of Telegraph Hill. They went forward in close conformity with the Sixth Corps upon their left, the 42nd Brigade being upon the left and the 43rd upon the right. Their movement during the day was a particularly fine one, and they not only took the strong position of Telegraph Hill, but they carried the British line to a point far to the east of it. Their whole advance was largely regulated by the situation upon their northern flank, and they were exposed to such an enfilade fire whenever they got at all ahead, that they found it impossible to act entirely upon their own.

Upon the left of the front was a strong German position called "The Harp," which was very gallantly carried by the 42nd Brigade. Sixteen tanks which were to have lent them a hand in this difficult operation failed for some reason to arrive in time, and the infantry had to advance with no help save their own stout hearts. The attack was carried out by the 9th K.R.R. with the 4th Royal Fusiliers of the Third Division acting upon their left, and their comrades of the 6th Oxford and Bucks upon their right. Their only serious opponents here as elsewhere were snipers and machine-gunners, but these were all of the best, and caused heavy losses before the whole objective with its garrison had been captured. By 9.15 in the morning it was entirely in British hands, and as the day wore on the division kept steadily improving their position, though still short of their final objective, that elusive line, which is so easy to draw and so hard to attain. In the evening, an attempt was made by the Fourteenth Division to struggle still further eastwards. This advance had no success, and so the forward units of the whole Seventh Corps dug in on the general line from Feuchy Chapel Road in the north to near Croisilles in the south, having after a desperate day's fighting achieved a gain which averaged two or three miles, and a total of nearly 2000 prisoners with a number of guns. Concerning these prisoners, it may be unsafe to generalise, but it is certain that many of them surrendered very readily. As to their general type the opinion of a commanding officer who handled many of them may be quoted : " The officers were mild persons, none of the bullet-headed, bristly-moustached, truculent Prussian type. The prisoners generally do not inspire one with respect. Braggarts and bullies in prosperity, in adversity they cringe."

Haldane's Sixth Corps was to the immediate left of the Seventh, and its operations were directed due east of Arras. The three front divisions, counting from the south, were the Third, the Twelfth South of England, and the Fifteenth Scottish, with the Thirty-seventh English in reserve. The troops of the assaulting divisions had been assembled for three days in the caves under Arras, but on the night of April 8 they were silently passed into the assembly trenches, an operation which was carried through with little interference or loss. The vile weather may have been a blessing in disguise, as it covered all the preparations from the German observation.

The right of the attacking line was formed by the

THE BATTLE OF ARRAS

76th Brigade of the Third Division, a unit which had distinguished itself greatly in previous fighting. The 8th and 9th Brigades were in close support. Its front was south of the Arras—Cambrai Road. To the left of the 76th Brigade the line was carried on by the 37th and 36th Brigades of the Twelfth Division. Their right rested on the Arras—Cambrai Road. To their left were the 44th and 45th of the Fifteenth Division. Their left rested upon the Scarpe. Nothing could have gone more smoothly than the advance, which kept well up with the barrage. Only at Observation Hill was vigorous resistance encountered, and the German barrage was so belated that it fell upon empty trenches after the stormers had left them. The line of infantry as it swept forward in its irresistible advance was formed, counting from the south, by the 10th Welsh Fusiliers, the 1st Gordons, the 6th Queen's, the 7th East Surreys, the 11th Middlesex, the 7th Sussex, the 8/10th [1] Gordons, the 9th Black Watch, the 6/7th Scots Fusiliers, and the 11th Argyll and Sutherlands. To the courage which had always been their birthright, the infantry now added all the cool war wisdom which experience of many battles must bring with it, and all those devices for overcoming the scattered forts of the enemy and avoiding their machine-guns, which had been learned on the Somme and the Ancre, were now practised to keep down the losses of the assault.

The advance of the 76th Brigade had been to the south of the great high road which leads from Arras to Cambrai—a road which was destined to be second only to the Menin Road as a centre of hard fighting.

---

[1] Where two numbers are given for one battalion, it means that two battalions with these numbers have been telescoped into one.

CHAPTER II.

The Battle of Arras.

The Gordons led the attack and took the front line with a number of the Prussian 38th Regiment. The 10th Welsh Fusiliers then passed through the ranks of the Highlanders and captured Devil's Wood. So swift were these movements that the German barrage was always in the rear. Having thus secured the first objective, the 9th Brigade, strengthened by the 2nd Suffolks, stormed forward to the next line of defence. The 4th Royal Fusiliers on the right took Nomeny, Spring, and Lynx Trenches, when the Suffolks passed through them and took Neuilly Trench. The 12th West Yorkshires took Tilloy village. The 13th Liverpool, after being held up on the left, carried the line forward and, by getting its machine-gun on to the roof of Tilloy Château, dominated the country to the extreme discomfort of the German snipers. Besides these numerous trenches and strong points, the 9th Brigade helped to take the fortified position known as The Harp, an exploit in which they were much assisted by a couple of tanks. Here a considerable number of prisoners were made, including most of a battalion of the 162nd Regiment, together with its commander.

It will save confusion if we follow the fortunes of each division for the day, regardless of what is going on upon its flank, as it is impossible to understand a narrative which switches continually from one portion of the line to another. The whole operation of the Sixth Corps was somewhat behind the time appointed, as each division had met with some delays, but the advance towards the third objective was begun about one o'clock in this southern area. The 8th Brigade had now taken up the running, and the 9th had fallen into support. Reinforced by the two reserve

THE BATTLE OF ARRAS

battalions of the 76th Brigade, the victorious advance was resumed, the 2nd Royal Scots and 7th Shropshires carrying the Bois des Bœufs to the south of the Cambrai Road, together with five guns which had been concealed in it. To those who had experienced what the capture of a wood meant in the Somme fighting, it was indeed a promise for the future that this considerable plantation should offer so slight a resistance. The 8th Brigade fought its way onwards for another mile or more until it had attained the line of Feuchy Chapel. Here the German resistance had thickened and the artillery fire had increased in the same ratio as the British had weakened. A halt was called, therefore, and the infantry consolidated their advanced position. An attempt by the Gordons and the 8th Royal Lancasters to reach the extreme final objective was checked in the evening by a very heavy fire upon both flanks.

In the centre, the Twelfth Division had met with strong resistance at several points, which caused the assault to fall behind the barrage. These centres of German resistance were usually isolated houses or small redoubts, so that it was possible in many cases to mask them and to push onwards. No village or large fixed defence lay in their path, and in spite of a check for some time at the estaminet upon the Cambrai Road, they were able to line up with their comrades to the south upon the second objective about half-past twelve o'clock. At this point the 35th Brigade passed through the advanced lines and moved to the front. A number of difficult positions were taken, including Observation Hill, and the ground was so thoroughly cleared that the assailants were able to go forward with the assurance that their wounds would not be in the back. It was found, however, as they neared the line of the third German position, that considerable stretches of wire had been imperfectly cut, and that the machine-gun fire was so severe as to make the final assault impossible. The infantry dug in, therefore, and waited for further support from the guns, many of which were already on the move. The 9th Essex upon the right actually reached the Feuchy Chapel Work and held their grip of it, keeping in line with the 8th Brigade upon the south.

The Fifteenth Division to the north of the corps' front had before them the very strong position called the Railway Triangle, where the line to Lens branches away from the line to Douai. This formidable place was attacked by the Scotch infantry, and after a severe struggle it was captured about 11.30 save for its eastern side, which was finally taken later in the morning, the artillery aiding the assailants by some extraordinarily good shooting. The advance was then resumed, and the division found itself shortly after noon in the line of the second objective. Six brigades of field artillery had followed closely upon the heels of the infantry and managed, in spite of the unfavourable state of the ground, to take up a position to cover the further attack. When one recalls the dreadful weather and the shell-pocked state of the countryside, it was a remarkable feat upon the part of the gun-teams to get their pieces so rapidly forward. Several tanks came forward also, and did good work not only upon this front, but at Tilloy and The Harp.

The Fifteenth Division was now somewhat behind the others, but shortly after two o'clock the 46th Lowland Brigade advanced upon the third objective.

These splendid soldiers brushed aside every obstacle, and when fired upon at short range by German guns rushed onwards with a yell and captured the battery. By 4 P.M. they had fully reached their final line and had pushed out their patrols some hundreds of yards to the eastwards. This fine advance, which was the only one to reach the extreme limit upon this front, was carried out by the 7th Scots Borderers, 10th Scots Rifles, and 12th Highland Light Infantry, with the 10/11th Highland Light Infantry mopping up behind them.

At 7 P.M. an attempt was made by the two southern divisions to get forward from the Feuchy Chapel Line and gain a position level with the 46th Brigade. Evening was setting in, however, the men were weary and the difficulties manifold, so that no progress was made, both the Third and the Fourteenth Divisions suffering additional losses in the attempt.

The Thirty-seventh Division, composed entirely of English troops, North, South, and Midland, had moved up in the rear of the fighting line, and in the middle of the afternoon it found itself in the German second line system, while the corps' mounted troops had followed behind the Fifteenth Division, as far as the Railway Triangle. As evening fell, the Thirty-seventh Division pushed forward with the intention of reaching the extreme point attained by the Fifteenth Division and then swinging to the right in the hope of capturing Monchy. The advance seems, however, to have taken a direction rather too much to the south, with the result that instead of finding the opening made by the 46th Brigade they came upon the more contracted Feuchy line held by the

Twelfth and Third Divisions. Here they were held up by a field of wire as their comrades had already been, and the two brigades concerned—the 111th upon the left and the 112th upon the right—remained in line with the 35th and the 8th Brigades, the units being considerably intermingled. The 63rd Brigade, however, which was now a brigade of the Thirty-seventh Division, though the reader will associate it with the Twenty-first Division in the past, was able to keep its true direction, and before night had finally established itself at the north end of Orange Hill well up to the third objective and in touch with the 46th Brigade. The corps' cavalry also pushed forward along the south bank of the Scarpe, capturing three 8-inch howitzers upon the way, and halting opposite Fampoux, where they were in touch with the Fourth Division upon the northern bank of the river.

Such was the splendid day's work of Haldane's Corps. It is true that in the south the uncut wire had made it impossible for them to reach their ultimate objective, but they had in the space of the one Easter day captured the villages of Feuchy and of Tilloy, the strong redoubts of The Harp and the Railway Triangle, gained some thirty-six square miles of ground, and taken 2000 prisoners with 60 guns. It was a most notable achievement. We shall now pause on the evening of this first day of battle and we shall go back to reconstruct the operations upon the northern bank of the Scarpe.

The Seventeenth Corps (Fergusson) was upon the left of the Sixth. Its right-hand unit, Lukin's Ninth Division, consisting of two Scottish and one South African brigade, was operating upon the immediate north of the Scarpe. This division was to attack with

THE BATTLE OF ARRAS 37

three brigades in line, the 26th on the right, 27th on the left, and South Africans between. Upon the left of the Ninth was Nicholson's Thirty-fourth Division, drawn largely from Scotland and Tyneside, the same fine division which had been the very pivot upon which the battle of July 1 had turned. Upon the left of the corps was the Fifty-first Highland Territorial Division which had distinguished itself so greatly at Beaumont Hamel five months before. It may be said, therefore, that the fighting line of the Seventeenth Corps upon this great day was predominantly Scottish, but Lambton's veteran Fourth Division was in immediate support. The whole battle-front was from the right bank of the Scarpe near Arras up to the post known as the Commandant's House, just south of Thelus. There were no villages over the greater part of this front, but there were great numbers of fortified farms and strong posts of every description, besides the usual lines of wired trenches. The ground was in successive ridges and a big tactical obstacle existed in the Lens—Arras railroad in its alternate cuttings and embankments. The long eager line of Highlanders, Tynesiders, and South Africans rolled over every obstacle, and by ten o'clock had mastered all the first objectives, which were the three lines of German trenches. In the south the Ninth Division, led by a well-known South African Imperial soldier, had carried first Blangy and then Athies by storm. There was a time when the 26th Brigade upon the right was hung up, but with fine initiative the right flank of the Transvaal Regiment worked down along the railway cutting and helped to clear the front of its neighbours. In the centre, the Thirty-fourth Division, after a short check at a network

CHAPTER II.

The Battle of Arras.

of trenches called "The Pump," had reached its allotted positions. In the north the clansmen, who as Territorials were sprung from the very soil of the Highlands, had swiftly advanced to the south of Thelus and had covered the right wing of the First Canadians while they captured that village. It was victory all along the line, and victory without those excessive losses which have made many of our greatest successes as tragic as they are glorious. The artillery barrage had been found to be a powerful antidote against the deadly machine-guns. "When our barrage lifted off the railway cutting, the machine-guns had been silenced and all the gunners were found to be dead." Such was the report of a South African officer.

Allusion has been made to the check caused by the strong point called "The Pump" and the trenches called the Kleemanstellung just east of it. Some detail should be added in this matter, for it retarded the attack of the flanks of two divisions, and the delay caused by it had the effect that the Canadians on the left and the Ninth upon the right were further forward in the late afternoon than part of the Fifty-first and the Thirty-fourth, which might have caused a dangerous situation. The Thirty-fourth Division had advanced upon a three-brigade front, which consisted from the south of the 101st, the 102nd, and the 103rd. On the north of the 103rd was the 152nd Brigade of the Fifty-first Division with the Seaforths as the flank battalion. This pestilent strong point, armed with well-served and well-concealed machine-guns, lay between the two brigades and held up the flanks of both, inflicting considerable losses not only on the Seaforths, but

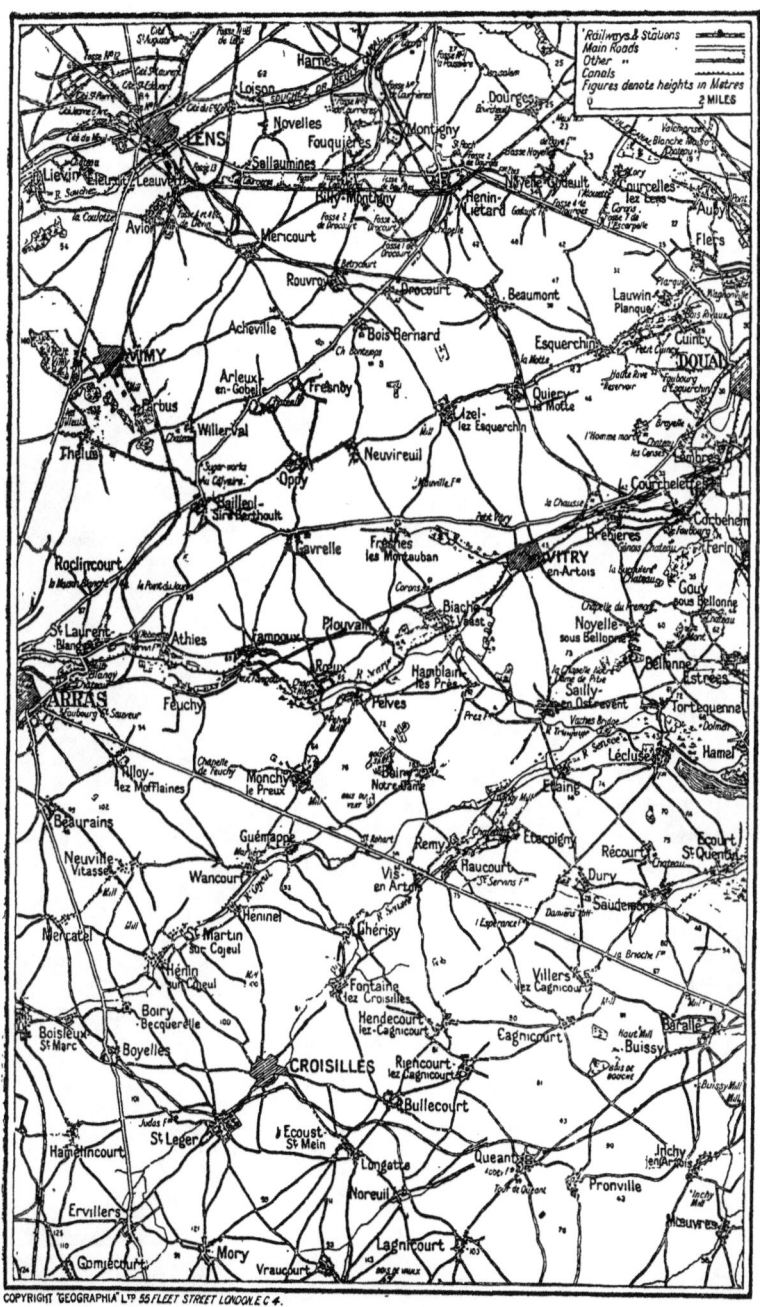

THE ARRAS FRONT

THE BATTLE OF ARRAS 39

on the 25th Northumberland Fusiliers, who were on the left of the Thirty-fourth Division. For a considerable time the advance was held. The 27th reserve battalion of the Northumberland Fusiliers were sent up, and one of its companies, led with a fine mixture of valour and cunning, carried the place by storm. The whole line then got forward, but the losses had been heavy, including Colonel Hermon of the 24th Northumberland Fusiliers. In the evening it was found that the final objective had not yet been fully attained at this quarter of the field, for it had been marked at a farm called Maison de la Côte, from which the front line was still a thousand yards distant. A brilliant little attack, however, by the 103rd Brigade, in the early morning of April 10, captured the whole position. Besides the check at The Pump, there had been another on the Fifty-first divisional front at a post called the "Deutsche Haus." The consequence of this was a loss of the barrage and a delay which led to the isolated left of the Fifty-first losing direction entirely and wandering round in a half-circle. The circumstances were so complex that it was not until next morning that they could be cleared up. Had the Germans had the spirit for a counter-attack, they would certainly have found a considerable gap in the line.

These events were in the northern area of the Seventeenth Corps. In the southern portion, at about eleven o'clock, the reserve division came forward, and, passing through the weary ranks of the Ninth, pushed on along the northern bank of the river. The advance had already been a splendid one, the Ninth Division having 2000 prisoners to its credit, but this

CHAPTER II.
The Battle of Arras.

movement of the Fourth Division against an enemy who was already badly shaken was a very fruitful one. The 12th Brigade was nearest the Scarpe, with the 11th upon the left, while the 10th moved forward in close support. Two obstacles faced the division, the straggling village of Fampoux upon the bank of the river, and the Hyderabad Redoubt, a considerable fort to the north of the village. The 12th Brigade moved swiftly forward in the nearest approach to open warfare that had been seen for years. The 1st Royal Lancasters were on the right of the swift flexible line, the 2nd Lancashire Fusiliers in the centre, and the 2nd Essex upon the left. The brigade fought its way in the teeth of a very hot fire to the outskirts of Fampoux, where the reserve battalion, the 2nd West Ridings, passed through the King's Own and carried the village in splendid style late in the evening at the point of the bayonet. It is a remarkable fact that the wire in front of the village had not been cut by the artillery, and the infantry passed in single file through the gaps in it, after disposing of the only German machine-gunner who offered resistance. At the same time the 11th Brigade kept pace upon their left flank—the Hampshires to the left and Somersets to the right, while the 1st Rifle Brigade, passing through them, rushed the strong position of the Hyderabad Redoubt, and the East Lancashires formed a defensive flank. Communication was at once opened across the Scarpe with Haldane's Corps upon the south side. By this fine advance of the Fourth Division the right of the Seventeenth Corps had got considerably further forward than the centre, so that a defensive line had to be formed sloping back from this advanced point. This was the position

THE BATTLE OF ARRAS 41

upon the evening of the first day of battle, and it was destined to remain so in the south for many a day to come, for the formidable Chemical Works lay immediately to the east on either side of the Arras—Douai railway track, and these were to prove a very grave obstacle to a further advance on this line. Meanwhile, 3500 prisoners with 50 captured guns testified to the success of the Seventeenth Corps.

Following upon this brief sketch of the work done by the Seventh, Sixth, and the Seventeenth Corps upon the first day of the Battle of Arras, we must now turn to the splendid achievement of the Canadian Corps upon the left. The reputation of the Canadians as brilliant soldiers, as dashing in attack as they were steady in defence, had already been solidly established by a long series of military feats beginning with the ever-memorable second battle of Ypres and continuing on to the capture of Courcelette and the fine fighting of the Somme. Hitherto, they had acted in comparatively small bodies, but now the whole might of Canada was drawn together in the four fine divisions which lay facing the historic Vimy Ridge—a long gradual slope which reaches a height of more than 450 feet at the summit. They were arranged in their numerical order from the south, the First (Currie) being in touch with the Fifty-first British Division, while the Fourth (Watson) had upon its left Holland's First Corps, which was not engaged in the first day's operations. The front covered by the Canadians was from the south end of the Ridge to the Souchez River, close to Lens. Nothing could have been more magnificent or more successful than their advance, the Second and Third Divisions (Burstall and Lipsett) attaining their full objectives

CHAPTER II.

The Battle of Arras.

CHAPTER II.

The Battle of Arras.

at every point, and the First doing the same after a short check. There was no rebuff save in the extreme north of the line. Sweeping onwards with irresistible fury, they overran three lines of German trenches, including the famous La Folie Farm, captured the village of Farbus, and secured the splendid total of 70 officers and 3500 men as prisoners, the same number as were taken by their British comrades to the immediate south. They not only crowned the redoubtable ridge, but they made their way down the eastern slope and established their line beyond it. Many of the German infantry were captured in the great chalk excavations in which they had taken refuge, two large tunnels in particular —the Volker and the Prinz Arnault Tunnels—being crammed with men. Incredible incidents happened in these subterranean burrows, where small bodies of Canadian moppers-up were faced suddenly by large numbers of armed Germans in hiding. In one well-authenticated case four Canadians bluffed and captured 2 officers and 70 men from a Bavarian unit who were found in such a pocket, an incident which meant a V.C. for Major Macdowell. When the Kaiser in prophetic mood had spoken about what would happen when his Bavarians met the British, such an incident was far from his thoughts. It should be mentioned that the Fifth British Division was in close support of the Canadians, and that the 13th Brigade of this division was incorporated with the Second Canadians upon that day. It was used in conjunction with the 6th Canadian Brigade on its right to take the final objectives, the eastern slopes of the Ridge, just north of Farbus Wood, which they did successfully with slight losses.

THE BATTLE OF ARRAS 43

During the night of the 9/10th April there was fighting at several points, notably at the north end of the Vimy Ridge. Here the Fourth Canadian Division had some difficulty in holding its ground against several strong counter-attacks of the Germans. It is probable that no body of troops in the whole battle had a harder task, or stuck to it more tenaciously, than this Fourth Canadian Division. Hill 145, which was an outlier of the Ridge, was very strongly held and desperately defended, so that it would have turned any but first-class troops. The final clearing of this point was effected upon April 10, and led to further operations in conjunction with British troops to the north, which will be afterwards described.

The second day of the Battle of Arras, April 10, was spent partly in the consolidation of the ground gained and partly in increasing the area now occupied. The troops were in high heart, for although the full extent of the victory had not yet been realised, it was already known that at least 10,000 prisoners and 100 guns had fallen into their hands, figures which showed that the battle had been the most serious military disaster which had yet befallen the enemy. A fuller enumeration taken some days later gave 13,000 men, 3 howitzers, 28 heavy guns, 130 field-guns, 84 trench-mortars, and 250 machine-guns as the total capture. It may be mentioned that over 1000 prisoners were taken from each of the six different German divisions already enumerated, which disposes of their mendacious assertion that only two divisions occupied their front. It was certainly the greatest blow delivered by the British Army up to that date, and the only other day's fighting at all comparable in its results was the French attack upon the Champagne

CHAPTER II.

The Battle of Arras.

April 10.

front on September 25, 1915, where the number of prisoners was greater but the capture of guns was less.

The Battle of Arras may be considered as having been in truth a one-day battle in the same sense as the succeeding Battle of Messines, for in each case the attack was delivered in order to gain a definite objective, which was the ridge from which observation could be obtained. The extreme limit of advance had not, however, been reached either in the south or in the north, and so in both these areas hard fighting continued, due partly to the efforts of the British to enlarge their gains and partly to the rally of the Germans and their attempts at counter-attack. There was no concentration of troops or guns, however, upon the side of the British, and no attempt at any considerable advance. We shall first follow these operations in the south where they centred chiefly round the village of Monchy and Wancourt in the areas of the Sixth and Seventh Corps. These we shall weave into a connected narrative, after which we shall return to the Vimy region and trace the movements which led to hard fighting in that quarter.

In the Seventh Corps to the south the Fifty-sixth Division of London Territorials had, as already described, enlarged the area which it had taken the day before in the Neuville Vitasse sector. The general curve of the line was such that it was not possible for the units of the Seventh Corps to get forward until the Sixth Corps to the north had won some ground, but upon the afternoon of the 12th a very fine advance was made, by which the 169th Brigade stormed Heninel. The Cojeul River was crossed by the

THE BATTLE OF ARRAS

Fourteenth Light Division, and the heights upon the eastern bank were occupied. The 41st Brigade of this unit had now come into the line. The first attempt upon the heights failed with heavy losses. Next morning it was found that Hill 90 had been evacuated, and they were able to advance and seize Wancourt. This brought the left flank of the Seventh Corps up to the right flank of the Sixth Corps, and ensured close co-operation in those operations to the north which will presently be more fully described. This storming of the German position in this section was the more important as the troops were faced by the new Hindenburg Line. It was well known that an alternative line from Drocourt to Quéant existed some miles to the eastward, but none the less the fall of the front section at a period when much of its wire was still intact proved to the Germans how impossible it was to hold off British troops by mere passive obstacles. The tanks were of great assistance to the assailants in this difficult operation. Upon April 13 and 14 the Twenty-first Division, with the aid of the 19th Brigade from the Thirty-third Division, carried forward the line to the high ground about 1000 yards east of the stream at Henin, astride of that portion of the Hindenburg Line. Here all further attempts to advance were stopped by fresh German troops, until the operations were renewed upon April 23. This advance of the Twenty-first Division upon April 13 and 14 was in connection with a general movement of Snow's Corps, but neither the Fifty-sixth London Territorials in the centre nor the Fiftieth North Countrymen on the left, both of them enfiladed from the north, could make much progress beyond the line of Wancourt Tower, and there was little to

Chapter II.
The Battle of Arras.
April 10.

CHAPTER II.

The Battle of Arras. April 10.

show for a hard day's work. The Thirty-third Division (Pinney) now took over the front from the Twenty-first.

The immediate task which lay before the Sixth Corps upon April 10 was to get the Third and Twelfth Divisions forward to the same line which the Fifteenth Division had reached. It will be remembered that the 46th Brigade of the latter division, together with the 63rd Brigade from the supporting Thirty-seventh Division, had pushed on as far as Orange Hill, half a mile farther eastward than the Feuchy Line which formed the front of the two southern Divisions. Six brigades of field artillery had been hurried up, and with the help of these guns, aided by trench-mortars, the wire which held up the advance was partly blown away. The Third and Twelfth Divisions were then able to move forward and to make one line with the Fifteenth—an operation which was completed by midday, the 8th Brigade doing some brilliant work. The strongly fortified village of Monchy, elevated above the plain, lay immediately in front of the Sixth Corps, and its capture was their next task. With this object in view, the 63rd Brigade was swung round from the north and worked its way south and east, getting into touch with the other brigades of the Thirty-seventh Division, which passed through the newly captured third objective and occupied the ground upon the west of the village. A general advance was then made on each side of the village, the 112th Brigade occupying La Bergère upon the Cambrai road due south of Monchy, while the 1/11th Brigade, with the 9th and 10th Royal Fusiliers in the lead, in the face of a considerable opposition, pushed onwards until it gained a footing on the out-

THE BATTLE OF ARRAS 47

skirts of the village and on the high ground to the north of it, where the 154th Company R.E. dug a temporary line. This was the position on the evening of April 10, while the British line had been strengthened by the presence of the 7th Brigade of Cavalry from the Third Cavalry Division, who were following closely behind the Thirty-seventh Division. In all these operations the weather greatly impeded progress, as it prevented the advance of the guns needed to break down wire and other obstacles.

During the night of April 10 the Twelfth Division was withdrawn into reserve, and the advance was resumed in the early morning by the remaining divisions and the cavalry. At 5 A.M. the infantry was closing in upon Monchy under a heavy fire. The line of advance extended right across the Cambrai road, the 76th Brigade finding itself opposite to the village of Guémappe. Here they were exposed to a very heavy fire of machine-guns, and this famous brigade sustained heavy losses, which were increased by a second attempt to get forward in the afternoon. The 76th Brigade finally entrenched itself some half a mile to the west of Guémappe and waited for developments. The 8th Royal Lancasters were particularly hard hit in their attack.

In the meantime the 111th Brigade of the Thirty-seventh Division had advanced directly upon Monchy, and after severe fighting, in which the splendid infantry struggled onwards in the face of every possible difficulty of German resistance and of driving snow-storms, the place was carried by assault. The three regiments of cavalry from the 8th Brigade, the Royal Horse Guards, 10th Hussars, and Essex Yeomanry, advanced at a gallop and did splendid service by taking part in the attack, following closely upon the infantry, and helping to consolidate the village. By nine o'clock in the morning the 13th K.R.R. and 13th Rifle Brigade, greatly aided by a very active and efficient tank, had driven their way to the farthest houses upon the eastern side. About 150 of the garrison remained in their hands, while very many lay dead among the ruins of the shattered buildings. The cavalry, who lost their brave leader, General Bulkeley Johnson, emerged on the eastern side of the village and lost heavily at that point, especially in horses, some 500 of which were hit. They had the satisfaction, however, of getting their light guns fairly on to the Germans, as they streamed across the open. One who was present says: "The cavalry filled the gap between us and the 112th Brigade. They lost heavily, and their conduct was magnificent." The new gain was instantly consolidated by the Colonel of the Rifles.

The Fifteenth Division upon the left of the Thirty-seventh had been fighting its way forward upon the north, endeavouring to keep in line with the Thirty-seventh. It had got somewhat ahead of the Fourth Division, however, which was to the north of the Scarpe, and in consequence had to face the whole fire from the strong village of Rœux, which held them up. The general line of the corps that night was La Bergère, Monchy, and then the line of the Monchy—Fampoux road as far as the Scarpe. To the north of the Scarpe there had been no forward movement, as the Chemical Works to the east of Fampoux presented an obstacle which was beyond the immediate scope of Sir Charles Fergusson's operations.

On the night of April 11 the Thirty-seventh

THE BATTLE OF ARRAS 49

Division, which had suffered considerably in the capture of Monchy, and the Fifteenth which had lived up to its reputation during fifty-six hours of incessant fighting under most inclement conditions, were withdrawn for a short rest, while the Twelfth Division returned into the line, and the Seventeenth took the place of the Thirty-seventh. April 12 was spent in consolidation and in bringing up heavy howitzer batteries along the Cambrai road, and placing them in positions between Feuchy and Tilloy where they could support the coming operations.

From the time that the British had captured the village, both it and the whole front line in that area had been subjected to a most severe German bombardment, which tried the troops extremely, but did not prevent them from repulsing several attempts at counter-attack, none of which reached the front trenches. On the night of April 12 the Twelfth Division, which was considerably worn from its exertions, was drawn out and was replaced by the famous Twenty-ninth Regular Division, which had gained such honour and suffered such losses at Gallipoli and on the Somme. There was no forward movement upon April 13 in the region of Monchy, but farther south the 9th Brigade, which had taken the place of the 76th in front of Guémappe, endeavoured to reach that village, but were met and checked by the same murderous machine-gun fire which had held up their comrades, a fire which came both from the hamlet itself and from the high ground to the south which lay within the area of the Seventh Corps. The 1st Northumberland Fusiliers and 12th West Yorks, which led the attack, both suffered severely.

As no large movement was contemplated upon

CHAPTER II.

The Battle of Arras.

April 12.

E

CHAPTER II.

The Battle of Arras.
April 14.

this front it was now held by only two divisions, the Twenty-ninth to the south and the Seventeenth to the north, covering the whole broad area from the north of the Cojeul River to the south of the Scarpe. At 5.30 upon April 14 both divisions advanced in order to test the German strength and, if possible, to push them farther back from Monchy. It was an unsuccessful day, and yet it was one of those failures which will be remembered where facile successes have been forgotten, for it brought with it one episode which elicited in the highest degree the historical qualities of British infantry. It had been arranged that the 88th Brigade, consisting of the 2nd Hants, 4th Worcesters, 1st Essex, and the Newfoundland Regiment, should attack due east of Monchy, while another brigade of the Twenty-ninth Division should advance to their right, and the Seventeenth Division guard their flank upon the left. Both of the flank attacks failed, however, and the result was that the storming line of the 88th Brigade, consisting of the Essex men on the left and the Newfoundlanders on the right, found themselves in possession of the German trenches on Infantry Hill, east of Monchy, but with both wings exposed and with so terrific a barrage behind them that they were practically cut off from assistance. This might have mattered little under ordinary circumstances, since two such battalions might be counted upon to hold their ground, but by an evil chance their advance had coincided with a considerable German counter-attack from the Bois du Sart, made by a whole Bavarian division with the intention of retaking Monchy. The result was a Homeric contest in which two battalions held up a whole division, shattered a considerable attack, and

THE BATTLE OF ARRAS 51

were practically annihilated in doing so. Of some companies not a single man returned and yet few were ever reported as prisoners in Germany. No more gallant feat of arms has been performed in the war. The 2nd Hants and 4th Worcesters in support did their best to help their comrades, and sustained considerable losses themselves in the attempt, but they were never able to reach the real front line, and it is undoubtedly true that the two battalions alone received and broke the full strength of the Bavarian Division, which was entirely fresh, having taken no part in any previous fighting. It was difficult in the barrage and confusion—the ground being unreconnoitred— to direct reinforcements to the points where they were so urgently needed, but a lieutenant of the Essex passed through the German barrage and managed to bring up one company of the 2nd Hants, who came too late to retrieve the fight, but were able to take up the defence of the northern flank and to prevent the Germans from getting round in that quarter. Small parties of the enemy got up to the fringes of the village, but the edge had been taken completely from their assault, and in spite of the heavy barrage, the staff of the brigade headquarters, who were the only troops available, were sufficient to hold them off; Colonel Forbes Robertson doing particularly good work with a Lewis gun. No German set foot in Monchy. Of the headquarter staff there were only nine survivors, each of whom was decorated.

Apart from the attack so heroically repelled, a second had developed to the south-east of Monchy which was driven back by rifles and machine-guns. The total German losses during the day must have been very heavy, and they had nothing to show for

CHAPTER II.

The Battle of Arras.
April 14.

52 THE BRITISH CAMPAIGN, 1917

CHAPTER II.
The Battle of Arras.
April 14.

it, though the British casualties amounted to some 4000, chiefly in the Twenty-ninth Division.

It must be admitted that the Germans, who had been strongly reinforced in men and in guns, were fighting with great resolution on this front, and their defence and counter-attacks were equally gallant.

From this date onwards until April 22, there was no particular forward movement, and every effort was concentrated upon the improvement of defences and communications. There were no fresh German counter-attacks, but there was constant and heavy bombardment upon both sides, the Germans pouring shells into Monchy and raking every road which led to the front, while the British overwhelmed Guémappe, Rœux, and Pelves with their fire. The only change of troops was that upon the night of April 19 the Fifteenth Scottish Division, after its short rest, pushed in upon the right of the Twenty-ninth Division, taking over the ground between La Bergère on the north and the Cojeul River on the south. The order of battle of the Sixth Corps was therefore from the north the Seventeenth, Twenty-ninth, and Fifteenth Divisions.

We shall now retrace our steps to glance at what had been going on since the first day of the battle upon the front of the Seventeenth Corps to the immediate north of the Scarpe. It has already been recorded how the flank unit, the Fourth Division, after relieving the Ninth Division found itself faced with the strongly-fortified Chemical Works and the village of Rœux. The position was a very formidable one, as future tragic experiences were to prove. Two brigades of the Ninth Division, the 27th Lowlanders upon the left and the South Africans upon the right, were ordered to pass the line of the Fourth Division

THE BATTLE OF ARRAS 53

and to endeavour to carry the place by assault. The attempt was not successful, though it was urged with great valour. The wastage of the division had already been such that neither brigade numbered 2000 bayonets. The average strength of the South African regiments was about 400 men. As a result, the attack was wanting in weight, and was repulsed with considerable loss, which fell chiefly upon the 1st Cape and 2nd Natal battalions in the front line of the South Africans. The attackers endured heavy losses in debouching from the narrow exits of Fampoux under fire, and they were afterwards faced with 700 yards of open ground swept by bullets. In spite of this, some of the stormers did actually penetrate the German lines, as was proved later by the discovery of their bodies.

To the north of this section of fierce fighting the line, which had sagged upon the evening of April 9, had been brought level upon April 10 by the readjustment of the Fifty-first Division, and by the attack of the 103rd Brigade of Tyneside Scottish upon the Maison de la Côte position. From that time the British front was firm in this region, and a strong counter-attack of four German battalions, who could be seen streaming westwards in lines of motor 'buses, was broken to pieces upon the night of April 11 by the steady rifle-fire of the 27th Northumberland Fusiliers who occupied the front trenches.

Facing this section of the line was the village of Bailleul which was abandoned by the Germans, and was taken over by Pereira's Second Division, who had relieved the Highland Territorials upon April 13. Shortly afterwards the Sixty-third Naval Division took over from the Thirty-fourth. These two divi-

CHAPTER II.

The Battle of Arras.
April 13.

sions belonged to the Thirteenth Corps (M'Cracken), which from now onward occupied a space in the line between the Seventeenth to the south and the Canadians to the north. The strong villages of Oppy and of Gavrelle lay now in front of the British in this quarter, but the German line was destined to remain unbroken for a considerable period. An attack was made upon Gavrelle by the 190th Brigade, the landsman unit of the Naval Division, but this was only partially successful. Farther to the north the Second Division had no better fortune against Oppy, which was attempted more than once. The further advance against these places will be found recorded further on, where it will fit into its place among the other incidents of the renewed general attack upon April 23.

The Canadians in the Vimy Ridge area were occupied during three days of dreadful weather in consolidating their new positions, and in pushing the Germans out of that northern portion which they still held. The Fourth Canadian Division had suffered much from machine-gun fire from Hill 145 in the Souchez district, but this was taken upon April 10. There was still a good deal of work to be done, however, at that end of the line, and upon April 12 a joint attack of Canadians and British cleared the ground in this quarter. Attacking at dawn in a snowstorm, the resolute Canadian infantry drove their way over the northern limits of Vimy Ridge, capturing among other positions an outlier of the Vimy Ridge, the venomous little hill called The Pimple, which had been a thorn in their side. At the same time the Twenty-fourth British Division moved forward nearly opposite to Lens, the river Souchez separating them from the Canadians. The immediate obstacle which

THE BATTLE OF ARRAS 55

faced the British troops was a scattered wood, the Bois-en-Haches, which was most gallantly attacked by the 73rd Brigade. The front line in this fine advance was formed by the 9th Sussex on the left and the 2nd Leinsters upon the right, supported by the 13th Middlesex and 7th Northamptons. Both the Sussex and the Irish battalions, especially the latter, had heavy losses, but they never faltered until their objective was won. Upon April 13 there was a general forward movement along the whole Canadian line, in the course of which they occupied Willerval in the south and both Vimy and Givenchy-en-Gohelle in the north. On the same date the 15th and 95th Brigades of the British Fifth Division took over from the Fourth Canadian Division from the Souchez River to south of Givenchy-en-Gohelle. These two brigades actually took over on the move forward, and did not stop until they had reached a line Cité-des-Petits-Bois to the Vimy—Lens Road just short of La Coulotte.

The Twenty-fourth Division in the north joined in this attack as, to a limited extent, did the Sixth Division upon its left. It may be explained that both of these divisions, together with the Forty-sixth in support of them, formed Holland's First Corps. The Twenty-fourth Division advanced upon a three-brigade front, the 72nd, 17th, and 73rd Brigades in that order from the left, sweeping forward in one line. Complete success attended their efforts. Angres, Lievin, and Cité St. Pierre were all stormed and occupied. The 17th Brigade, which had been strengthened by the inclusion of the 1st Marine Battalion, did particularly well, for it was faced by two dangerous strong points called Crook and Crazy, both of which were carried, the 3rd Rifle Brigade

Chapter II.

The Battle of Arras.

April 13.

being conspicuous in each operation. Some days later, the Forty-sixth Division took over from the Twenty-fourth and the new line was firmly held, the area of the Forty-sixth being from the Souchez River in the south to Fosse 12 de Lens in the north. Farther to the north the Sixth Division had made some progress, but had not been able to surmount the old enemy, Hill 70, the long, clear glacis of which had cost the British such losses at Loos. The Twenty-fourth Division had lost 3000 men in these operations, but their services had been of great value, for the grip upon Lens was appreciably tighter, and according to Sir Douglas Haig's despatch it was the capture of this position which prevented the Germans from attempting the retaking of the positions which they had lost. The British Army was close to the great mining centre, one of the springs of wealth in France. Ominous explosions and dense plumes of dark smoke seemed to show that it was a spring which would be sealed for many a day. So precipitate had been the German retreat in this area that candles were found burning in the dug-outs, meals were half consumed, and large stores of engineering materials and grenades were left behind.

Pausing for a moment at this instant, with the line advanced from three to six miles along the whole front, one may take a glance at the practical results of this great battle. As a mere military triumph it was a considerable one, since the total booty in the immediate battle came by this date to some 14,000 men and 180 guns. Its strategical result was to win the high ground along the whole of a front which had been considered impregnable, and so to give both better observation and drier foothold to the army.

THE BATTLE OF ARRAS

It was clear that it must entail a prolongation of the same operation to the north, and this was manifested two months later at the victory of Messines. That again pointed to a fresh prolongation towards the higher ground round Ypres, which led to the severe but successful fighting in the autumn. Thus the Arras Battle was the prologue to the whole campaign of 1917.

It is impossible, even in so brief an account as this, to turn away from this great victory without a word as to the splendid service of the airmen, and the glorious efforts by which they secured the supremacy over their brave adversaries. The air, the guns, the infantry—those are the three stages which lead from one to the other in a modern battle. Starting with every possible disadvantage, our knight-errants of the air, as without hyberbole they may well be called, by a wonderful mixture of reckless dare-devil bravery and technical skill brought their side to victory. The mixture of the Berserk fighter and of the cool engineer, as ready with the spanner and oil-can as with the pistol and machine-gun, is indeed a strange product of modern tactics. No mention of these grand men, most of them hardly more than boys in their years, could be complete which did not specially name one who is likely to remain as a great memory and inspiration in the Service, Captain Albert Ball, a gallant youth whose bravery and modesty were equally beautiful. He brought down not less than forty-three German planes in single combat before meeting his own glorious end.

Whilst this battle had been raging along the Arras front, the great southern curve which marked the eventual halting-place of the German retreat was

CHAPTER II.

The Battle of Arras.
April 2-12.

the scene of continual fighting, which attained no great intensity save at Bullecourt, but smouldered all along the line, as the British drove in the outlying German posts and impinged upon the main Hindenburg position from Croisilles to St. Quentin. Detail of these smaller operations hardly comes within the scale of this narrative, but some indication of their nature and sequence may be given. On April 2 had been the successful advance upon Ecoust, Noreuil, Louverval, and Doignies, which was carried out to the immediate south of the Seventh Corps area by the left of Gough's Fifth Army. The troops engaged were the British Divisions — the Seventh, Fifty-eighth, and Sixty-second upon the left near Croisilles, the Fourth Australians at Noreuil, and the Fifth Australians at Doignies and Hermies. This brought the army in this section up to the front Hindenburg Line, which the Australians with little support behind them proceeded at once to break, a most valiant but rather rash undertaking, as it was clear that the task was one which required the massed batteries of several army corps to bring it to success. The idea was to connect up with the flank of the Third Army in its new positions and the Sixty-second British Division advance on the left for the same purpose. The attack, which began upon April 12, was directed against the line at a point between Bullecourt village upon the left and Lagnicourt upon the right. A broad apron of barbed wire covered the whole German front, and the only means of piercing it, in the absence of heavy gun power, was by the crushing force of tanks. The attack was delivered across the snow in the early morning by men many of whom had never seen snow

THE BATTLE OF ARRAS 59

in their lives until they entered the war zone. In some places the tanks broke the wire, but for the greater part the infantry—West Australians and New South Welshmen on right, Victorians on left—with extraordinary gallantry and with considerable loss worked its way through it, taking the village of Riencourt. On the farther side, however, they were met with repeated bombing attacks which continued through the morning and afternoon with such pertinacity that the Australian supply of bombs was exhausted. There were only three tanks, and though they behaved with the greatest audacity they were all put out of action. The artillery support being inadequate, the infantry had to fall back, and one considerable party, some 700 in number, were unable to get through the wire, so that after doing all that men could do they were compelled to surrender. Several of these men escaped later with fresh tales of that German brutality to prisoners which has been their constant policy, with a few honourable exceptions, since the first days of the war. When the large national issues have been settled or forgotten, these smaller villainies will leave Germans as outcasts among the civilised nations of the earth, with no living men save the murderers of Armenia with whom they can hold equal converse. This temporary repulse upon the Hindenburg Line by no means disheartened the Australians, who argued that if with so little support they could effect so much, a more deliberate assault could hardly fail of success. Within three weeks, as will be shown, they were to prove the truth of their contention.

In the meantime, a considerable German attack had been prepared which fell upon the Australian line

Chapter II.
The Battle of Arras.
April 12.

in the early morning of April 15. Two Guards Divisions and two ordinary divisions took part in it, so that it was no small matter. The outposts were weak and a number of the field-guns had been brought well forward into the front line, so that the first onset crashed through the defences and brought about a situation which might have been dangerous. The front line rallied, and with the aid of supports advanced so swiftly upon the Germans that they had little time to injure the guns which had come for the moment into their power. The front of the attack was nearly six miles, from Hermies to Noreuil, with its centre at Lagnicourt, and all along this extended position the stormers had rushed forward in heavy masses into the Australian line. It was easier to break than to destroy, for every scattered post spat out bullets from rifles and Lewis guns, fighting viciously until it was either submerged or rescued. In some posts, notably that of Subaltern Pope, an old warrant-officer of the Navy from West Australia, the men fired away every cartridge and then all died together, stabbing and thrusting with their bayonets into the grey clouds which hemmed them in. Seventy German dead were found round his position. In front of Lagnicourt, the Germans had the advanced guns in their hands for nearly two hours, but they had been dismantled by the gunners before they were abandoned, and the Prussian Guardsmen had apparently no means of either moving or of destroying them. All of them, save five, were absolutely intact when retaken. A rush of Queenslanders and New South Welshmen drove back the intruders, retrieved the guns, and followed the fugitives into Lagnicourt. Large numbers of the Germans were shot down in their retreat, especially in their efforts to get back through the gaps in their own wire. Both sides took several hundred prisoners in this action, but the German losses were heavy, and nothing at all was gained.

The units which have been mentioned, the Seventh Fifty-eighth, and Sixty-second Divisions, with the Fourth and Fifth Australian Divisions, constituted for the moment the whole of Gough's Fifth Army. To its south, extending from the right of the Australians at Hermies down to the junction with the French at St. Quentin, lay Rawlinson's Fourth Army, which consisted at this period of the Fifteenth Corps (Du Cane) upon the left, with the Twentieth, Eighth, and Forty-eighth Divisions in the line. To the south of this was the Third Corps with the Fifty-ninth, Thirty-fifth, and Thirty-second Divisions in the line. Their general instructions were to push the enemy back so as to gain complete observation of the Hindenburg system. The Twentieth Division pushed up into Havrincourt Wood, and gradually by many skirmishes cleared it of the enemy, an operation which extended over some time, but was not accompanied by any hard fighting.

A sharp little action, already described, was fought at the extreme south of the British line upon April 13, in which the Thirty-second Division was engaged. This unit captured Fayet, which is only one mile north of St. Quentin. At the same time, the two divisions upon the left, the Thirty-fifth and the Fifty-ninth, advanced and captured the ground in front of them. After some fighting, these two divisions occupied the Gricourt—Pontruet line. This section of the line ceased after April to concern the

CHAPTER II.

The Battle of Arras.

April 15.

CHAPTER II.

The Battle of Arras.
April 13.

British commanders, for the St. Quentin end of it was taken over by the French, while the trenches north of that were occupied by Canadian and Indian cavalry, so as to release fresh divisions for the operations in the north.

The full objects of the Arras battle, so far as they could be attained, had been reached after a week of fighting. Had he only himself to consult, Sir Douglas would have assumed a strict defensive from that time onwards and begun at once to transfer his forces for those operations which he had planned in Flanders. It was essential, however, that he should hold and use up as many German divisions as possible in order to help the French offensive which was about to start in the south. How successful the British General had been already in this design is shown by his own statement that after this week of fighting the Germans had twice as many divisions opposite to him as they had at the beginning, and were driven into constant counter-attacks which cost them heavy losses. The whole aftermath of the Battle of Arras, extending until the end of May, is to be judged from this point of view, and though we may be inclined to wince at the heavy losses and the limited results, we have to bear in mind continually the wider strategic meaning of the operations.

CHART OF
ORDER OF BATTLE—ARRAS
April 9, 1917

LENS		VIMY			FARBUS	THELUS	OPPY		GAVRELLE	FAMPOUX RŒUX	SCARPE RIVER		BLANGY	FEUCHY	MONCHY	GUÉMAPPE WANCOURT	CROISILLES
46	24	4	3	2	1	51	34		9	15	12	37	3	14	30	56	21
6									4								

1st C. (Holland)	Canadian Corps (Byng)	17th C. (Fergusson)	6th C. (Haldane)	7th C. (Snow)
			ARRAS	

First Army (Horne)	Third Army (Allenby)	Gough's Fifth Army

Reserve of First Army

13th C. (Congreve) { 63, 31, 5, 2 }

Reserve of Third Army

18th C. (Maxse) { 33, 50, 17, 29 }

{ I, II, III } Div. Cav.

CHAPTER III

OPERATIONS IN THE ARRAS SECTOR FROM APRIL 23 ONWARDS

Advance of April 23—Middlesex and Argyll—Grand fighting of the Fifteenth Division—H.A.C. at Gavrelle—Operations of May 3—The Gavrelle Windmill—Loss of Fresnoy—Capture of Rœux—The long fight at Bullecourt.

UPON April 16 the great French offensive had broken out upon the Aisne, directed against the line of Chalk Downs which the British had learned to know so well in 1914, and aiming at that ancient road, the Chemin des Dames, which some of the First Division had actually reached in that year. The attack was very successful in the outset, a haul of prisoners and guns being secured which brought their victory to a level with that at Arras. After a time, however, the defence became too strong for the attack, and the French losses became very serious. Whilst they were gathering their strength for a fresh blow, which was brilliantly delivered later in the year, it was necessary for Sir Douglas to keep up his pressure to the north, and to engage guns and troops which should, according to his original plan, have been diverted long ago to the Flemish front. This had the effect of delaying the operations there, and this in turn brought us into the premature rainy season which began upon

OPERATIONS IN THE ARRAS SECTOR 65

August 1 and lasted with very few breaks for the rest of the autumn. Thus the circumstances at this date, unavoidable as they were, had a malign effect upon the year's campaign, which was greatly increased by the wild proceedings of the new Russian rulers, if the organisers of anarchy can be known by such a name. These preposterous people, who began their career of democracy by betraying all the democracies of the world, and exemplified their morality by repudiating the loans which had been made to Russia in her need, reduced the armies to such a state of impotence that they were useless as allies, so that the Latin and Anglo-Saxon races had to fight with the full weight of the military autocracies. This fact made the situation both upon the Italian and upon the Western fronts infinitely more serious than it would otherwise have been, since not only the men, but the munitions of the Germans, could be concentrated upon their undoing.

Upon April 23 there was a renewal of the advance all along the British line, which took for its objectives, counting from the south, Bois du Vert, Bois du Sart, Pelves, Rœux, Gavrelle, Oppy, Acheville, etc.

Upon this date, Snow's Seventh Corps in the south had the Thirty-third Division upon its right, the Thirtieth in the centre, and the Fiftieth upon the left. It was a day of hard fighting and of very limited gains, for General Snow experienced all the disadvantages which the attack has against the defence, when there is no overwhelming artillery to blast a road for the infantry. All three divisions made some progress in the early hours of dawn, but the whole of the two northern divisions and the centre of the Thirty-third Division were soon

CHAPTER III.

Operations in the Arras Sector. April 23.

F

held up and were finally driven back to their starting-point by very heavy machine-gun fire. About 11 A.M. a heavy German counter-attack, preceded by a terrific shower of shells, came rolling down the Cojeul Valley, driving back the Fiftieth Division after their very fine initial advance. The obstacle in front of the troops was nothing less than the Hindenburg front line, so that they might well find it a difficult nut to crack. The Thirtieth Division fell back in touch with the Fiftieth, but the Thirty-third managed to hold on to its gain of ground on the flank which had brought it into the German front line south of the Sensée River.

The position at this part of the line had become serious, and was ever more so as the evening passed into night, for the forward position of the Thirty-third Division had exposed its whole left flank, its advanced units were cut off, and the Germans, pushing back the Lancashire men of the Thirtieth Division, had worked forward to an extent which threatened the guns. If the advance continued, the Thirty-third Division must either fall back under most difficult conditions or be overwhelmed. General Pinney held his ground, and was comforted in doing so by the sounds all night of a brisk rifle-fire upon his front, though it was impossible to ascertain what troops were in so isolated a position. With the first light of morning, two battalions of the 19th Brigade, the 20th Royal Fusiliers and 2nd Welsh Fusiliers, were pushed forward to clear up the situation. They came after advancing 1200 yards upon the remains of two grim, battle-stained companies, one of the 1st Middlesex and one of the 2nd Argyll and Sutherland Highlanders, who had spent some fifteen hours in the heart of the enemy's advance, seeing their attacks sweeping past them, but keeping as steady as two rocks in a stream. Apart from the other hardships of their position, they had endured the whole of the British barrage put down to stop the German advance. This stout defence not only screened the face of the Thirty-third Division, but to some extent covered the flank of the Thirtieth—a striking example of what may be accomplished by a small body of determined men who refuse to despair, be the situation ever so desperate. In their shell-holes were found a score or so of German prisoners whom they had held in their clutch. Lieutenant Henderson of the Highlanders received the V.C. over the fine stand made by his troops, and Lieut. Archibald of the same battalion, together with Captain Belsham and Lieut. Rutter of the Middlesex, received decorations for valour, as did many of their brave followers. It was a deed which was worthy of the famous 91st and of the old Die-Hards of Albuera. Altogether upon this day the Thirty-third Division gained great distinction, and, as a visible sign of its prowess, 750 prisoners from the German Sixty-first Division.

The attack, so far as the Sixth Corps was concerned, was launched in the early morning of April 23, with the 44th and 45th well-tried Scottish Brigades upon the right; on their left were the 88th and 87th Brigades of Regulars, and farther north still was the 51st Brigade with one battalion of the 50th. The remaining brigades were in reserve, with the Third Division in support behind them.

The advance was met by an extremely heavy machine-gun fire and by a desperately destructive barrage of heavy artillery. In spite of this, the

68 THE BRITISH CAMPAIGN, 1917

CHAPTER III.
Operations in the Arras Sector.
April 23.

infantry made good progress at several points. The Highlanders of the 44th and the Lowlanders of the 45th Brigades faced the deadly fire with equal bravery, and had soon established themselves to the north and partly to the east of Guémappe. The Twenty-ninth Division had also made a fine advance, being screened from the flank fire which told heavily upon their comrades to north and south. By nine o'clock they had reached the line which had been marked out as their objective, and though the Germans came swarming down from Pelves, they could not budge them from their new positions. On the British left, however, the advance had failed, for the guns in Rœux on the north side of the Scarpe commanded their flank, and the 51st Brigade was unable to get forward in the north, and only slightly in the south. The German counter-attacks developed so strongly in the course of the morning that the Fifteenth Division had to fall back from their advanced positions, taking up a line due north of Guémappe, where it was in very close touch with the Germans in front and with the 88th Brigade upon the left. Both brigades of the Twenty-ninth Division, thrown out in a large semi-circle, held fast to their ground all day. At six in the evening the support brigade of the Fifteenth Division, the 46th Brigade, advanced and again won the forward line, including the village of Guémappe; but the Seventeenth Division upon the left was unable to get forward. The 46th Brigade, as night fell, found its isolated position so precarious that it fell back a little so as to get into closer touch with the right of the Twenty-ninth Division, but still held on to the village. It was a long and hard day's fighting, in which both

OPERATIONS IN THE ARRAS SECTOR 69

parties gave and took severe blows. The German resistance was very strong from the first, and though a fair amount of ground was gained, it was at a considerable cost, which was only justified by the fact that the enemy in their counter-attacks suffered even more heavily. At nightfall, a portion only of the first objective had been won. Bavarian and Scot had fought till they were weary round Guémappe, and never had the dour tenacity of our northern troops been more rudely tested. It was a fine exhibition of valour on both sides, but the village stayed with the Scots.

CHAPTER III.

Operations in the Arras Sector. April 23.

The Seventeenth Corps on the other side of the Scarpe had very similar experiences upon this day of battle as their neighbours in the south. The Thirty-seventh Division was on their left and the Fifty-first upon the right. The Thirty-seventh pushed their line forward to their final objective, which did not contain any particular village. This advanced line they were able to hold. The Fifty-first Division, charging forward with the old Celtic fire, carried the Chemical Works by assault, and the Corona Trench beyond them; but after a desperate day of alternate advance and retreat, their final line was to the west of the Chemical Works. It was a very hard day's work upon this sector, and the losses upon both sides were very heavy.

The Thirteenth Corps upon the same day had attacked Oppy and Gavrelle to the north, with the result that the Sixty-third Division captured the latter. Oppy had proved to be, for the time, in-violable; but the assault upon Gavrelle was brilliantly successful, the village being stormed with a splendid rush, in spite of the most deadly fire, by the 189th and

190th Brigades of the Sixty-third Naval Division. The German losses were greatly increased upon this occasion by their unsuccessful counter-attacks, which spread over several successive days, and never made an impression. It is on record that one gathering of 2000 men, collected in a hollow, was observed and signalled to the guns, with the result that they were simply shot to pieces by a sudden concentration of fire. An officer who observed this incident has made a statement as to the complete nature of the catastrophe. More than 1000 prisoners were taken on this front, and nearly 3000 in all. To the north of the line the Fifth Division also advanced on the German position, the chief attack being carried out by the 95th Brigade, having the Electric Generating Station as its objective. In this operation the 1st Cornwalls particularly distinguished themselves. The result of the advance was a mere readjustment of the line, for the 15th Brigade upon the right was stopped by uncut wire, though the Germans were actually seen holding up their hands in the trenches. Seeing the attack at a standstill, the Germans brought up their machine-guns and drove it back. Upon the immediate north of the Fifth Division, the Sherwood Forester Brigade of the Forty-sixth Division was brought to a stand in front of Hill 65 and Fosse 3, two strong positions bristling with machine-guns. The 6th and 8th Foresters suffered heavily in this attack, 9 officers and 200 men being killed, wounded, or taken. Farther still to the north, the Sixth Division had moved towards the Dynamite Magazine and Nash Alley, but here also the attack was held by the defence. On the whole, in spite of the prisoners and in spite of Guémappe and

OPERATIONS IN THE ARRAS SECTOR 71

Gavrelle, it was doubtful if the gains made up for the losses upon the day's balance.

A second day of hard fighting was destined to follow that of April 23, though the advance began later in the day. In the area of the Seventh Corps some advance was made in the centre and two field-guns were captured. The Sixth Corps also went forward again. The front attacked was strong, the fire heavy, and the attacking troops had again and again been through the furnace, which had only tempered their courage, but had woefully consumed their numbers. The Fifteenth Division in the south got forward some distance and dug themselves in on the new line. The Twenty-ninth also made some gains, but were unable to retain them, and fell back upon their old line. In the movement some of the parties to flank and rear were overwhelmed, and 250 men, including 3 officers, were taken. In the north, the Seventeenth Division held its old line, and did not join in the advance. After nightfall the Twelfth Division came into line again, relieving the weary Twenty-ninth. Farther north the Seventeenth Corps and the First Army were driving back counter-attacks.

The next day (April 25) saw the long struggle still renewed. In the early morning the 50th and 52nd Brigades of the Seventeenth Division went forward and made some progress, as did the indomitable Fifteenth Division in the south. It was clear, however, that the forces available for attack were not strong enough to attain any considerable result in this portion of the line. The Fifteenth, however, were not to be denied, and with extraordinary tenacity they made a sudden night attack upon April 26, and

Chapter III.

Operations in the Arras Sector. April 24.

for a time got possession of a strong German post, called Cavalry Farm, which barred the way. The enemy counter-attacked in the early morning of April 27 and re-occupied the Farm, but the Scotsmen held firmly to the trenches immediately south of it. At this date the Seventeenth drew out of the line and the Third came in again in the centre of the Corps front, while the Twelfth moved to the left. They were just in time to meet a strong German night attack upon April 27, which broke before the rifle and machine-gun fire of the infantry at the point of contact between the two divisions. The German losses were heavy, and they left a few prisoners behind them.

April 28 had been fixed for a forward movement of Fergusson's Seventeenth Corps on the north of the Scarpe, so the Twelfth Division on the south bank advanced in sympathy with it. This attack gained possession of part of Bayonet Trench, a formidable line which crossed the front, but a further attack was unable to clear the whole of it, on account of the very severe machine-gun fire down the Scarpe Valley.

It was a day of hard fighting to the north of the Scarpe, which only affected the line of the Sixth Corps to the extent that the Thirty-fourth Division failed to carry the Chemical Works on the north bank of the river. It was the possession by the enemy of this position and of the village of Rœux to the east of it which was so fatal to all advances south of the Scarpe, as the guns from these places enfiladed the southern line. But for this the Twelfth Division might have reached their whole objective. The Thirty-fourth Division made another attempt upon Rœux in the middle of the night, but again

OPERATIONS IN THE ARRAS SECTOR 73

without success, and the Second Division farther north had no better luck in front of Oppy.

Although the progress had been very limited at the southern end of the line, there were better results to the north. The Canadians, whose staying power in this long-drawn fighting was as remarkable as their valour, had taken Arleux, together with a considerable section of trench upon either side of it. This fine assault was opposed by wire, by sunken roads, and by a desperate hand-to-hand encounter amid the ruins, all of which failed to hold the Canadian infantry. On their right the 5th and 6th Brigades of the Second Division were heavily engaged in front of Oppy and Oppy Wood with some success at first, but this was neutralised by a strong German counter-attack. Some progress had been made also by the Thirty-seventh Division upon the left, and by the Thirty-fourth Division to the right of the Seventeenth Corps to the north of Gavrelle, and on the slopes of the long incline known as Greenland Hill between Gavrelle and Rœux. In these two days of defensive fighting the German bulletins claimed a victory, but the fact that they had lost ground and nearly 1000 prisoners was sufficient to show how hollow was the pretence. Their losses were greatly increased by the continual unsuccessful counter-attacks which they threw against the new positions in the Oppy line, which had now reached the edge of the village. Gavrelle village was attacked no less than seven times, and each time the stormers were completely repulsed.

One particular deed of valour connected with these operations demands some fuller exposition. The front of the German line which had been breached

Chapter III.

Operations in the Arras Sector. April 28.

CHAPTER III.

Operations in the Arras Sector.

April 23.

between Gavrelle on the south and the Bailleul-Gavrelle railway upon the north, was a narrow one, and the Naval Division had penetrated here to a depth of nearly 1000 yards, thus creating a narrow salient into the German defences with its apex at a fortified windmill. The 4th Bedfords, supported by the 7th Royal Fusiliers, were responsible for this advance. The attacks at the north had failed. Thus the troops in the salient had a most difficult task in holding the position in view of the determined counter-attacks, which had continued with hardly a check from April 23, when the salient was formed. The pressure fell upon the 190th Brigade, and very especially upon the 7th Royal Fusiliers and the 1st Honourable Artillery Company.

The orders had been given to endeavour to widen the base of the salient by bombing up the German trenches to the northward, and this work was committed to Major Osmond of the H.A.C. The attack was to be carried on in two parallel lines—the one up the original front trench and the other up the original support trench. Three young lieutenants—Pollard, O'Brien, and Haine—led the bombers, and they came away with a rush which would have gladdened the hearts of the many generations of soldiers who have served in this ancient corps. The railway to the north was their limit, and they had almost reached it when Haine's party found itself held up by a fortress containing 200 of the Fusilier Guards. He sat down before it, repulsed a severe counter-attack, sent back for trench mortars, and upon April 28, after a rest during which the 1st Marine Battalion maintained and enlarged the line, he attacked it in due form. After a short but vigorous

OPERATIONS IN THE ARRAS SECTOR 75

bombardment, he captured it with two machine-guns and fifty of the garrison. He was ordered to leave a platoon in the captured post, but they, in turn, were besieged by an attacking force of the German Guards coming down-trench, and driving in the extreme right of the Second Division in the north. The platoon, or what was left of it, blew up the guns and retreated upon the main body of their Company, who were assembled, under Haine, just south of the railway. There they established a block and remained fast, while Pollard threw out his bombers on the left to form a defensive flank.

Whilst the Royal Marines had held the line they had endeavoured to push the Germans to the north and had lost heavily in the venture. They—or the scanty remains of them—were now relieved by the 4th Bedfords and 7th Royal Fusiliers. Encouraged by this strengthening of the general line, the indefatigable Haine, whose company now numbered only thirty-five men, assembled his miniature siege-train, beleaguered the fort once more, and captured it for the second time with its garrison. Pollard with his men then pushed past, and took the northern objective which had already cost so dearly. Having seized it, he called to his aid men of the Bedfords, the 7th Fusiliers, and of the 22nd Royal Fusiliers of the Second Division to hold the new line. The battle swung and swayed for a time as the Germans made successive efforts, but the whole Naval Division front and part of the Second Division front was cleared. The total trench line taken by Pollard was about a mile; and 1000 yards of this he cleared with the help of four bombers, while Haine repelled no fewer than fourteen attacks. Altogether it was a remarkable

CHAPTER III.

Operations in the Arras Sector. April 23.

76   THE BRITISH CAMPAIGN, 1917

CHAPTER III.
Operations in the Arras Sector.
May 3.

example of what audacity and initiative can do, and both these young officers obtained the V.C. for their determined valour, while Major Osmond, in local charge of the operation, won his D.S.O.

May 3 was a day of general battle upon the British front, the attack being arranged to help the coming French advance due upon May 5. The main action raged from Vimy in the north to the Scarpe, while to the south of the Scarpe the Sixth Corps and Seventh Corps still continued their indefatigable struggles to get forward past the Monchy-Guémappe line on to Pelves and Cherisy. The upshot of the long day's fighting was the capture of Fresnoy by the Canadians at one end of the line, and of a part of the new German line by the Australians at the other end. The Oppy position was also enlarged and strengthened, and progress was made all along the front as far south as Croisilles. Nearly a thousand additional prisoners were taken by the Seventh Corps.

The operations in the southern area upon May 3 were carried out by the hard-worked Twenty-first Division upon the right, the Eighteenth in the centre, and the Fourteenth on the left. Good progress was made all along the line, which extended in the evening roughly from the St. Rohart Factory through a point 1000 yards west of Cherisy to the west edges of Fontaine. All three divisions had hard fighting, and all three lived up to their high reputations. At one time, the 53rd Eastern County Brigade of the Eighteenth Division had actually entered and passed Cherisy, but the pressure of the counter-attacks and of the guns was too strong, and they had to relax their grip. In commenting upon this achievement, General Snow remarked: " I have never met

OPERATIONS IN THE ARRAS SECTOR 77

a division which so persistently pushed its way forward during the intervals between heavy fighting, and the ground (over 1000 yards) won in this manner stands to its credit." The 8th Norfolk and 10th Essex did particularly well. In the Fourteenth Division the 42nd Brigade was in close touch with the Londoners on their left, while the 44th were on the right. The first 1500 yards' advance of this division was easy going, but here as elsewhere the darkness caused loss of touch and some confusion, which was not improved by the severe fire into which the troops came with the breaking of the dawn. It is a dismal experience at any time to trudge through that leaden sleet, but most dismal surely in that cold ghostly hour of early morning. The 8th Rifle Brigade and 7th K.R.R. did all that men could do, and held a flank for the Eighteenth Division when they advanced upon Cherisy, but when at last the latter was forced back the Fourteenth Division retired also, and found themselves by 10.30 in the morning little advanced from where they started.

The exertions and losses of the 42nd Brigade upon the left of the divisional front were not less than those upon the right, nor had they anything solid to show for them. Their advance was led by the 5th Oxford and Bucks upon the right, with the 9th Rifle Brigade upon the left. The Oxfords with great gallantry captured a position called New Trench, and endeavoured to consolidate it, but after sustaining a shattering fire from every sort of missile, and after having lost 300 men, they were charged by six or seven waves of infantry, each wave being about 150 strong. Their numbers and the volume of their fire were not sufficient to stop such an advance,

Chapter III.

Operations in the Arras Sector. May 3.

and the remnants fell back after having taken heavy toll of their assailants.

The advance to the immediate south of the Scarpe was started at an hour before dawn, and was carried out by the Fifty-sixth, Third, and Twelfth Divisions of the Sixth Corps in the order named from south to north. This attack from the onset met with the same terrific machine-gun fire which had limited all our gains and made them so costly upon this front. On the extreme right the 69th Brigade made a most dashing advance, passing through Cavalry Farm in the darkness, and making good their footing in the German system of trenches to the east of it. In this quarter the gain of ground was permanent, but the 167th Brigade upon the left was not so successful, and was held up by wire and machine-guns, as was the 8th Brigade upon its left. All the leading battalions in this quarter sustained crushing losses, especially the 1st London, the 7th Middlesex, and the 2nd Royal Scots. For some reason the British artillery preparation seems to have been entirely inadequate. "As soon as the first wave topped the ridge between our front line and the German trench, it was obvious that the latter had never been adequately dealt with, and had apparently escaped the barrage, as it was full of infantry standing shoulder to shoulder, and waiting for our men to come on. In consequence, while isolated groups got forward, the great bulk of our men were attacked by a withering fire, and pinned down into shell holes from which they were unable to emerge until after darkness."

The hostile shelling in all this St. Rohart area was almost incessant during the day, and of so heavy a volume that it was such as had hardly ever been witnessed by any one present. "If we had another day of it I verily believe we should have been reduced to idiocy." So wrote a brave veteran who endured it. It was therefore clear that the British counter-battery work had been at fault. Add to this that the start before dawn had the same effect as in other parts of the line, causing clubbing of units with loss of direction, and it must be admitted that the experience of the soldiers upon May 3 was not a happy one. Deverell's Third Division upon the left of the Fifty-sixth found much the same conditions and could make little progress. On the extreme left, however, the 36th Brigade of the Twelfth Division, the same unit which had done so well at Ovillers, made a fine advance, gaining the position known as Scabbard Trench. They lost it temporarily to a counter-attack, but it was again taken and permanently held by the 7th Sussex. The fact that the corresponding point on the north bank of the Scarpe had not yet been taken by the flank unit of the Seventeenth Corps made it impossible to get farther forward in this quarter. The difficulty of the Twelfth Division, which had made the farthest advance in the morning, was that they had gone forward in the darkness, and had lost direction and touch with each other, while leaving behind them scattered parties of German infantry. The result was that when the Germans began their counter-attacks the front British lines were practically surrounded, and several small parties of the 37th Brigade were cut off. One little post of the 6th Buffs was entirely isolated a thousand yards ahead of the British line, but held off the enemy all day, and 15 men, the survivors out of 40, made their way back in the evening, scrambling through

German trenches and shooting down all opposition. By that time the whole right of the Twelfth Division had been forced back to its original line, but the left still held firm in Scabbard Trench. The division had 2000 casualties in this day's fighting.

The 169th Brigade had in the meanwhile maintained a difficult position with very great gallantry. This position had been always isolated upon the left, but it was covered upon the right by the successful advance of the Fourteenth Light Division to the south of the Cojeul River. About mid-day, however, a strong German advance forced the Fourteenth Division back to their original line, with the result that the right flank of the 169th Brigade became exposed. It was only when there seemed an imminent possibility of being cut off that this gallant brigade, which contained the 2nd London, Victorias, Westminsters, and London Rifle Brigade, was compelled to drop back to their original line. It was a barren and bloody day in this section of the line, save for the limited gain upon the south of the Scarpe. Two machine-guns and 100 prisoners were the meagre trophies of a long day's fighting. Yet in estimating results, one must never lose sight of that necessity for constant action which is the only method by which the side which has the stronger reserves can assert its eventual superiority in a war of attrition.

To the north, the Fourth Division gained ground east of the Chemical Works and penetrated into Rœux, but were driven out once more, the 10th and 11th Brigades, especially the 1st Somersets and 2nd Seaforths, having very heavy losses. The Ninth Division got well forward upon their left, some of them over-shooting their objective—Uit Trench—and being cut off. Very heavy counter-attacks in the afternoon broke upon this and upon the other sections of the Third Army. In the evening, both the Fourth and Ninth Divisions with gallant pertinacity tried to get forward again in the hope that their advanced posts might still be rescued, but they had no success. A hundred prisoners were taken, but at least as many were lost, including Highlanders, West Ridings, and Lancashire Fusiliers, victims of their own push and valour.

To the north of the Ninth Division, two divisions of the Thirteenth Corps, the Thirty-first to the south and the Fifth to the north, had beaten furiously against the German line upon the Oppy—Gavrelle sector. The efforts of these divisions were greatly handicapped, as in the case of others, by the very early hour at which the action had begun, and by moonlight in the earlier hours, which exposed the assembly of the troops. Starting in pitch darkness the brigades lost touch and direction, so that they were unable to reach their objectives with the speed and precision which is so necessary if barrages and machine-guns are to be avoided. The 92nd East Yorkshire Brigade of the Thirty-first Division advanced upon Oppy Wood, and found itself among trees in the darkness with criss-cross lacings of barbed wire from the branches in every direction, and a heavy fire beating on their ranks. The obstacles would have been difficult in day-time, but were impossible at night. The battalions got completely mixed up, and finally a strong German attack drove them back to their trenches, in spite of a most strenuous resistance, notable for many deeds of valour, for one of which, the single-handed attack upon a

Chapter III.

Operations in the Arras Sector.
May 3.

machine-gun, Lieutenant Harrison of the 11th East Yorks received a posthumous Victoria Cross.

The 93rd West Yorkshire Brigade had got off well and had reached its objective, but this successful German attack exposed the 16th West Yorkshires, who were the flank battalion, to pressure upon its left rear, so that they had eventually to fall back. This exposed the 15th and part of the 18th West Yorkshires, who were now holding Gavrelle village and the trenches to the immediate north of it. For a time things were very critical, and the windmill which commanded the village was retaken by the enemy. The Colonel of the 15th West Yorks collected sixty men of his battalion and held splendidly to the east side of the village for the whole day. One company of the 18th Durhams under Lieutenant Hitchings was sent to retake the windmill, which they did, but were driven out again by the shattering fire of the enemy. They re-formed at the foot of the slope and attacked and recaptured the mill once more, only to be driven out for the third time. Again they took the mill, and this time they drove back the German counter-attack and held on to the position. Sixty out of a hundred in the British ranks had fallen, but when the battle painter of the future is in search for a subject, he will find none better than that of the forty survivors under their boy leader, wearied, blood-stained, but victorious in their shot-torn mill. The whole Gavrelle position was now held, the 93rd being strengthened by two battalions from the 94th York and Lancaster Brigade.

The one outstanding success of the day was the capture of Fresnoy by the First Division of Canadians, which was carried out with the usual dash and gallantry

OPERATIONS IN THE ARRAS SECTOR 83

of this veteran unit, whose worth had now been proved upon so many battlefields. The fighting was the more severe as the village was full of German troops mustered for an attack. Fresnoy was, however, most difficult to hold, as the enemy had retained trench systems both to the north and to the south of it. Shortly after its capture the First Canadians were drawn out of the line for a rest, and the Thirteenth Corps extended to the left, so as to take over its front and to connect with the Second Canadians.

In the early dawn of May 8 the garrison of the village was driven out by a powerful attack from three German divisions. This attack fell at the point of contact between the left of the British and the right of the Canadians, and was so severe that both were pushed back. The 95th Brigade of the Fifth Division, which had moved down from the Lens area, was the particular one which bore the brunt upon the British line, and the two front battalions, the 1st East Surreys and 12th Gloucesters, lost heavily under the terrible concentrated shellfire which a survivor who had tested both described as being "as bad as Longueval." For some reason the artillery support was deficient, and the S.O.S. signals were unanswered. The infantry were driven out by the German rush, and a gallant counter-attack led by a Major of the Gloucesters, with some of their men and some of the 1st Cornwalls, failed to recover the position. The Canadians made no less desperate efforts, but it was impossible to stand against the concentrated bombardment. "You could not see for mud in the air," says an observer. Fresnoy became once more a part of the German line. The price paid, however, was a very heavy one, for it was only the second attacking division, who were the famous 5th Bavarians, which effected a lodgment after the leading division had been broken and driven back with very heavy losses by the rapid fire of the defenders. Upon the British side a large proportion of the small garrison was killed or wounded, while 300 were taken. The 1st Devons came up in the evening and the line was reconstructed about 600 yards to the rear of the old one. It was determined, however, to push it forward at once, and in the early morning of May 9 the Fourth Canadians upon the left, the Devons in the centre, and the 15th Brigade upon the right, pushed on once more, and established the line close to the village, which still remained in the hands of the enemy.

Up to this point the new British offensive which had started upon April 9, and had now come practically to an end, had yielded the splendid results of 400 officers and 19,100 men prisoners, 98 heavy guns, and 159 field-pieces captured, together with 227 trench mortars, 464 machine-guns, and other material.

The battle of May 3, which had ended by some gain of ground, and by the capture of nearly 1000 prisoners (as against some 300 which were lost upon that day), was the last general action along the new line, though it was followed by numerous local engagements.

On May 10, in the dusk of the evening, the lull upon the Scarpe was broken by a most successful attack by the Fourth Division upon Rœux Station, the Cemetery, the Chemical Works, and finally the village itself, every one of these points being taken by storm. The value of this success may be judged by the fact that this was the ninth assault upon the position, a fact which gives an index both of the

OPERATIONS IN THE ARRAS SECTOR 85

pertinacity of British infantry and of the steadfast courage of the successive German garrisons. The 10th Brigade, led by that man of many wounds and honours, de Wiart, took the village itself, the Dublin Fusiliers and the newly formed battalion, made from dismounted Household Cavalry, doing good service. Berners' 11th Brigade had advanced upon the left and captured all their objectives, the 1st Hants taking the Château, whilst the 1st East Lancashires and the 1st Rifle Brigade got the Chemical Works, the scene of so many combats. The place was defended by the 362nd Brandenburgers, who were nearly all killed or taken, the prisoners being over 500 in number. The Fourth Division handed over Rœux to the 51st Highland Territorials, who successfully held it during a very desperate counter-attack upon the night of May 13. The incessant and costly counter-attacks of the Germans in all these regions proved how vital they considered these lost positions.

On May 11 there was another sharp little action which improved the British position. Upon that date the 168th Brigade of the Fifty-sixth Division made a sudden attack at nightfall upon Tool Trench, an awkward position which ran along a small spur and had been a cause of loss in the previous attack. It was captured with a rush, together with a handful of prisoners and six machine-guns. This position was consolidated and permanently held. On the same night the 169th Brigade on the right advanced its line between Cavalry Farm and the Cojeul River. Next day an attempt was made to carry forward this success along the northern portion of the corps line, but was met with so heavy a barrage that it was not possible to carry it out.

CHAPTER III.

Operations in the Arras Sector. May 10.

CHAPTER III.

Operations in the Arras Sector. May 16.

The strain upon the divisions during this continuous fighting had been so great that it was found necessary to give them all the rest and relief possible. With this object in view, the Sixth Corps front was held now by only two divisions, the Fifty-sixth upon the right and the Twenty-ninth on the left. In order to cover the whole line, the Corps mounted troops were advanced and were placed in the trenches upon the south of the Scarpe, which were less vulnerable since the capture of Rœux by the Fourth Division.

In the dim light of the very early morning of May 16, after a heavy shell-fall, a new division of the enemy was thrust forward just north of the Scarpe. In a long day's fighting it was practically destroyed, for though in its first ardent advance it flowed over the shot-shattered advance posts, it was finally held, and then after a long tussle was shot out of its new positions by the rifles and Lewis guns, until before evening it was back whence it started. In this brisk action thousands of the assailants were killed or wounded with nothing to show for it save the substantial losses which they inflicted. This very severe attack fell mainly upon the Fifty-first Division, who showed once more that British formations, even if penetrated, are very far from being defeated.

On May 18 there was a spirited local operation by the 8th Middlesex of the 167th Brigade, in which they made a very gallant bombing attack upon that portion of Tool Trench which was not yet in British hands. The opposition, however, was so strong that no permanent good could be effected. On the next day there was a further attempt to get forward, both by the 167th and by its neighbour, the 87th Brigade. The fire was too deadly, however, and the advance

OPERATIONS IN THE ARRAS SECTOR 87

was not successful. This failure seems to have been due to a knowledge on the part of the enemy as to the coming assault, for the machine-gun fire and the barrage opened in full force at the very moment when the leading line of infantry sprang over the lips of their assembly trenches.

CHAPTER III.

Operations in the Arras Sector. May 20.

May 20 marked a successful advance of the Thirty-third Division on the right of the Seventh Corps, against the Hindenburg Line in the Sensée Valley and southwards towards Bullecourt. On this occasion there was no preliminary bombardment and no creeping barrage. A mist helped the 98th Brigade to deploy unobserved under the bulge of the chalk hills that rise to the south of the Sensée Valley. When this mist rose the Germans had a fine, though transitory, view of British tactics, for the battalions were advancing as upon an Aldershot field day. The 100th Brigade worked down the Hindenburg Line north of the river, crossed it, and joined hands with their comrades on the south. It was a complete surprise, and counter-attack was checked by the volume of the British gun-fire which tore up the whole rear of the German defences. The result was the capture of more than a mile of the front line on either side of the Sensée River, with half a mile of the support line, and 170 prisoners, with many machine-guns. The losses in this well-managed affair were well under a thousand.

For ten days after this the southern front was quiet, and the only change consisted in the withdrawal of the Fifty-sixth and the substitution of the Thirty-seventh Division. On May 30 a minor operation was carried out upon a small section of German trench by the 88th Brigade,

CHAPTER III.
Operations in the Arras Sector.
May 30.

assisted by the 8th East Lancashires from the 112th Brigade. This attack had some partial success, but was eventually driven out of the captured position by a strong counter-attack, with the result that a small body of the 3rd Middlesex Regiment, some thirty in number, were isolated and taken or slain. Greater success, however, attended the next operation, which was an attack upon June 14 upon Infantry Hill, which included Hook Trench and Long Trench. This very successful advance was carried out by the 1st Gordons and 2nd Suffolks, the two regular battalions of the 76th Brigade. The whole position was stormed by a surprise attack and 180 prisoners were taken. A counter-attack was broken up by the British artillery. The losses of the storming battalions were well under 400 men. Two days later the Germans again made a strong effort to thrust back the British advance, but again they failed with considerable loss, save at the more advanced posts which they occupied. A British attempt next morning to regain these lost posts was not successful. Upon June 18, the anniversary of the great day when Germany and Britain fought together for freedom, there was a fresh attack to retake Hook and Long Trench. It surged up to and into the trenches, but could not disperse the sturdy men of Suffolk, who held them. The German wave lost its momentum and broke up into pools, which soon were swept back with the ebbing tide. Nearly 200 prisoners were taken in this spirited affair.

The Seventeenth Corps had a brisk day upon June 5, which extended into three days of fighting. On this date the Ninth Division upon the right and the Thirty-fourth upon the left moved forward suddenly in the evening, covering the space between Rœux and Gavrelle. The attack was directed against a dangerous network of trenches called Curly, Charlie, and Cuthbert, which guarded the rising slope known as Greenland Hill. The brunt of the fighting was borne by the 27th or Lowland Brigade in the south, and by the 102nd Tyneside Brigade in the north. In the latter brigade the 20th and 21st Northumberland Fusiliers carried the trenches opposite to them, while the Scottish infantry kept pace with them upon the right. After hard fighting the whole front German position fell into the hands of the stormers, who had to defend it against a long series of desultory counter-attacks, which lasted until June 7, when the enemy finally gave up the attempt to regain the ground which he had lost. Six officers and 217 men were captured, and the German losses in killed were very heavy, each front battalion reckoning that there were between three and four hundred enemy dead scattered in front of it. It was a spirited local action attended by complete success.

It is necessary now to go back in point of time and pick up the narrative at the northern end of the line.

On Thursday, May 24, the operations at Lens, in abeyance since April 23, broke out once more, when the Forty-sixth Division, which had extended its left so as to occupy much of the ground formerly held by the Sixth Division, made an attempt upon Nash Alley and other trenches in front of it. The attack was made by the 137th Stafford Brigade, and was launched at seven in the evening. The objectives with twenty-eight prisoners were easily secured. It was found impossible, however, to hold the captured ground, as every German gun within range was turned upon it, and a furious succession of assaults wore down the defenders. Captain McGowan beat off five of these onslaughts before he was himself blown to pieces by a bomb. Every officer being down, Major MacNamara came forward from Headquarters to take command, and in the morning withdrew the detachment, an operation which was performed with great steadiness, the men facing back and firing as they retired. Major MacNamara was himself killed in conducting the movement. There were incessant skirmishes, but no other outstanding action for some time in the north of the line, so we must again return to the extreme south and follow the fortunes of the Australians and their British comrades upon the Bullecourt sector.

The operations of the Australians and of the British divisions were renewed upon May 3 in front of Bullecourt and Lagnicourt, the scene of the brave but unsuccessful attack of April 11, when the Australian infantry with little support penetrated the Hindenburg Line. On this second occasion the British gun-power was very much heavier and cleared a path for the attack, while laying down an excellent barrage. The original advance was in the first glimmer of daylight, and by 6.30 it had penetrated well into the Hindenburg Line, the wire having been blown to pieces. The advance made its way by successive rushes to the right of Bullecourt village, where it clung for the rest of the day, the infantry engaged being almost entirely men from Victoria. Laterally by their bombing parties they extended their hold upon the two front lines of German trenches to the right, in which quarter the attack had originally been held up. In the meantime the 62nd Yorkshire Territorial Division had fought their way up to the village and were engaged in desperate hand-to-hand fighting among the shattered brick houses. An English aviator, flying at a height of only 100 feet or so, passed up and down the Australian battle-line helping with his machine-gun, and finally dropping a message, "Bravo, Australia!" a few moments before a bullet through the petrol tank brought him at last to earth. The greeting of this brave lad might well have been the voice of the Empire, for the Australian infantry wrought wonders that day. The British division having been held at Bullecourt, the result was that the Australians projected as a salient into the Hindenburg Line, and that they were attacked on both flanks as well as in front, but they still held on not only for May 3, but for two days that followed, never losing their grip of the trenches which they had won. On the right the Germans made counter-attacks which have been described by the admirable Australian Official Chronicler as being done in "School of Seals" formation, where a hundred grey-backs all dived together from one shell crater to another. None of these attacks got up, owing to the rapid and accurate rifle fire which met them. The German bombing attacks down the trenches were met by showers of trench-mortar bombs, which broke them up. The Germans had trench-mortars also, however, and by their aid they made some of the right-hand positions untenable, but West Australian bombers restored the fight, and the New South Welshmen added further to the gains. In vain a battalion of Prussian Guards and a column of picked storm-troops beat up against that solid defence. The

CHAPTER III.

Operations in the Arras Sector. May 3.

CHAPTER III.

Operations in the Arras Sector. May 3.

position once taken was always held. The Seventh Division had relieved the Sixty-second, and had tightened its grip upon the outskirts of Bullecourt, and from this time onwards its daily task was on the one hand to push farther into the ruins and to eradicate more of the scattered German posts, and on the other to move out upon the right and get close touch with the Australians so as to cover one side of their dangerous salient. Each object was effected in the midst of fighting which was local and intermittent, but none the less very desperate and exhausting. During a week continual counter-attacks moving up from Riencourt broke themselves upon either the British or Australian lines. The 9th and 10th Devon battalions of the 20th Brigade, and their comrades of the 2nd Borders and 2nd Black Watch, were especially hard pressed in these encounters. With inexorable pressure they enlarged their lines, however, and by May 17 the British Fifty-eighth Division of London Territorials (Cator), which had taken over the work, could claim to have the whole of Bullecourt in their keeping, while their brave Oversea comrades had fairly settled into the gap which they had made in the Hindenburg front line. Though the operations were upon a small scale as compared with great battles like Arras, no finer exploit was performed upon the Western front during the year than this successful advance, in which the three British divisions and the Australians shattered no less than fifteen attacks delivered by some of the best troops of Germany. Sir Douglas Haig, who is not prodigal of praise, says in his final despatch: "The defence of this 1000 yards of double trench line, exposed to attack on every side, through two weeks

OPERATIONS IN THE ARRAS SECTOR 93

of constant fighting, deserves to be remembered as a most gallant feat of arms." The losses were naturally heavy, those of the three British divisions—the Seventh, Fifty-eighth, and Sixty-second—being approximately the same. They had been opposed by Guards Regiments and Brandenburg Grenadiers, the very cream of the Prussian Army, and had rooted them out of their carefully prepared position.

CHAPTER III.

Operations in the Arras Sector. May 3.

CHAPTER IV

THE BATTLE OF MESSINES

June 7, 1917

Plumer's long vigil—The great mines—Advance of Australians—Of New Zealanders—Of the Twenty-fifth Division—Of the Irish Divisions—Death of Major Redmond—Advance of Nineteenth Division—Of the Forty-first Division—Of the Forty-seventh Division—Of the Twenty-fourth Division—General results.

<small>Chapter IV.
The Battle of Messines.
June 7.</small>

THE operations upon the Somme in the autumn of 1916 had given the British command of the high ground in the Somme district. The next move was to obtain a similar command in the continuation of the same high ground to the north. This was accomplished from Arras to Lens in the great battle which began upon April 9, 1917. After the complete conquest of this Vimy position, the next step was obviously to attack the prolongation of the same ridge in the Ypres direction. This was carried out with great success upon June 7 in the Battle of Messines, when nine miles of commanding country were carried and permanently held, from the neighbourhood of Ploegstrate in the south to Hill 60 and Mount Sorel in the north. Thus many spots which will for ever be associated with the glorious dead—Hill 60 itself, with its memories of the old 13th and 15th Brigades; Wytschaete, where the dismounted troopers fought

THE BATTLE OF MESSINES

so desperately in the fall of 1914; Messines, sacred also to the memory of the cavalry and of the British and Indian infantry who tried hard to hold it; finally the long, gently sloping ridge which was reddened by the blood of the gallant London Scots when they bore up all night amid fire and flame against the ever-increasing pressure of the Bavarians—all these historic places came back once more into British keeping. It is this action, so splendid both in its execution and in its results, which we have now to examine, an action which was a quick sequel to the order of the German command that " the enemy must not get Messines Ridge at any price."

For two thankless years Sir Herbert Plumer, the officer who in his younger days had held on in such bulldog fashion to the country north of Mafeking, had been the warden of the Ypres salient. His task had been a peculiarly difficult and responsible one—indeed, many a military critic might have said *a priori* that it was an impossible one. The general outline of the British trenches formed a loop rather than a salient, and there was no point in it which could not be shot into from behind. Add to this that all the rising ground, and therefore all the observation, lay with the enemy, and that the defending troops were very often skeleton divisions which had come up exhausted from the south. Taking all these circumstances together, one can understand the facts which turned General Plumer's hair white during these two years, but never for an instant weakened the determination of his defence. There was no one in the Army who did not rejoice, therefore, when it was learned that the Second Army had been chosen for the next attack, and that the long-suffering Plumer was at last to have a chance of showing that he could storm a line as well as hold one.

The Battle of Messines.

Preparatory to the attack, some twenty great mines had been driven into the long, low hill, which is really little more than a slope, attaining a height of 250 feet at the summit. These mines contained 600 tons of explosives, and had been the work of constant relays of miners during many months. These tunnelling companies of miners, drawn from all sorts of material and officered by mining engineers and foremen, did some splendid work in the war, and the British finally outfought the Germans under the earth as completely as they did both on it and above it. The accumulation of guns was even greater than at Arras, and they were packed into about half the length of front, so that the effect of the massed fire when it broke out in the morning of June 7 was crushing to an extent never before known in warfare. What with the explosions of the mines and the downpour of shells, the German front line, with its garrison, may be said to have utterly disappeared, so that when at 3.20 in the first faint flush of a summer morning the infantry dashed forward to the attack, the path of victory had already been laid out before them. Let us examine the general composition of the British line before we follow the fortunes of the various units.

General Plumer's Army had been moved down the line so as to cover all its objectives, and Gough's Fifth Army from the south had been put in to the north of it, occupying the actual salient. This Army was not in the first instance engaged. The Second Army consisted of three Corps. The northern of these was Morland's Tenth Corps, which was in the

THE BATTLE OF MESSINES

region of St. Eloi. This Corps consisted, counting from the north, of the Twenty-third, Forty-seventh and Forty-first Divisions with the Twenty-fourth in reserve. Upon its right, facing Wytschaete, was Hamilton Gordon's Ninth Corps, containing from the north the Nineteenth, Sixteenth, and Thirty-sixth Divisions, with the Eleventh in reserve. Still farther to the right was the Second Anzac Corps (Godley) facing Messines with the Twenty-fifth British Division, the New Zealanders, and the Third Australians in line from the north, and the Fourth Australians in reserve. This was the British battle-line upon the eventful dawn of June 7, 1917.

To take the work of individual units, we shall begin with the Third Australian Division (Monash) upon the extreme right. The men, like their comrades all along the line, had endured very heavy shelling in their assembly trenches, and sprang eagerly forward when the word to advance was given. The First and Second Australian Divisions had given so splendid an account of themselves already in the Hindenburg Line, that it was no surprise to find that their mates were as battleworthy as any troops in the Army. The whole country in front of them was drenched with gas, which hung heavy with the mists of morning, but the weird lines of masked men went swiftly onwards in open order through the poison region, dashed over the remains of the German trenches, crossing the small river Douve upon the way, and then pushing on from one shot-shattered building to another, keeping well up to the roaring cloud of the barrage, occupied without a hitch the whole of their allotted position. With a single pause, while Messines was being occupied upon their left, the leading line of

H

CHAPTER IV.

The Battle of Messines.

Victorians and Tasmanians drove straight on for their ultimate goal, sending back a stream of captured prisoners behind them. Only at one trench was there a sharp hand-to-hand fight, but in general so splendid was the artillery and so prompt the infantry that the enemy had never a chance to rally. It was a perfect advance and absolutely successful. Some indications of counter-attacks came up from the Warneton direction during the afternoon and evening, but they were beaten out so quickly by the shrapnel that they never came to a head. Half-a-dozen field-guns, as well as several hundred prisoners, fell to the lot of the Australians.

Upon the immediate left of the Australians was the New Zealand Division (Russell), which had done so splendidly at the Somme. Their Rifle Brigade had been given the place of honour exactly opposite to Messines, and by eight o'clock they had occupied the village and were digging in upon the farther side. Thirty-eight machine-guns and a number of prisoners were the trophies of their advance. There was no severe fighting, so well had the mines and the guns together done their work; but the men who stormed the village found numerous cellars and dug-outs still occupied, into which they swiftly penetrated with bayonet or bomb. In one of these regimental headquarters was found a message from General von Laffert ordering the 17th Bavarian Regiment to hold the village at all costs. It is certainly extraordinary how these unfortunate and gallant Bavarians were thrust into every hot corner, and if the reason lies in the fact that their Prince Rupprecht had the honour of commanding the German Army of Flanders, then it is an honour which will leave its grievous trace upon

THE BATTLE OF MESSINES 99

his country for a century to come. It is an extraordinary historical fact that the Bavarians, who were themselves overrun and crushed by the conquering Prussians in 1866, should have paid without demur the enormous blood tribute to their conquerors in a cause in which they had no direct interest, since no annexation of Briey metals or Belgian lands would bring prosperity to Bavaria.

CHAPTER IV.

The Battle of Messines.

The losses of the New Zealanders in their fine advance were not heavy, but they had a number of casualties that evening and next morning in their newly consolidated position, which included unfortunately Brigadier-General Brown, one of the finest officers in the force, who was killed by a burst of shrapnel.

Upon the immediate left of the New Zealanders was the Twenty-fifth (Bainbridge), a sound, hardworking British Division, which had a fine and a very long record of service upon the Somme. The task allotted to this division was a formidable one, consisting of an attack upon a 1200-yard front, which should penetrate 3000 yards and cross nine lines of German trenches, the concealed Steenebeek Valley, and crush the resistance of a number of fortified farms. In spite of these numerous obstacles, the advance, which was well-covered by General Kincaid-Smith's guns, was splendidly successful. The 74th Brigade was on the right, the 7th upon the left, with the 75th in reserve. Observers have recorded how at the very instant that the men surged forward under their canopy of shells, six miles of S.O.S. rockets rose in one long cry for help from the German line. From the right the British wave of stormers consisted of the 2nd Irish Rifles, the 13th

Cheshire, the 3rd Worcesters, and the 8th North Lancashires, veterans of Ovillers and the Leipzig Redoubt. Keeping close behind a barrage of sixty guns, they flooded over the enemy trenches, just missing the answering barrage which came pattering down behind them. These troops advanced without a check to the line of the Steenebeek, where the work was taken up by the second wave, consisting of the 9th Lancs., 11th Lancashire Fusiliers, 10th Cheshires, and 1st Wilts, the order being taken from the right. For a time there was a dangerous gap between the Wiltshires and the flank of the Ulstermen to the left, but this was bridged over, and the advance rolled on, with a constant capture of prisoners and machine-guns. Only at one point, named Middle Farm, was there a notable resistance, but the Lancashire Fusiliers and Irish Rifles combined to crush it. All this attack had been carried out in a dim light, half mist and half dust-laden from explosions, where obstacles were hardly seen until they were reached, and where it took fine leading and discipline to preserve direction, so that numbers of men lost touch with their own battalions and went forward as best they might. These are the times when shirkers have their chance and when the true individual quality of troops is most highly tested. Out of touch with officers on either side, the British advanced and the Germans surrendered.

On the capture of all the first objectives the 8th South Lancashires and 11th Cheshires of the 75th Brigade passed through the victorious ranks of their fellow brigades and pushed on against the strong October system of trenches beyond. The 8th Borders followed closely behind, consolidating the ground won

THE BATTLE OF MESSINES 101

by the forward line. It was still only four in the morning. As the 75th Brigade swept forward, it found the 1st New Zealand Brigade upon its right, and the 107th Ulster Brigade upon its left, all moving swiftly in one great line. By eight o'clock all immediate opposition had been beaten down, and the full objectives were being consolidated by the 106th Field Company Royal Engineers, five field-guns having been added to the other trophies. These might have been got away by the enemy had not the machine-guns knocked out the gun teams. The 110th and 112th Brigades of British artillery had been pushed up after the infantry, and though some delay was caused by the unfortunate destruction of Major Campbell and his whole battery staff by a single shell, the batteries were in action within the German lines by 11 A.M.

About midday a counter-attack began to develop along the front of the Second Anzac Corps, involving both British, New Zealanders, and Australians, but the blow already received had been too severe, and there was no resilience left in the enemy. The attempt died away under a withering fire from rifles and machine-guns. By 2 P.M. all was quiet once more.

The British effort was not yet at an end, however. The long summer day was still before them, and there was a good reserve division in hand. This was the Fourth Australian Division (Holmes), two brigades of which passed through the ranks of the Twenty-fifth and New Zealand Divisions, about 3.15 P.M. Their objective was a further system of trenches 500 yards to the east and well down the other slope of the Messines Hill. The advance of each brigade was admirable, but unfortunately they diverged, leaving a dangerous gap between, in which for two days a party of the enemy, with machine-guns, remained entrenched. At the end of that time two battalions of the 13th Australian Brigade, the 50th and 52nd, carried the place most gallantly by storm and solidified the line.

Passing from the area of the Anzac Corps to that of the Ninth Corps, we come first upon Nugent's Thirty-sixth Ulster Division, which had not reappeared in any battle since its day of glory, and of tragic loss in front of Thiepval. It was now, by a happy chance or by a beneficent arrangement, fighting upon the right flank of the Sixteenth Southern Irish Division (Hickie) and the two may be treated as one, since they advanced, step by step, in the same alignment up the bullet-swept slope, and neither halted until they had reached their full objectives. The Ulstermen went forward with the 107th Brigade of Irish Rifles upon the right in close touch with the Twenty-fifth Division, while the 108th was on the left, keeping line with their fellow-countrymen, both Irish divisions dashing forward with great fire and resolution.

The Sixteenth Irish Division for the purpose of the attack consisted of four brigades, having been strengthened by the addition of the 33rd Brigade from the Eleventh Division. In the attack, the 47th Brigade was upon the right and the 49th upon the left. If some further detail may be permitted in the case of men who were playing so loyal a part at a time when part of Ireland had appeared to be so disaffected, it may be recorded that the Irish line counting from the right consisted of the 6th Royal Irish, the 7th Leinsters, the 7/8th Royal Irish Fusiliers, and the 7th Inniskilling Fusiliers. These battalions sprang up

THE BATTLE OF MESSINES

the Wytschaete slope, closely followed by their second line, which was formed by the 1st Munster Fusiliers, 6th Connaught Rangers, 2nd Royal Irish and 8th Inniskillings. In this order, in close touch with the Ulstermen upon their right and the English Nineteenth Division upon their left, they swept up the hill, their Celtic yell sounding high above the deep thunder of the guns. The explosion of the huge mines had a disconcerting effect at the first instant, for great masses of *débris* came showering down upon the men in the advanced positions, so that the dense smoke and the rain of falling earth and stones caused confusion and loss of direction. The effect was only momentary, however, and the eager soldiers dashed on. They swarmed over Wytschaete village and wood, beating down all resistance, which had already been badly shaken by the accurate fire of General Charlton's guns. It was in the assault of the village that that great Irishman, Major Willie Redmond, fell at the head of his men. "He went in advance when there was a check. He was shot down at once. As he fell, he turned towards his men and tried to say something. No words came, but he made an eloquent gesture with his right arm towards the German line, and the Irish swept forward." The profound gratitude of every patriot is due to him, to Professor Kettle, to Mr. Stephen Gwynn, M.P., and to all those Nationalists who had sufficient insight to understand that Ireland's true cause was the cause of the Empire, and that it was the duty of every Irishman of all shades of opinion to uphold it in arms. *O si sic omnes!* An Irishman could then hold his head higher to-day!

By 3.45 A.M. the first objective had been taken, and by five the second, save in front of the Leinsters,

CHAPTER IV.

The Battle of Messines.

where there was a stout resistance at a German machine-gun post, which was at last overcome. It was at this period that a dangerous gap developed between the retarded wing of the right-hand brigade and the swiftly advancing flank of the left, but this opening was closed once more by seven o'clock. By 7.30 the third objective had been cleared by the 1st Munsters on the right and the 2nd Irish Rifles on the left, for the second line had now leap-frogged into the actual battle. By eight o'clock everything had fallen, and the field-guns of the 59th and 113th Brigades R.F.A. had been rushed up to the front, well-screened by the slope of the newly conquered hill. The new position was swiftly wired by the 11th Hants and Royal Engineers.

There now only remained an extreme line which was, according to the original plan, to be the objective of an entirely new advance. This was the Oostaverne Line, so called from the hamlet of that name which lay in the middle of it. Its capture meant a further advance of 2000 yards, and it was successfully assaulted in the afternoon by the 33rd Brigade, consisting of the 7th South Staffords, 9th Sherwoods, 6th Lincolns, and 6th Borders. It has been frequently remarked, and Guillemont might be quoted as a recent example, that both Englishmen and Irishmen never fight better than when they are acting together and all national difference is transmuted suddenly into generous emulation. So it was upon the field of Messines, for the advance of the 33rd Brigade was a worthy continuation of a splendid achievement. Keeping pace with the 57th Brigade of the Nineteenth Division to their north, they dashed aside all obstacles, and by 5.45 were in complete possession of the farthest

THE BATTLE OF MESSINES

point which had ever been contemplated in the fullest ambition of the Generals.

The enemy had been dazed by the terrific blow, but late in the evening signs of a reaction set in, for the German is a dour fighter, who does not sit down easily under defeat. It is only by recollecting his constant high qualities that one can appreciate the true achievement of the soldiers who, in all this series of battles—Arras, Messines, and the Flanders Ridges—were pitch-forking out of terribly fortified positions the men who had so long been regarded as the military teachers and masters of Europe. Nerved by their consciousness of a truly national cause, our soldiers fought with a determined do-or-die spirit which has surely never been matched in all our military annals, while the sagacity and adaptability of the leaders was in the main worthy of the magnificence of the men. As an example of the insolent confidence of the Army, it may be noted that on this, as on other occasions, all arrangements had been made in advance for using the German dumps. "This should invariably be done," says an imperturbable official document, "as the task of rapidly getting forward engineer stores is most difficult."

A line of mined farms formed part of the new British line, and upon this there came a series of German bombing attacks on June 8, none of which met with success. The 68th Field Company of the Engineers had inverted the position, turning the defences from west to east, and the buildings were held by the Lincolns and Sherwoods, who shot down the bombers before they could get within range even of the far-flying egg-bomb which can outfly the Mills by thirty paces, though its effect is puny in comparison

CHAPTER IV.

The Battle of Messines.

106   THE BRITISH CAMPAIGN, 1917

CHAPTER IV.

The Battle of Messines.

with the terrific detonation of the larger missile. From this time onwards, the line became permanent. In this long day of fighting, the captures amounted to 8 officers and 700 men with 4 field-guns and 4 howitzers. The losses were moderate for such results, being 1100 men for the Irish and 500 for the 33rd Brigade. Those of the Ulster Division were also about 1000.

Upon the left of the Irishmen the advance had been carried out by Shute's Nineteenth Division. Of this hard fighting division, the same which had carried La Boiselle upon the Somme, the 56th Lancashire Brigade and the 58th, mainly Welsh, were in the line. The advance was a difficult one, conducted through a region of shattered woods, but the infantry cleared all obstacles and kept pace with the advance of the Irish upon the right, finally sending forward the reserve Midland Brigade as already stated to secure and to hold the Oostaverne Line. The ground to be traversed by this division, starting as it did from near Wulverghem, was both longer and more exposed than that of any other, and was particularly open to machine-gun fire. Without the masterful artillery the attack would have been an impossibility. None the less, the infantry was magnificently cool and efficient, widening the front occasionally to take in fortified posts, which were just outside its own proper area. The 9th Cheshires particularly distinguished itself, gaining part of its second objective before schedule time and having to undergo a British barrage in consequence. This fine battalion ended its day's work by blowing to shreds by its rifle-fire a formidable counter-attack. The Welsh battalions of the same 58th Brigade, the 9th Welsh Fusiliers, 9th Welsh, and 5th South Wales Borderers fought their

THE BATTLE OF MESSINES 107

way up through Grand Bois to the Oostaverne Line with great dash and gallantry. The village of that name was itself taken by the Nineteenth Division, who consolidated their line so rapidly and well that the German counter-attack in the evening failed to make any impression. Particular credit is due to the 57th Brigade, who carried on the attack after their own proper task was completed.

We have now roughly sketched the advance of the Ninth Corps, and will turn to Morland's Tenth Corps upon its left. The flank Division of this was the Forty-first under the heroic leader of the old 22nd Brigade at Ypres. This unit, which was entirely English, and drawn mostly from the south country, had, as the reader may remember, distinguished itself at the Somme by the capture of Flers. It attacked with the 122nd and 124th Brigades in the line. They had several formidable obstacles in their immediate front, including the famous Dammstrasse, a long causeway which was either trench or embankment according to the lie of the ground. An estaminet upon this road was a lively centre of contention, and beyond this was Ravine Wood with its lurking guns and criss-cross of wire. All these successive obstacles went down before the steady flow of the determined infantry, who halted at their farthest line in such excellent condition that they might well have carried the attack forward had it not been prearranged that the Twenty-fourth, the reserve division, should pass through their ranks, as will presently be described.

To the left of the Forty-first was the Forty-seventh London Territorial Division containing the victors of Loos and of High Wood. The effect of

Chapter IV.
The Battle of Messines.

the mines had been particularly deadly on this front, and one near Hill 60 is stated by the Germans to have taken up with it a whole Company of Wurtembergers. The position attacked by the Londoners was on each side of the Ypres—Comines Canal, and included some formidable obstacles, such as a considerable wood and a ruined country-house named "The White Château." Again and again the troops were held up, but every time they managed to overcome the obstacle. Around the ruined grandeur of the great villa, with all its luxuries and amenities looking strangely out of place amid the grim trimmings of rusty wire and battered cement, the Londoners came to hand-grips with the Prussians and Wurtembergers who faced them. In all 600 prisoners were sent to the rear.

To the left of the Forty-seventh London division, and forming the extreme flank of the attack, was the Twenty-third Division (Babington) of Contalmaison fame, a unit which was entirely composed of tough North of England material. It was in touch with the regular Eighth Division upon the left, this being the flank division of the Fifth Army. The latter took no part in the present advance, and the Twenty-third had the task of forming a defensive flank in the Hooge direction, while at the same time it attacked and conquered the low ridges from which the Germans had so long observed our lines, and from which they had launched their terrible attack upon the Canadians a year before. No long advance was expected from this division, since the object of the whole day's operations was to flatten out an enemy salient, not to make one upon our own side. Sufficient ground was occupied, however, to cover the advance farther

THE BATTLE OF MESSINES 109

south, and without this advance it would have been impossible for the supporting division to carry on, without exposing its flank, the work which had been done by the two divisions upon the right. At 3.10 in the afternoon, the Twenty-fourth Division under General Bols, an officer whose dramatic experience in the La Bassée fighting of 1914 has been recounted in a previous volume, advanced through the ranks of the Forty-first and Forty-seventh Divisions at a point due east of St. Eloi, its attack being synchronised with that upon the Oostaverne line farther south. The operation was splendidly successful, for the 73rd Brigade upon the left and the 17th upon the right, at the cost of about 400 casualties, carried that section of the Dammstrasse and the whole of the historic, blood-sodden ground upon either side of it, so rounding off the complete victory of the Second Army. So close to the barrage was the advance of the infantry, that the men of the 1st Royal Fusiliers and 3rd Rifle Brigade, who led the 17th Brigade, declared that they had the dust of it in their faces all the way.

It only remains to be added that on the extreme left of the line the Germans attempted a counter-attack while the main battle was going on. It was gallantly urged by a few hundred men, but it was destined to complete failure before the rifles of the 89th Brigade of the Thirtieth Division (Williams). Few of these Germans ever returned.

It was a one day's battle, a single hammer-blow upon the German line, with no ulterior operations save such as held the ground gained, but the battle has been acclaimed by all critics as a model and masterpiece of modern tactics, which show the highest power of planning and of execution upon the part of Sir Herbert Plumer and his able Chief-of-Staff. The main trophy of course was the invaluable Ridge, but in the gaining it some 7200 prisoners fell into British hands, including 145 officers, which gives about the same proportion to the length of front attacked as the Battle of Arras. The Germans had learned wisdom, however, as to the disposition of their guns in the face of "the unwarlike Islanders," so that few were found within reach. Sixty-seven pieces, however, some of them of large calibre, remained in possession of the victors, as well as 294 machine-guns and 94 trench mortars. The British losses were about 16,000. The military lesson of the battle has been thus summed up in the words of an officer who took a distinguished part in it: "The sight of the battle-field with its utter and universal desolation stretching interminably on all sides, its trenches battered out of recognition, its wilderness of shell-holes, *débris*, tangled wire, broken rifles, and abandoned equipment, confirms the opinion that no troops, whatever their morale or training, can stand the fire of such overwhelming and concentrated masses of artillery. With a definite and limited objective and with sufficient artillery, complete success may be reasonably guaranteed." It is the big gun then, and not, as the Germans claimed, the machine-gun which is the Mistress of the Battle-field. The axiom laid down above is well proved, but it works for either side, as will be shown presently where upon a limited area the weight of metal was with the Germans and the defence with the British.

So fell Messines Ridge. Only when the British

ORDER OF BATTLE
MESSINES
June 7, 1917

THE DAMMSTRASSE   WYTSCHAETE   MESSINES

8   30   23   47   41   19   16   36   25   N.Z. 3rd (Aust.)
              24   11   4th (Aust.)

         10th C. (Morland)   9th C. (Hamilton Gordon)   2nd Anzacs (Godley)

                        Second Army
                         (PLUMER)

Fifth Army
(GOUGH)

stood upon its low summit and looked back upon the fields to westward did they realise how completely every trench and post had been under German observation during these years. No wonder that so much of the best blood of Britain has moistened that fatal plain between Ypres in the north and Ploegstrate in the south. "My God!" said an officer as he looked down, "it is a wonder that they let us live there at all." "It is great to look eastwards," said another, "and see the land falling away, to know that we have this last height and have wrested it from them in three hours." It was a nightmare which was lifted from the Army upon June 7, 1917.

CHAPTER V

OPERATIONS FROM JUNE 10 TO JULY 31

Fighting round Lens—Good work of Canadians and Forty-sixth Division—Action on the Yser Canal—Great fight and eventual annihilation of 2nd K.R.R. and 1st Northamptons—An awful ordeal—Exit Russia.

THE Battle of Messines was so complete and clean-cut within its pre-ordained limitations that it left few readjustments to be effected afterwards. Of these, the most important were upon the left flank of the Anzac Corps, where, as already narrated, some Germans had held out for some days in the gap left between the two forward brigades of the Fourth Australians. These were eventually cleared out, and upon the night of June 10 the 32nd Brigade of the Eleventh Division extended the front of the Ninth Corps to the south, and occupied all this sector, which had become more defensible since, by the energy and self-sacrifice of the 6th South Wales Borderers, a good road had been driven right up to it by which stores and guns could proceed.

It was determined to move the line forward at this point, and for this purpose the Twenty-fifth Division was again put in to attack, with the 8th Borders on the left and the 2nd South Lancs on the right, both of the 75th Brigade. The objective was

CHAPTER V.

Operations from June 10 to July 31.

a line of farmhouses and strong posts immediately to the east. The men were assembled for the attack in small driblets, which skirmished forward and coalesced into a line of stormers almost unseen by the enemy, crouching behind hedges and in the hollows of the ground. At 7.30 in the evening, before the Germans realised that there had been an assembly, the advance began, while the New Zealanders, who had executed the same manœuvre with equal success, kept pace upon the right. The result was a complete success within the limited area attacked. The whole line of posts, cut off from help by the barrage, fell into the hands of the British in less than half-an-hour. The enemy was found lying in shell-holes and improvised trenches, which were quickly cleared and consolidated for defence. After this second success, the Twenty-fifth Division was drawn out, having sustained a total loss of about 3000 during the operations. Their prisoners came to over 1000, the greater number being Bavarians.

For a time there was no considerable action along the British line, but there were large movements of troops which brought about an entirely new arrangement of the forces, as became evident when the operations were renewed. Up to the date of the Battle of Messines the Belgians had held the ground near the coast, and the five British Armies had lain over their hundred-mile front in the order from the north of Two, One, Three, Five, and Four. Under the new arrangement, which involved a huge reorganisation, it was the British Fourth Army (Rawlinson) which came next to the coast, with the Belgians upon their immediate right, and an interpolated French army upon the right of them. Then came Gough's

Fifth Army in the Ypres area, Plumer's Second Army extending to the south of Armentières, Horne's First Army to the south end of the Vimy Ridge, and Byng's Third Army covering the Cambrai front, with dismounted cavalry upon their right up to the junction with the French near St. Quentin. Such was the general arrangement of the forces for the remainder of the year.

CHAPTER V.

Operations from June 10 to July 31.

Save for unimportant readjustments, there were no changes for some time along the Messines front, and little activity save at the extreme north of that section on the Ypres—Comines Canal. Here the British gradually extended the ground which had been captured by the Forty-seventh Division, taking some considerable spoil-heaps which had been turned into machine-gun emplacements by the Germans. This supplementary operation was brought off upon June 14 and was answered upon June 15 by a German counter-attack which was completely repulsed. Some brisk fighting had broken out, however, farther down the line in the Lens sector which Holland's First Corps, consisting of the Sixth, Twenty-fourth, and Forty-sixth Divisions, had faced during the Battle of Arras. This sector was rather to the north of the battle, and the German line had not been broken as in the south. These divisions had nibbled their way forward, however, working up each side of the Souchez River until they began to threaten Lens itself. The Germans, recognising the imminent menace, had already blown up a number of their depots and practically destroyed everything upon the surface, but the real prize of victory lay in the coal seams underground. Huge columns of black smoke which rose over the shattered chimneys and winding gears showed that even this, so far as possible, had been ruined by the enemy.

Operations from June 10 to July 31.

On June 8, the Forty-sixth Division carried out a raid upon so vast a scale that both the results and the losses were greater than in many more serious operations. The whole of the 138th Brigade was concerned in the venture, but the brunt was borne by the 4th Lincolns and 5th Leicesters. On this occasion, use was made upon a large scale of dummy figures, a new device of the British. Some 400 of these, rising and falling by means of wires, seemed to be making a most heroic attack upon an adjacent portion of the German line, and attracted a strong barrage. In the meanwhile, the front trenches were rushed with considerable losses upon both sides. When at last the assailants returned, they brought with them twenty prisoners and a number of machine-guns, and had killed or wounded some hundreds of the enemy, while their own losses came to more than 300. A smaller attack carried out in conjunction with the 11th Canadian Brigade upon the right also gave good results.

On June 19, the 138th Brigade, moving in conjunction with the Canadians, took and consolidated some of the trenches opposite them. Unhappily, their position did not seem to be clearly appreciated, as some of our own gas projectors fell in their new trench, almost exterminating a company of the 5th Leicesters. The sad tragedy is only alleviated by so convincing if painful a proof of the powerful nature of these weapons, and their probable effect upon the Germans.

The combined pressure of the Forty-sixth Division and of the Fourth Canadians began now to close in upon Lens. Upon June 25 the 6th South Staffords, with the brave men of the Dominion operating to the south of them, pushed the Germans off Hill 65. Upon June 28 there was a further advance of the 137th and 138th Brigades, which was much facilitated by the fact that the Canadians upon the day before had got up to the village of Leuvette upon the south. A number of casualties were caused by the German snipers after the advance, and among the killed was M. Serge Basset, the eminent French journalist, who had followed the troops up Hill 65.

A successful advance was made by the Forty-sixth Division and by the Canadians upon the evening of June 28, which carried them into the village of Avion and ended in the capture of some hundred prisoners. This operation was undertaken in conjunction with the Fifth Division near Oppy, upon the right of the Canadians. Their advance was also attended with complete success, the 95th and 15th Brigades clearing by a sudden rush more than a mile of German line and killing or taking the occupants. To the north of them both the 4th Canadians and the 46th Midlanders carried the success up the line. The advance was an extraordinary spectacle to the many who looked down upon it from the Vimy heights, for a violent thunderstorm roared with the guns, and a lashing downpour of rain beat into the faces of the Germans. They were tired troops, men of the Eleventh Reserve division, who had already been overlong in the line, and they could be seen rushing wildly to the rear before the stormers were clear of their own trenches. An unfired and brand-new machine-gun was found which had been abandoned by its demoralised crew. The flooded fields impeded

CHAPTER V.
Operations from June 10 to July 31.

the advance of the Canadians, but the resistance of the enemy had little to do with the limits of the movement.

Upon June 30 the 6th North Staffords and 7th Sherwood Foresters made a fresh advance and gained their objectives, though with some loss, especially in the case of the latter battalion. This operation was preparatory to a considerable attack upon July 1. This was carried out upon a three-brigade front, the order being 139th, 137th, 138th from the north. The 139th were in close touch with the Sixth Division, who had lent two battalions of the 71st Brigade to strengthen the assailants. The objective was from the Souchez River in the south, through Aconite and Aloof Trenches, to the junction point of the Sixth Division, north-west of Lens. The day's fighting was a long and varied one, some ground and prisoners being gained, though the full objective was not attained. The dice are still badly loaded against the attack save when the guns throw their full weight into the game. The Lincoln and Leicester Brigade in the south had the suburb of Cité du Moulin as their objective, and the 4th Lincolns next to the Canadians got well up; but the 5th Lincolns on their left were held up by wire and machine-guns. Through the gallantry of Sergeant Leadbeater one party penetrated into the suburb and made a lodgment in outlying houses, although their flank was entirely in the air. As the day wore on, the line of the 138th Brigade was driven in several times by the heavy and accurate shell-fire, but was each time reoccupied by the enduring troops, who were relieved in the morning by the 4th and 5th Leicesters, who spread their posts over a considerable area. One of these small posts, commanded by Lieutenant Bowell, was forgotten, and held on without relief, food, or water until July 5, when finding himself in danger of being surrounded this young officer effected a clever withdrawal —a performance for which he received the D.S.O.

Whilst the 138th Brigade had established itself in the fringes of Cité du Moulin, the Stafford men upon their left (137th Brigade) had captured Aconite Trench and also got among the houses. A number of the enemy were taken in the cellars, or shot down as they escaped from them, the Lewis guns doing admirable work. About one o'clock, however, a strong attack drove the Stafford men back as far as Ague Trench. The support companies at once advanced, led by Major Graham of the 5th North Staffords, who was either killed or taken during the attack, which made no progress in face of the strong masses of German infantry. The result of this failure was that the remnants of two companies of the 5th North Staffords, who had been left behind in Aconite Trench, were cut off and surrounded, all who were not killed being taken. In spite of this untoward result, the fighting on the part of the battalions engaged had been most spirited, and the conflict, after the fall of most of the officers and sergeants, had been carried on with great ardour and intelligence by the junior non-commissioned officers.

On the left, the Sherwood Forest Brigade (strengthened by the 2nd Regular battalion of their own regiment) advanced upon the Lens—Liévin Road and the network of trenches in front of them. It was all ideal ground for defence, with houses, slag-heaps, railway embankments, and everything which the Germans could desire or the British abhor. The

CHAPTER V.

Operations from June 10 to July 31.

brigade had advanced upon a three-battalion front, but as the zero hour was before dawn, and the ground was unknown to the Regular battalion upon the right, the result was loss of direction and confusion. Separated parties engaged Germans in isolated houses, and some very desperate fighting ensued. In the course of one of these minor sieges, Captain Chidlow-Roberts is said to have shot fifteen of the defenders, but occasionally it was the attackers who were overpowered by the number and valour of the enemy. The Germans tried to drive back the British line by a series of counter-attacks from the Lens—Bethune Road, but these were brought to a halt during the morning, though later in the afternoon parties of German bombers broke through the scattered line, which presented numerous gaps. The losses of the Sherwood Forester Brigade were considerable, and included 5 officers and 186 men, whose fate was never cleared up. Most of these were casualties, but some remained in the hands of the enemy. The total casualties of the division in this action came to 50 officers and about 1000 men.

This hard-fought action concluded the services of the North Midland Division in this portion of the front. It had been in the line for ten weeks, and under constant fire for the greater part of that time. The strength of the battalions had been so reduced by constant losses, that none of them could muster more than 300 men. Upon July 2 the Forty-sixth Division handed over their line to the Second Canadians and retired for a well-earned rest. Save for two very fruitful raids in the Hulluch district in the late autumn, this Division was not engaged again in 1917.

The Germans had strengthened the defence of Lens by flooding the flats to the south of the town, submerging the Cité St. Augustin, so that the Fourth Canadians on the right of the Forty-sixth Division could not push northwards, but they had advanced with steady perseverance along the south bank of the Souchez, and got forward, first to La Coulotte and then as far as the village of Avion, which was occupied by them upon June 28—a date which marked a general move forward on a front of 2000 yards from the river to Oppy. Meanwhile, the Sixth Division had also pushed in upon the north and northwest of Lens, which was closely invested. The First Canadian Division relieved the Sixth Division early in July, so that now the pressure upon Lens was carried out by three Canadian Divisions, one to the north, one to the west, and one to the south of the town. No actual attack was made until the middle of August, but for the sake of continuity of narrative we may reach forward and give some short account of the operations upon that occasion. After constant pressure, and the drifting of a good deal of gas over the huge house-covered area which faced them, the Canadians made an attack upon August 15, which brought them into the very suburbs of the town, while advancing their line both to the north and to the south of it. Two Canadian divisions, the First upon the left and the Second upon the right, made the main attack, while the Fourth Division guaranteed their southern flank. The First Division found itself in what was practically the old British line, as it was defined at the end of the Battle of Loos in September 1915, nearly two years before. This veteran division had not far to go to find its enemy, for the German

CHAPTER V.

Operations from June 10 to July 31.

trenches were not more than 120 yards away. Flooding over them after a heavy discharge of flaming oil drums, the Canadians swept with little loss up that deadly slope of Hill 70, sacred to the memory of the Scots of the Fifteenth Division and of many other brave men who found their last rest upon it. The 3rd Brigade upon the left and the 2nd upon the right topped the low hill and charged roaring down into the Cité St. Auguste beyond. There was a fierce fight at Cinnebar Trench and the other points which made up the German second line. The enemy infantry stood up stoutly to the push of bayonet, and there was some bloody work before the line was finally taken and consolidated by the Canadians. The Second Division in the meanwhile, advancing with the 5th Brigade upon the left and the 4th upon the right, had carried their charge right up to the edge of the city itself, and had established themselves among the shattered houses. As the 5th Brigade rushed forward, they encountered a body of German infantry advancing as if to an attack, so that for a few glorious minutes there was close bludgeon work in No-Man's-Land before the German formation was shattered and the stormers rushed on. A counter-attack developed about mid-day in front of the First Division, and the grey-clad troops could be clearly seen marching up in fours, breaking into artillery formation and finally deploying in line, all after the most approved British fashion—a fact which was explained later by the discovery in the dug-outs of official copies of a translation of the latest Aldershot regulations—surely a most unexpected result of the clash of the two nations, and one which is a compliment to our military instructors. The British methods of defence, however, proved upon this occasion to be more efficient than those for attack, and the Germans were shot back into the rubble-heaps behind them. The losses of the Canadians in this advance were not heavy, save in the 5th Brigade, which had in front of it a network of trenches in front of Cité St. Emile, and carried a hard task through with great valour and perseverance. From this time forward the advanced line was held, and it was only the deflection of the Canadian Corps to the north which prevented them from increasing their gains at Lens.

The seven weeks of comparative peace between the conclusion of the Battle of Messines and the beginning of those long-drawn operations which may be called the Battle of the Ridges, was broken by one tragic incident, which ended in the practical annihilation of two veteran battalions which held a record second to none in the Army. As misfortunes of this sort have been exceedingly rare in the progress of the war, it may be well to narrate this affair in greater detail than the general scale of this chronicle would justify.

Strickland's First Division had taken over the sector which was next the sea, close to the small town of Nieuport. The frontage covered was 1400 yards and extended to Lombardzyde, where Shute's Thirty-second Division carried the line along. The positions had not been determined by the British commander, but were the same as those formerly occupied by the French. It was evident that they were exceedingly vulnerable and that any serious attempt upon the part of the Germans might lead to disaster, for the front line was some six hundred yards beyond the Yser River, and lay among sand

CHAPTER V.

Operations from June 10 to July 31.

dunes where the soil was too light to construct proper trenches or dug-outs. The river was crossed by three or four floating bridges, which, as the result showed, were only there so long as the enemy guns might choose. The supporting battalions were east of the river, but the two battalions in the trenches were to the west, and liable to be cut off should anything befall the bridges behind them. It was indeed a very difficult situation both for Strickland and Shute, for the Germans had complete local supremacy both in guns and in the air.

Upon July 10, the day of the tragedy, the two battalions in front were the 2nd King's Royal Rifles, next the sea, and the 1st Northamptons, upon their right. The Brigadier of the 2nd Brigade had been wounded only a few days before, and a new man was in local command. The story of what actually occurred may be told from the point of view of the Riflemen, who numbered about 550 on the day in question. Three companies, A, D, and B, in the order given from the left, were in the actual trenches, while C Company was in immediate support. The night of July 9–10 was marked by unusually heavy fire, which caused a loss of seventy men to the battalion. It was clear to Colonel Abadie and his officers that serious trouble was brewing. An equal shellfall was endured by the Northamptons on the right, and their casualties were nearly as heavy. So weakened was A Company in its post along the sand dunes that it was drawn into reserve in the morning of July 10, and C Company took its place. During this night an officer and twenty men, all Rhodesians, from B Company, were pushed forward upon a raid, but lost nine of their number on their return. From 8.50

in the morning until 1 P.M. the fire was exceedingly heavy along the whole line of both battalions, coming chiefly from heavy guns, which threw shells capable of flattening out any dug-out or shelter which could be constructed in such loose soil. For hour after hour the men lay motionless in the midst of these terrific ear-shattering explosions, which sent huge geysers of sand into the air and pitted with deep craters the whole circumscribed area of the position. It was a horrible ordeal, borne by both battalions with the silent fortitude of veterans. Many were dead or shattered, but the rest lay nursing the breech-blocks of their rifles and endeavouring to keep them free from the drifting sand which formed a thick haze over the whole position. The two supporting battalions across the canal, the 2nd Sussex and 1st North Lancashire, were also heavily shelled, but their position was more favourable to taking cover. There was no telephone connection between the Rifles' Headquarters and the advanced trenches, but Lieutenant Gott made several journeys to connect them up, receiving dangerous wounds in the attempt. About twelve, the dug-out of B Company was blown in, and a couple of hours later that of C Company met the same fate, the greater part of the officers in each case being destroyed. An orderly brought news also that he had found the dug-out of D Company with its inmates dead, and a dead Rifleman sentry lying at its door. As the man was staggering and dazed with shell-shock, it was hoped that his message was an exaggeration. The telephone wire to the rear had long been cut, and the doomed battalions had no means of signalling their extreme need, though the ever-rising clouds of sand were enough to show what they were enduring. No message of any sort seems to have reached them from the rear. The fire was far too hot for visual signalling, and several pigeons which were released did not appear to reach their destination. With sinking hearts the shaken and dazed survivors waited for the infantry attack which they knew to be at hand. There were really no means of resistance, for, in spite of all care, it was found that the all-pervading sand, which nearly choked them, had put out of gear the mechanism of all the machine-guns and most of the rifles. The divisional artillery was doing what it could from the other side of the Yser, but the volume of fire from the heavies was nothing as compared with the German bombardment. To add to the misery of the situation, a number of German aeroplanes were hawking backwards and forwards, skimming at less than 100 feet over the position, and pouring machine-gun fire upon every darker khaki patch upon the yellow sand.

Both the battalion commanders behaved with the utmost intrepidity and coolness. Of Colonel Abadie of the Rifles, it was said by one of the few survivors: " He inspired all with the utmost confidence. He did everything in his power and was splendid the whole time." Great hopes were entertained that some diversion would be effected by the gunboats upon the flank, but for some reason there was no assistance from this quarter. Hour after hour passed, and the casualties increased until the dead and wounded along the line of both battalions were more numerous than the survivors. At 3 P.M. the regimental dug-out of the Rifles showed signs of collapse under the impact of two direct hits. Those who could move betook themselves to an unfinished tunnel in the sand in which a handful of Australian miners were actually working. These men had changed their picks for their rifles, and were ready and eager to help in the defence of the position. In little groups, unable to communicate with each other, each imagining itself to be the sole survivor, the men waited for the final German rush. At 7.15 it came. A division of German marines made the attack, some skirting the British line along the seashore and approaching from the flank or even from the rear. As many Riflemen as could be collected had joined the Australians in the tunnel, but before they could emerge the Germans were dropping bombs down the three ventilation shafts, while they sprayed liquid fire down the entrance. The men who endured this accumulation of horrors had been under heavy fire for twenty-four hours with little to eat or drink, and it would not have been wonderful if their nerve had now utterly deserted them. Instead of this, every one seems to have acted with the greatest coolness. "The Colonel called to the Riflemen to sit down, and they did so with perfect discipline." By this means the spray of fire passed over them. The entrances were blown in, and the last seen of Colonel Abadie was when, revolver in hand, he dashed out to sell his life as dearly as possible. From this time the handful of survivors, cut off from their Colonel by the fall of part of the roof, saw or heard no more of him. The few groups of men, Rifles or Northamptons, who were scattered about in the sandy hollows, were overwhelmed by the enemy, the survivors being taken. Four officers, who had been half-buried in the tunnel, dug their way out, and finding that it was now nearly dark and that the Germans were all round them, proceeded to make their way as best they could back to the bank of the river. An artillery liaison officer made a gallant reconnaissance and reported to the others that there was a feasible gap in the new line which the enemy was already digging. The adjutant of the battalion, with the second-in-command, and his few comrades, who included an Australian corporal, crept forward in the dusk, picking their way among the Germans. Altogether, there were 4 officers, 20 Australians, and 15 Riflemen. One of the Australians, named McGrady, was particularly cool and helpful, but was unfortunately killed before the party reached safety. Even at this crisis the military code was strictly observed, and the confidential documents of the battalion carefully destroyed by the adjutant. As the British emerged into the gloom from one end of the tunnel, a party of Germans began to enter at the other, but were so skilfully delayed by two Riflemen, acting as rearguard, that they were unable to stop the retreat. The men streamed out at the farther end under the very noses of their enemies, and crept swiftly in small parties down to the river, which at this point is from 70 to 100 yards broad. Across their path lay a camouflage screen some twelve feet high, which had been set on fire by the shells. It was a formidable obstacle, and held them up for some time, but was eventually crossed. Here they were faced by the problem of the broken bridges, and several were shot while endeavouring to find some way across. Finally, however, the swimmers helping the others, the greater number, including the four Rifle officers, got safely across, being nearly poisoned by gas shells as they landed upon the farther side. Of the Northamptons, it would appear that only one officer, Captain Martin, made his escape, though badly wounded. Colonel Tollemache was heard calling out to his men : "It may be the last time, but fight like Englishmen!" He and all his staff became casualties or prisoners. The Northampton front was not more than forty yards from that of the Germans, and the rifle-fire of the latter swept the parapet to such an extent that it was impossible to stop the rush. A private who was No. 1 of a machine-gun, with two other men, who knew nothing of the mechanism, rushed a gun out upon the flank and held up the grey wave for a minute or so before being submerged, while a sergeant also distinguished himself by a determined resistance and by finally crossing the Canal to explain the situation to those in command there.

So ended an experience which can have had few parallels even in this era of deadly adventure. Of the Riflemen, it was found next day that 3 officers and 52 men had rejoined their brigade. If so many got away it was largely due to the action of Rifleman Wambach, who swam the canal with a rope in his mouth, and fixed it for his more helpless comrades. Even fewer of the Northamptons ever regained the eastern bank. "Like the Spartans at Thermopylae the men of Northampton and the Riflemen had died where they had been posted. Heroism could do no more." Out of about 1200 men, nearly all, save the casualties, fell into the hands of the victors. Every officer seems to have behaved with the utmost possible gallantry, and not least the battalion surgeon, Captain Ward, who stood by his wounded until both he and

CHAPTER V.
Operations from June 10 to July 31.

they fell into the hands of the Germans. Such was the deplorable affair of Nieuport, a small incident in so great a war, and yet one which had an individuality of its own which may excuse this more extended account. The total German advance was 600 yards in depth, upon a front of three-quarters of a mile.

The attack had extended to the eastward upon the farther side of the Geleide Creek, but here the positions were more favourable for defence, as there were supports available and the communications had not been broken. It is a most significant sign of the enormous respect which the German authorities entertained for the British Army, that this limited action in which only two weak British battalions were overwhelmed was solemnly announced by them in their official bulletin to be "a great and magnificent victory." When one remembers how the British in turn would have dismissed so small an action as a mere incident in the campaign, had they been the victors, it is indeed a most memorable tribute. The main cause of the defeat, apart from the faulty position, appears to have been that the infantry took over the new line more quickly than the artillery, and that the French heavies had withdrawn before the British heavies were ready for action. A British officer, afterwards released, was informed by the Germans that they had 182 batteries concentrated upon the position, while there were only 13 ready for the defence.

It was hoped in Germany and feared in Britain that the new position gained by the Germans at the north of the Yser River would enable them to outflank the British defences at Lombardzyde, and to destroy the 97th Brigade, which lay to the north of the river. The situation certainly looked most alarming in the map, and no military critic could have imagined that the position could be held. The British soldier has a way of doing, however, what the lecture-rooms would denounce, and after some very desperate fighting the lines were maintained. The attack was not on so overwhelming a scale as on the left, but it was severe and long continued, from 7.30 P.M. till the evening of July 11. The enemy had at one time won three lines of defence, but they were eventually thrust back, General Shute feeding his fighting line from his reserves until he had the upper hand. The main strain fell upon the 11th Borders and 16th H.L.I., but as the action went on the 17th Highland Light Infantry, 15th Lancashire Fusiliers, and 16th Northumberland Fusiliers were all in turn involved. It was a real infantry fight, often in the dark and sometimes at close grips, and it ended with the line as it was before the attack commenced. The severity of the action may be judged by the fact that the brigade had nearly a thousand casualties. From this time the line remained unchanged until the great Battle for the Flanders Ridges turned the thoughts of both parties to larger issues.

Before we enter upon an account of that terrific and protracted engagement, one should mention a brisk action which was fought by those stark fighters the New Zealand Division, upon the Warneton front, to the immediate south of the Messines area. There is a small ruined village, hardly rising to the dignity of a mention upon the maps, called La Basseville, which was held by the Germans under the very noses of the men with the red hatbands. Upon the night of July 27 the Wellington battalion, a name of good military omen, captured this place with some of its Bavarian garrison. In the early morning the Germans came again with a rush, however, and regained the place. The New Zealanders attacked once more in the night of July 31, so that their venture may appear to have been in connection with the larger operations in the north. Once more the village was captured by the Wellington and Auckland infantry with some fifty more prisoners and seven machine-guns. The Germans lost heavily in killed, and the losses were doubled or trebled by their gallant but unsuccessful counter-attacks, which were undertaken often by such limited groups of men that they seemed the results less of reasoned tactics than of desperation. From this time La Basseville passed into the British system.

This month of July was signalised by the last efforts of the Russian Army so long as it remained a serious force. Under Brusiloff and Korniloff they made an attack upon the Austro-German lines, but after initial successes they were paralysed by the growing disaffection and disorganisation of the soldiery, who had all the want of discipline of the old French republicans without the fiery valour and patriotism. From this time onward Russia played no real military part in the great war, save as the betrayer of Roumania, the deserter of Serbia, and the absorber of such ill-spared supplies as she could get from her former allies.

CHAPTER VI

THE THIRD BATTLE OF YPRES

July 31, 1917

Attack of July 31—Advance of the Guards—Of the Welsh—Capture of Pilkem—Capture of St. Julien by Thirty-ninth Division—Advance of Fifty-fifth Division—Advance of Jacob's Second Corps—General results.

It had been accepted as an axiom at this stage of the war that no great operation could be in the nature of a surprise—an axiom which, like most other axioms, was shown later in the year to have some startling exceptions. To pack the base of the historic Ypres salient with guns, and to assemble within and behind its trenches the storming troops for a great advance was, however, an operation which could not possibly be concealed. British aircraft might have an ascendency in observation, but that did not prevent the German fliers from being both daring and skilful. All camouflage, therefore, was thrown aside, and throughout the month of July Sir Douglas Haig openly assembled his forces for the widening or destruction of the iron bands which had so long constricted us in this northern area. The Fifth Army gathered for the venture, still commanded by Sir Hubert Gough, the victor of Thiepval. On his left,

Chapter VI.

The third Battle of Ypres. July 31.

opposite Bixschoote, on the edge of the inundations, was a French army under General Antoine, a genial giant who impresses those who meet him as a mixture of Porthos and d'Artagnan. The general rôle of the French Army was to cover the British from counter-attack from the north, especially from Houthulst Forest, in the depths of which great reserves might lurk, for it covers no less than 600 acres. Upon the right, and engaged in a subsidiary degree in the operations, was the Second Army, under Sir Herbert Plumer, fresh from the triumph of Messines.

The direction of this new attack against the ridges of Flanders was the logical sequence from the preceding operations of the year. The high ground of the Ancre had been taken late in 1916. The high ground of Vimy fell into British hands in April. In June the Germans had been driven in one strenuous day from the high ground of Messines. The whole line of ridges from end to end was in British hands save only those which girt in Ypres and dominated it from the north and north-east. It is true that these so-called ridges were often little more than undulations, but they meant firmer ground, artillery observation, self-concealment, and everything which makes for military advantage. For these reasons Sir Douglas Haig turned his strength now in that direction. After his successive advances he might say with Wellington: "Knowing well that if we laid our bloody hands upon a town it was fated to fall." The men who took Ciudad Rodrigo or stormed the dreadful breach of Badajos could teach nothing in hardihood and contempt of death to those who carried Guillemont or Ovillers.

In attacking a salient like that of Ypres and in

THE THIRD BATTLE OF YPRES

endeavouring to flatten it out, it is obvious that the efforts must be made at the sides rather than in the centre, since success in the latter case would simply mean a larger salient. Of the two sides of the Ypres salient the success of Messines had already relieved the pressure in the south, and this area was clearly less important than the north, since it was farther from the sea. It was evident that any considerable success upon the northern side would advance the British line towards Bruges, and an occupation of Bruges would surely mean the abandonment by Germany of the Flemish coast. For these reasons the effort of the British was chiefly directed towards the north-east, a tract of ground which was difficult when dry, but which became grotesque in its difficulties when it rained and the small low-lying streams or "beeks" which meandered through it spread out into broad marshy bottoms. These all-pervading morasses, when ploughed up with innumerable shell-holes, were destined to form an almost insuperable military obstacle. In attacking at such a point Sir Douglas could only hope that the weather would abide as a neutral, but as a fact, now as so often before, its action was bitterly hostile. Up to the very day of the advance it smiled deceitfully only to break into a month of rain from the very hour of the attack. If Berlin needs one more monument in her meretricious "Sieges-Allee," she may well erect one to the weather, which has saved her cause as surely as the geese of old saved Rome.

So notorious were the British preparations, culminating in the usual terrific bombardment, that the approaching conflict was discussed in the German papers weeks before it occurred. Their preparations

CHAPTER VI.

The third Battle of Ypres.

July 31.

CHAPTER VI.

The third Battle of Ypres.
July 31.

had been gigantic, and took a new form which called for corresponding ingenuity upon the side of the stormers if it was to be successfully countered. The continuous trench had, save in the old system, been discarded as offering too evident a mark for the shattering guns. The ground was held by numerous disconnected trenches, and strong points arranged in depth rather than in breadth, so that the whole front should form one shock-absorber which would yield at first, but must at the last bring any pressure to a stand. Scattered thickly among these small posts there were concrete forts, not unlike the Martello towers of our ancestors, but sunk deeply into the ground, so as to present a small mark to gun-fire. These forts were made of cement and iron with walls so enormously thick that a direct hit from anything less than a six-inch gun could not possibly harm them. The garrisons of each were composed of twenty or thirty men, with two or three machine-guns. There was usually no visible opening, the entrance being approached by a tunnel, and the windows mere slits which gave a broad traverse for a machine-gun. They were contrivances which might well hold up an army, and it was a fine example of British adaptability as well as courage that they were able to make progress against them. The days of the gallant bull-headed rush were over, and the soldiers had learned in a cruel school that the fighting man must be wary as well as brave.

At four o'clock in the morning, in the first grey light of a rainy morning, under a canopy of grey sweeping clouds, and in a fog-girt landscape of bedraggled fields and brown patches of mire, the French and British infantry sprang forward with splendid

THE THIRD BATTLE OF YPRES 137

alacrity upon this dangerous venture which should culminate in taking the last dominant ridge upon the British front from those who had held them so long.

The French attacked upon the extreme left of the line, and had an extremely difficult task, which they accomplished with a dash and spirit which won the unstinted admiration of their British comrades. In front of them was the canal, but they had succeeded in throwing across some troops in the days before the battle. It was fitting that they should advance the line in this sector, for they were starting from the very spot to which their comrades had been pushed in the poison-gas battle of April 22, 1915, more than two years before. The ground in front of them was very marshy, and as a background to the German position loomed the great forest of Houthulst, which was known to be a strong gun position and place of arms. It was subjected, however, to such a shattering bombardment that it was nearly silent when the attack advanced, and the French poilus, pushing rapidly on from point to point, seized the village of Steenstraate, and finally the larger village of Bixschoote, establishing their line well to the north of that point. It was a most valorous advance, and if no detail can be given of it save this passing mention, it is because it belongs to that weighty and wonderful volume which shall record the glorious military deeds of France, a volume which can only be written with proper appreciation and knowledge by a French pen.

The British line of battle was formed by five corps, the Fourteenth (Cavan) to the north, the Eighteenth (Maxse) upon its right, the Nineteenth (Watts) upon the right of that, the Second (Jacob) came next, and then upon the southern edge of the

Chapter VI.

The third Battle of Ypres.

July 31.

CHAPTER VI.
The third Battle of Ypres.
July 31.

area, and hardly engaged in the main fighting, was the Tenth (Morland). Each corps had two divisions in the line and two in reserve. We will take each in turn, starting from the north. It should be noted that the four first corps made up Gough's Fifth Army, and that the Tenth Corps was the only part of Plumer's Army to be engaged.

Cavan's Fourteenth Corps was next to the French, with the Guards in immediate touch with our allies, and the Thirty-eighth Welsh Division upon its right. The Twentieth and the Twenty-ninth Divisions were in support. We shall now follow the splendid advance of the Guards, a division which more and more as the war progressed reasserted its position as the very cream of the Army.

On the days preceding the action a number of bridges had been thrown across the canal, and the attacking brigades had been passed over this impediment, so that they were able to deploy rapidly and escape the German barrage which fell, for the most part, behind them. This most useful work was carried out by the 1st Guards Brigade, especially by the 3rd Coldstream and 1st Irish, who got across the first. This brigade was relieved, and on the day of battle the 3rd Brigade was upon the left in close liaison with the French, while the 2nd Brigade was on the right with their flank touching the Welshmen. Two "Hate Companies," as they were called, were thrown out on the divisional front, whose task it was to make special discharges of oil drums, thermite, and other missiles which might smooth the way for the advance of the infantry. At 4.24 the whistles of fate were heard shrilly all along the line, and the Guards rose up from

THE THIRD BATTLE OF YPRES 139

their wet assembly ditches, and went forward in their usual sedate and inexorable fashion. The front line of battle of the two brigades, counting from the French flank, were the 1st Welsh, 1st Grenadiers, 2nd Irish, and 1st Scots, while behind them in the second line were their comrades of the 2nd Scots, 4th Grenadiers, 1st Coldstream, and 3rd Grenadiers. Each platoon of the Irish carried a green flag adorned with the Irish harp.

CHAPTER VI.

The third Battle of Ypres. July 31.

The attack at first was so strong or the opposition so weak that in ten minutes the first-line objective had been gained. From this point the shock-absorber system began to act, a system which must prevail save where the attackers know when to suspend their effort so that the spring of resistance is never pressed back to the uttermost. The British generals had learned this lesson and the aims of any one day's battle were strictly limited. Thus, although the losses grew and the difficulties increased, the Guards were well within their powers, in gradually pushing forwards to the Steenbeek stream, which was the extreme limit assigned to them. As they advanced sections were told off to deal with the various concrete forts and other strong points, a method of attack which gave great scope for the initiative of individual junior officers or non-commissioned officers, and which was fruitful in acts of valour. About six o'clock the German machine-guns in Hey Wood held up the line for a time, and the 2nd Brigade had the chagrin of seeing some German guns limbering up and withdrawing in front of them, while their own barrage fell as an invisible steel curtain which covered them from seizure. It was remarked generally of the British barrage that though extremely accurate as a rule, it

Chapter VI.

The third Battle of Ypres. July 31.

still consisted too much of shrapnel and not enough of high explosives, so that it had not the shattering and uprooting effect which was needful. The Germans had read the lessons differently, for at this period of the war their barrage consisted almost entirely of 5·9 " crumps " with a small admixture of shrapnel.

By the early afternoon the front lines of the Guards had fulfilled their programme, and a number of prisoners, including the commanding officer and adjutant of the 73rd Hanoverians, had been conducted to the rear. The losses of the Guards had not been excessive, save in the right flank battalions, especially the 1st Scots, but they included many valuable officers killed or wounded, including Colonel Greer of the 2nd Irish, Colonel Romilly of the 1st Scots, and Colonel Lord Gort of the 4th Grenadiers. Among many deeds of valour which were added to the records of the division upon that morning there may be mentioned that of the heroic surgeon David Lees, who was decorated for passing five times through the barrage carrying wounded, and of the brave Irish priest, Father Knapp, who absolutely refused to take shelter when his men were exposed, and met his death rather than leave them. It is invidious, however, to mention brave men where all were brave. About three o'clock the 1st Guards Brigade passed through the ranks of their comrades and carried the advance forward to its limit. The order of their advance from the left was the 2nd Coldstream, with the 2nd Grenadiers on the right, while the 3rd Coldstream and 1st Irish took the corresponding places in the second line. The 2nd Grenadiers lost heavily from a flank fire, its difficulties and those of all the right flank being increased by the fact that the railway line,

THE THIRD BATTLE OF YPRES 141

dotted with German strong points, ran as the boundary between divisions. Captain Ritchie, of Loos fame, was among the casualties. The Grenadiers got so far ahead that the protective barrage became thin and erratic, hardly existing in many places. The whole brigade moved forward in close touch with the 113th Brigade of Welshmen upon their right. The latter after the final objective was reached were shelled for a time out of their position, so that the Irish and Grenadiers had to throw back a defensive flank, but the Welsh with dogged spirit came back to their work and re-established their line late in the evening. Their work will presently be described, but so far as the Guards are concerned it may be added that, with the help of the 55th and 76th Field Company R.E., all they took they kept, although the physical surroundings were appalling, for they found themselves for three days lying on the forward slope of a low ridge under heavy rain in deep puddles of water, exposed to German shelling and to the constant stinging of invisible German snipers. No conditions could have been more trying, but the Guards stuck it out with a quiet patient discipline which was as fine as the valour of their assault. "We are just lying in a snipe bog in the rain," wrote an Irish officer. Due dispositions were made for relief among the three brigades, and the line was held until a farther advance should become possible—an event which was continually postponed by the incredible weather.

Passing to the 38th Welsh Division upon the right of the Guards, their battle line consisted of the 113th Brigade upon the left, consisting entirely of battalions of Welsh Fusiliers, while the

CHAPTER VI.

The third Battle of Ypres.

July 31.

CHAPTER VI.
The third Battle of Ypres.
July 31.

114th Brigade, formed from the Welsh Regiment, was on the right. The order of the foremost battalions taken from the left was the 16th and 13th Welsh Fusiliers, with the 13th and 10th Welsh. The experiences of the division upon its advance were, as might be expected, not unlike those of the Guards. "It was still dark," says one graphic correspondent, "and all we had to guide us was our barrage moving forward like a living line of fire, from left to right as far as the eye could see." The first objective was captured with little loss, a fair number of prisoners being taken in the Caesar Support Trench. In attacking the second objectives the reserve line came through the front one, so that the order of the troops, taken again from the left in the 114th Brigade, was the 15th and 14th Welsh, while in the 113th Brigade, which had a less difficult task, there was a mere change of companies in the units already engaged. The opposition now became fiercer and the losses more severe. Marsouin Farm, and Stray Farm on the right, and the village of Pilkem upon the left poured bullets upon the advancing infantry, who slipped from shell-hole to shell-hole, taking such cover as they could, but resolutely pushing onwards. Again and again the machine-gun forts were isolated, surrounded, and compelled to surrender. The Welshmen had reached their second objective in the scheduled time. The 15th Welsh Fusiliers were now pushed into the firing-line upon the left, and the advance went forward. A gap had formed between the Welshmen and the Highlanders of the Fifty-first Division upon their right. In this gap lay Rudolph Farm, spitting fire from every cranny and window. A platoon of the 15th Welsh turned aside from their

THE THIRD BATTLE OF YPRES 143

path and captured or killed all who were in the German post. To the immediate left of this point lay another stronghold called Iron Cross. This was rushed by the 14th Welsh, at considerable loss to themselves, but twenty of the garrison were bayoneted, forty captured, and three machine-guns secured. Just beyond the Iron Cross was a German dressing-station which yielded forty more prisoners.

The 15th Welsh Fusiliers on the left had in the meanwhile a severe ordeal, for so heavy a fire poured upon them from the clump of trees known as Battery Copse that they were left with hardly an officer and with their protective barrage rapidly receding into the distance. The men were staggered for a time, but struggled forward again with fine resolution, and at last established themselves upon the same line as Iron Cross.

Whilst the fighting line had been getting forward as described, the 113th carrying among other obstacles the village of Pilkem, and both brigades, but especially the 114th, bursting through three separate battalions of the famous Käferlein regiment of the Guards, the reserve brigade had been keeping in close attendance in spite of the German barrage. Now two battalions of the 115th Brigade were slipped into the front, the 11th S.W. Borderers and the 17th Welsh Fusiliers. These fine fresh troops took up the running and made for the final objective, which was the Steenbeek stream. This was successfully reached, in spite of the ever-growing resistance, and the final line was formed with posts upon the farther side of the Steenbeek. Shortly after three o'clock a strong counter-attack broke upon this Welsh line, and for a time the Borderers were forced

CHAPTER VI.

The third Battle of Ypres. July 31.

CHAPTER VI.
The third Battle of Ypres.
July 31.

from the post at "Au bon gîte" which they had occupied and were thrown across the river. Aided by a good barrage of artillery and machine-guns the attack was finally beaten off, about a hundred Germans who had charged through the barrage being shot down by rifle fire. After this there was no attempt upon this day to disturb the new front of the Welsh Division, though upon August 1 in the afternoon there was some sign of a counter-attack, which was broken up by the British artillery before it could materialise. From then onwards the weather made further operations impossible. On August 6 the Twentieth Division took over this new line.

The advance of the Welsh Division, including as it did the two exploits of capturing the strongly fortified village of Pilkem, and of utterly scattering three battalions of one of the most famous regiments in the Prussian service, was worthy of the great reputation which they had won at Mametz Wood. The way in which the men followed up the barrage and tackled the concrete forts was especially worthy of mention. The Cockchafers mentioned above were the dandy regiment of Berlin, and their utter defeat at the hands of a brigade of the New Army must indeed have been bitter to those who remembered the cheap jests which had been made at that Army's expense. Four hundred prisoners from this regiment found their way to the cages. Altogether 700 prisoners were taken, nearly all Guardsmen from the Third Division. The Welsh had about 1300 casualties, including Colonels Radice, Norman, and Taylor. Among the dead was one, Private Ellis H. Evans of the 15th Welsh Fusiliers, whose position and importance were peculiarly Cymric, since he was the winner

THE THIRD BATTLE OF YPRES 145

of the Bardic chair, the highest honour of the Eisteddfod. An empty Bardic chair was afterwards erected over his grave. It is only in Wales that the traditions of Athens are preserved, and contests of the body and of the mind are conducted in public with equal honour to the victors.

To the south of Cavan's Fourteenth Corps lay Maxse's Eighteenth Corps, extending from the right of the Thirty-eighth Division to a point opposite to the village of St. Julien. Maxse's Eighteenth Corps consisted of four divisions, the Fifty-first supported by the Eleventh being upon the left, and the Thirty-ninth supported by the Forty-eighth upon the right. South of the St. Julien front they connected up with Watts' Nineteenth Corps to the south. It should be mentioned that the whole corps' front was occupied for some weeks before the battle by the 33rd Brigade, who at great strain and loss to themselves held this long stretch in the face of constant gassings and shellings, in order that the attacking divisions might be able to practise for the day of battle.

Taking the narrative once more from the north, the Fifty-first Highland Territorial Division (Harper), a unit which has seen an extraordinary amount of service during the war, advanced with the usual dash of these magnificent clansmen. Everything went down before their disciplined rush. There was no particular geographical point in the area which they conquered, but their whole front was covered by fortified posts, some of which fell with ease, while others put up a considerable resistance. Prominent among the latter was Rudolph Farm, which was on the line between the Thirty-eighth and Fifty-first Divisions, pouring a flanking fire upon each and holding

CHAPTER VI.

The third Battle of Ypres. July 31.

L

up the left of the Fifty-first. This post was eventually stormed by the Welsh. Finally the Highlanders, clearing the ground carefully behind them, reached their full day's objective, which was the line of the Steenbeek. Here they dug themselves in and beat off an enemy counter-attack.

On the right of the Highland Territorial Division was the Thirty-ninth Division, consisting of the 116th Sussex Brigade, the 117th Rifle and Sherwood Foresters Brigade, and the 118th mixed Territorial Brigade. The attack was undertaken by the 117th Brigade upon the north in touch with the Highlanders, and the 116th upon the south. Both of these brigades got forward in excellent style, but the position was strong and the losses were heavy. Canadian Farm was taken by the 117th Brigade, and the 116th also attained its full objective. Finally, the spare brigade, the 118th, passed through the ranks of the others, and fought their way into St. Julien, where no British foot had been placed since April 24, 1915, when the heroic remnant of the Canadians had been cut off and overpowered in its streets.

The operation would have been entirely successful had it not been for the attempt to advance beyond the village. This was carried out by the same brigade, the 118th, with the 6th Cheshires upon the right, the 1st Herts in the centre, and the 4/5th Black Watch upon the left. The Cambridge Battalion was in support. The attack was extraordinarily gallant, but was held up by uncut wire and very severely punished. No permanent gain was effected, but greater constancy has seldom been seen. The Hertfordshire men were particularly fine. Their Colonel Page and their

THE THIRD BATTLE OF YPRES 147

adjutant were both killed, and every combatant officer was on the casualty list, so that it was the serjeant-major who withdrew the 120 men who had gone forth as a strong battalion. The doctor was wounded, and only the chaplain was left, who distinguished himself by being the last man to recross the Steenbeek with a wounded man slung over his shoulder. Such was the experience of the Herts, and that of the Cheshires and of the Highlanders differed only in detail.

Chapter VI.
The third Battle of Ypres.
July 31.

A counter-attack along the whole corps' front was beaten back upon the evening of July 31, but the concentration of German artillery upon St. Julien was so terrific that it was found necessary next day to withdraw the 1st Cambs who garrisoned the village, the adjacent bridge over the Steenbeek being retained. Next day the village was reoccupied.

The Thirty-ninth Division, very hard hit by its victorious but strenuous service, was relieved upon August 4, after a terrible four days of constant rainfall and shell-fall, by the Forty-eighth South Midland Territorial Division, while a few days later their Highland comrades were relieved by the Eleventh Division. So battered was the Thirty-ninth Division that it was taken forthwith out of the line and its place in the corps was filled by the Fifty-eighth.

To return to the order of the advance, Watts' Nineteenth Corps, which was the next one to the south, consisted of the Fifty-fifth West Lancashire Territorials with the Thirty-sixth Ulsters upon the left, while the Fifteenth Scottish Division supported by the Fourteenth Light Division were on the right. Of these we will deal first with the attack of the men of Lancashire.

The advance was made by the 166th Brigade upon the left, and by the 165th upon the right. The first German line was rapidly carried, and the only serious fighting was at the strong point known as Pommern Redoubt, which held out for some time but was eventually captured about 10 A.M. The 166th Brigade, which covered the space between St. Julien in the north and the Wieltje—Gravenstafel Road in the south, was led by the 5th King's Royal Lancasters and the 5th North Lancashires, while the 165th Brigade, with their left upon the road and their right in touch with the Fifteenth Division, were composed entirely of battalions of the King's Liverpool Regiment, the 5th and 6th in front, the 7th and 9th in the second line. This brigade upon being counter-attacked used its liquid fire apparatus with good results. "From under the mantle of fire ran blazing Huns with heartrending cries, but I cannot say we had any sympathy for them. We remembered John Lynn and the other Lancashire lads who had been gassed and roasted round Ypres in the battles of other days, and we felt that the Huns were only being paid back in their own coin." The losses in the first stages of the advance were not severe and came chiefly from the machine-gun fire of the three strongholds of Bank Farm, Spree Farm, and Pommern Castle. The latter was very formidable, spouting bullets on three sides, so that the 165th Brigade was held up by it for a time. In the second stage of the attack the 164th Brigade with the 4th North Lancashires on their right and the 5th Lancs Fusiliers upon their left pushed through the ranks of their comrades and carried the advance on, taking Hindu Cott and Gallipoli, and finally reaching the

THE THIRD BATTLE OF YPRES 149

most advanced objective, whence they pushed out patrols to Toronto and Aviatik Farms. They were exposed to strong counter-attacks as will be shown.

This fine advance had been matched by Reed's Fifteenth Scots Division on the right. Of their conduct that day it can only be said that it was worthy of the reputation which they had gained at Loos and at the Somme. The Scottish bands who fought under Gustavus Adolphus in the Thirty Years' War left a renown in Germany which lingers yet, and it is certain that some memory of the terrible "Hell-hags," as they were called by the German soldiers, will preserve the record of Scotch military prowess so long as any of their adversaries are alive to speak of it. Two brigades led the advance, the 44th upon the right and the 46th upon the left. As in the case of the Lancashire men upon their left the first stages of the attack were easy. On getting past the German line, however, the full blast of fire struck the infantry from Douglas Villa, Frezenberg Redoubt, Pommern Castle, Low Farm, Frost House, and Hill 37. By ten o'clock, however, the second objectives had been taken. The 45th Brigade now pushed through, and though held up on the right by Bremen Redoubt, they attained the full objective upon the left, and kept in close touch with the 164th Brigade. The position, however, was perilous and, as it proved, impossible, for Watts' Corps was now well ahead of either of its neighbours. About two o'clock a violent German drive struck up against the exposed flank of the Fifty-fifth Division, causing great losses, especially to the 4th Royal Lancasters, some of whom were cut off. Another counter-attack beat against the left of the enfeebled

CHAPTER VI.

The third Battle of Ypres.
July 31.

45th Brigade. As a result the remains of the four front line battalions were pushed back some hundreds of yards, but at 5 P.M. the edge was taken off the attack and the German infantry were seen to be retiring. About I P.M. next day this attack was renewed down the line of the Ypres—Roulers Railway, and again the Fifteenth Division bore a heavy strain which forced it back once to the Frezenberg Ridge, but again it flooded forward and reoccupied its line. So severe had been the exertions and the losses of these two divisions that they were drawn out of the line as soon as possible, their places being taken by the 36th Ulsters upon the left and the 16th Irish upon the right.

We now come to Jacob's Second Corps lying to the south of the Nineteenth with its left resting upon the Ypres—Roulers Railway. It contained no less than five divisions, three of which were in the line and two in support. Those in the line, counting from the north, were the Eighth Regular Division with its left on the railway and its right at Sanctuary Wood, the Thirtieth Lancashire Division in the centre, and the Twenty-fourth Division opposite Shrewsbury Forest with its right resting upon the Zillebeke—Zandvoorde Road. In support was the Twenty-fifth Division upon the left, and the Eighteenth Division upon the right.

The Eighth Division advanced upon a two-brigade front, the 23rd upon the left and the 24th upon the right. Many strong posts including several woods faced the assailants, and from the beginning the resistance was very obstinate. None the less, in spite of numerous checks and delays, the advance was carried forward for half a mile and

THE THIRD BATTLE OF YPRES 151

captured the whole of the front line trenches without much loss, for the German barrage was slow and late whereas the British artillery support was excellent. Indeed it may be remarked that one of the features of the battle was the remarkable preparation by which General Jacob, with the aid of his two artillery leaders, managed to place nearly a thousand pieces into a line which was fully exposed to enemy observation. It was done at a considerable loss of men and guns, but it was absolutely essential to the advance.

Chapter VI.
The third Battle of Ypres.
July 31.

The low rising called the Bellewaarde Ridge was the first objective of the division and was easily taken. The two magnificent Regular brigades swept onwards with a perfect order which excited the admiration of spectators. As they passed over the curve of the ground they came into heavy fire from the farther rise near Westhoek, but it neither slowed nor quickened their gait. Hooge, Bellewaarde Lake, The White Château, all the old landmarks were passed. When the full objective had been reached after more than half a mile of steady advance the 25th Brigade passed through the ranks of their comrades and carried on until, as they neared Westhoek, they ran into a very heavy flank fire from Glencorse Wood in the south. This was in the area of the southern division, so that the 25th Brigade were aware that their flank was open and that the Thirtieth Division had not come abreast of them. They halted therefore just to the west of Westhoek, and as their flank remained open all day they had to content themselves with consolidating the ground that they had won and beating back two counter-attacks. The left of the division kept their station well forward upon the

152 THE BRITISH CAMPAIGN, 1917

CHAPTER VI.
The third Battle of Ypres.
July 31.

Ypres—Roulers Railway, with their left in close touch with the Scotsmen to the north. The division was relieved next day by the Twenty-fifth Division. All the battalions had done great things in the action, but some specially fine work was put in by the 1st Sherwood Foresters upon the left of the advance of the 24th Brigade. At one point it was necessary to cut through wire which held up the advance, and the gallantry of the wire-cutting detachment was such that the dying continued to snip at the strands, while even the dead contrived to fall forward in an attempt to screen with their bodies their living comrades. The losses were very heavy, but the historic old 45th Foot, the "old Stubborns" of the Peninsula, never in its long career carried through more gallantly in so fierce a fight. The 2nd Northamptons also increased their high reputation upon this arduous day, during which they took many prisoners.

The Thirtieth Division, which consisted, as will be remembered, to a large extent of "Pal" battalions from Liverpool and Manchester, advanced to the south of the Eighth. Sanctuary Wood and other strong points lay in front of the 90th and 21st Brigades which provided the first lines of stormers. The resistance was strong, the fire was heavy, and the losses were considerable, so that the assailants were held up and were unable to do more than carry the front trenches, whence they repulsed repeated counter-attacks during the rest of the day. In the initial advance the 2nd Scots Fusiliers, that phoenix of a battalion, so often destroyed and so often renewed, wandered in the dusk of the morning away from its allotted path and got as far north as Château Wood in the path of the 24th Brigade. This caused

THE THIRD BATTLE OF YPRES 153

some dislocation of the front line, but the Manchester men on the right of the Scots pushed on and struck the Menin Road as far forward as Clapham Junction. The 21st Brigade in the meantime had to pass a great deal of difficult woody ground and met so much opposition that they lost the barrage, that best friend of the stormer. Bodmin Copse was reached, but few penetrated to the eastern side of it. The strong point of Stirling Castle was, however, taken by the Manchesters of the 90th. It was the line of Dumbarton Lakes which proved fatal to the advance, and though two battalions of the 89th and finally the East Anglians of the 53rd Brigade from the supporting Eighteenth Division were thrown into the fight, the latter winning forward for some distance, they found that it was finally rather a question of holding ground than gaining it. The ultimate line, therefore, was across from Clapham Junction. Since neither of the divisions on either side was in any way held up, save perhaps at one point, it is probable that the southern advance would have been more successful but for the limited advance of the Thirtieth Division.

Upon August 2, much exhausted, they were drawn out of the line and the Eighteenth Division took their place, and held the Clapham Junction and Glencorse Wood, which their own 53rd Brigade had largely been instrumental in winning, against repeated attacks.

Upon the right of the Thirtieth Division was the Twenty-fourth, a famous fighting unit which was the only division able to boast that it had been present at Vimy Ridge, Messines, and Ypres—three great battles in the one year. The ground in front

CHAPTER VI.

The third Battle of Ypres.
July 31.

of this division was broken and woody, including Shrewsbury Forest and other natural obstacles. None the less good progress was made, especially upon the right, while the left was only retarded by the fact of the limited advance in the north. The advance was made upon a three-brigade front, the 17th upon the left, the 73rd in the centre, and the 72nd upon the right. The 17th, advancing with that fine battalion the 3rd Rifle Brigade alone in the front line, carried all before it at first, but found both flanks exposed and was compelled to halt. The 73rd, led by the 2nd Leicesters and the 7th Northamptons, were held up by a strong point called Lower Star Post in front of them. On the right the 72nd, with the 8th Queen's and the North Staffords in the lead, gained the house called the Grunenburg Farm, which marked the line of their immediate objective. There they dug in and held firmly, connecting up with the left of Plumer's Army to the south. Several unsuccessful counter-attacks were made in the succeeding days upon this point, in one of which on August 5 Colonel de la Fontaine of the 9th East Surreys was killed.

If the attack of the Second Corps upon this and other occasions met with limited success, it is to be remembered that the long clear slope leading to Glencorse and Inverness Woods upon either side of the Menin Road represented as impossible a terrain for an advancing force as could be imagined. When finally these woods were won, officers who stood among the tree-stumps and looked back were amazed to think that such ground could have been taken, and were filled with surprise that the Ypres salient could have been held so long under an observation

THE THIRD BATTLE OF YPRES 155

from which nothing could be concealed. When such positions are held by troops which have a world-wide reputation, in concrete fortifications, one should be surprised, not that the assailants should have failures but that they should have the dour resolution which brought them at last to success.

All the four corps already mentioned, covering the front from the junction with the French in the north to Shrewsbury Forest in the south, belonged to Gough's Fifth Army. Of Plumer's Second Army only a portion of the extreme left, consisting of Morland's Tenth Corps, was engaged upon July 31. The flank unit, the Forty-first English Division, was in the front line opposite Basseville, with the New Zealanders upon their right. There was no intention to advance the line to any distance in this locality, but the whole task assigned to the troops was completely carried out, and the front was pushed forward until it was level with the right of the Twenty-fourth Division. It has been explained by Sir Douglas Haig, however, that the attack in this quarter had never any serious intentions, and that it was in the nature of a feint in order to distribute the German reserve of men and guns. None the less the ground captured by the 123rd Brigade of the Forty-first Division represented a substantial gain, including the village of Hollebeke and all the broken and difficult country to the north of the bend of the Ypres—Comines Canal and east of Battle Wood. The advance along this portion of the front varied from 200 to 300 yards, while the New Zealanders at the right of the line covered the short area assigned to them in their usual workmanlike fashion, taking after a short fight the hamlet of La Basseville. On

CHAPTER VI.

The third Battle of Ypres.

July 31.

156 THE BRITISH CAMPAIGN, 1917

CHAPTER VI.
The third Battle of Ypres.
July 31.

the right of the New Zealanders were the Australians, whose movement, in accordance with the general plan was a small one, including the capture of a ruined windmill opposite their position. This was captured, retaken, and captured once again in a spirited little fight, and August 1 saw more fighting in this sector under very trying conditions of weather and ground.

We have now briefly reviewed the work of each of the twelve divisions which were in line upon the 31st of July. In some places success was absolute, in some it was partial, in none was there failure. Speaking generally it may be said that the Thirty-ninth, Fifty-first, Welsh, and Guards, had captured their full objectives, including the villages of St. Julien, Pilkem, and the Pilkem Ridge; that the Fifty-fifth and Fifteenth had carried the first and second lines, with the villages of Verlorenhoek and Frezenberg and the all-important ridge; finally that the units upon their right had captured the German first lines, including Hooge, Hollebeke, Stirling Castle, and a line of woods. Apart from the gain of important and dominant positions, 6000 prisoners and 133 officers were taken, together with 25 guns, exclusive of those which had been captured by General Antoine to the north. The progress of the French had been admirable, and they had not only reached their full objectives but had gone beyond them and seized the village of Bixschoote, driving back one severe German counter-attack which surged up to the point of junction between them and the Guards. With such results the first day of the third Battle of Ypres was undoubtedly a British victory, but it was a victory which was absolutely complete

THE THIRD BATTLE OF YPRES

in the north, and incomplete in the south. Only one British disaster occurred during the day, and that was in the appearance of that constant and formidable ally of the Central Powers, the autumn rain. That night it began, and for many weeks it continued in a dreary downpour upon a land which at the best of times is water-laden and soft. For two months to come it may be said that operations were really impossible, and that if they were occasionally driven forward by the fiery determination of the British leaders, they were undertaken at such a desperate disadvantage that large results were out of the question. Impassable mud and unfordable craters covered the whole German front, and a swimming collar might well have been added to those many appliances with which the patient British soldier was already burdened.

Chapter VI.

The third Battle of Ypres.

July 31.

CHAPTER VII

THE THIRD BATTLE OF YPRES

August 1 to September 6

Dreadful weather—German reaction—Attack of August 16—Advance of Cavan's Corps—Capture of Langemarck—Dreadful losses of the two Irish Divisions—Failure in the south—Splendid field-gunners—The Forty-second Division upon September 6.

<small>Chapter VII.
The third Battle of Ypres.
Aug. 1 to Sept. 6.</small>

FROM the evening of July 31 till that of August 1, there were intermittent and sporadic German attacks along the whole of the new line, which were the more dangerous as the wretched weather made it impossible for the aircraft to operate and the artillery support was therefore unreliable. None the less, the wet and weary infantry huddling in the puddles and ditches were not to be forced back. Only at St. Julien, as already described, was there a temporary loss of ground. In this quarter, the Thirty-ninth Division, especially the 118th Brigade, sustained very heavy losses, some of the battalions being almost annihilated for military purposes. For days in succession they lay in improvised trenches sodden and cold in the pitiless rain, and when the rising waters drove them out they were shot down by the enemy. None the less, the ground was held and the abandoned village was regained.

THE THIRD BATTLE OF YPRES 159

Another point at which the German reaction was particularly severe upon August 1 was near Bremen Redoubt and the Roulers Railway. Here at 3.30 P.M. the enemy attacked with great valour, the blow falling chiefly upon the 24th Brigade on the left of the Eighth and the 44th on the right of the Fifteenth Divisions. The 10th Gordons, 2nd Northamptons, and 1st Sherwood Foresters were for a time fighting for their lives, the regimental staff of the Gordons having to defend the burrow which served as Headquarters. The 7th Camerons were also engaged in this desperate conflict which was fought ankle-deep in mud and under driving rain-clouds. Finally a body of Highlanders under Captain Geddes of the Gordons made so fierce a charge that the Germans were driven back and abandoned the attempt in despair. Their advance, however, had been so sudden and so fierce that there was a time when the line was in grave danger. Captain Symon of the Camerons did great work also in the charge which turned the tide. Both Geddes and Symon were decorated for their valour.

From the first day of the battle the front had been quiet in the sector of the Second Corps, save for constant reciprocal bombardments, the Germans endeavouring to hinder consolidation, while the British prepared for an advance upon Glencorse and Inverness Woods. Upon August 10 an attempt was made to carry the line forward, the Twenty-fifth Division advancing upon the left opposite to Westhoek and the Eighteenth Division coming forward upon the right. The operation was a local one, but was attended with some success, the Twenty-fifth reaching their full objective and occupying the village of

CHAPTER VII.

The third Battle of Ypres.
Aug. 1 to Sept. 6.

Westhoek. This attack was carried out by the 74th Brigade, and was a model operation of the kind. Westhoek itself was rushed by the 2nd Irish Rifles, but the 11th Lancashire Fusiliers on the north did equally well, fighting their way to the advanced line and capturing several houses with their garrisons. The 9th North Lancashires had also a very fine day's work, but the 13th Cheshires, coming up in support, lost heavily from the barrage which had been too slow to catch the main attack. None the less the survivors made their way to the extreme line, where they joined up with some 7th Bedfords from the 54th Brigade to the south, and held a covering flank so as to block any attack upon Westhoek. The Cheshires did particularly well in this strenuous day's work, they and the Fusiliers having repeated hand-to-hand fights with the German counter-attacks. At one time a body of the Cheshires were quite cut off, but they held their own with determined bravery until their comrades rescued them. The Eighteenth Division were held up by the heavy flanking fire from Inverness Copse. The left of the advance got into the south-western edge of Glencorse Wood, touching the 74th Brigade south of Westhoek, but the right brigade could not get farther than the road east of Stirling Castle. On the whole, however, it was a good advance, and in the meantime the Twenty-fourth Division had drawn closer to Lower Star Post, the obstinate strong point which had held up the 73rd Brigade upon July 31. The Germans showed their resentment at these new advances by five counter-attacks on the evening of August 10, all of which, especially the last, were strongly pressed. These attacks were most strongly

THE THIRD BATTLE OF YPRES 161

made against the 76th Brigade upon the left, but by the exertions of the 106th and 130th Field Companies Royal Engineers, and their pioneers, the 6th South Wales Borderers, they had consolidated to such an extent that they held out against extreme pressure. The 7th Bedfords and 7th Queens in the front of the Eighteenth Division had also much to endure, and were pushed to the very edge of Glencorse Wood. All day the Irish Riflemen in Westhoek could see the Germans in small bodies dribbling over into the Hannebeek valley in front of them until in the evening a large force had accumulated. From ten in the morning the drift had been going on. The 10th Cheshires and 3rd Worcesters of the 7th Brigade had come up to thicken the attenuated line, but the danger was threatening, and rockets and pigeons were sent up to warn the guns. A very heavy barrage was laid down by them and stopped the attack. The enemy could be seen running for safety in every direction. At the same time an attack broke upon the 11th Lancashire Fusiliers to the north. An isolated house, which was occupied by a small party of this battalion, was so closely attacked that three Germans were shot as they clambered through the windows, but the North Countrymen stood fast, and forty-eight dead were picked up round this post in the morning. This ended the enemy's attempts to recover the lost ground. The fighting had been severe, and the British losses were heavy. For a second time within a year the 13th Cheshires had their commanding officer and every other officer of the battalion upon the casualty list. When one reads such figures one can ask with confidence whether all the exclusiveness of a special

CHAPTER VII.

The third Battle of Ypres.
Aug. 1 to Sept. 6.

M

caste with its codes of honour and appeals to violence can exceed the quiet courage of those civilian gentlemen who undertook the leading of our new armies.

Six field-guns with 8 officers and 300 men were taken in this Westhoek operation. The enemy consisted of the German Fifty-fourth Reserve Division, and all accounts agree that both in defence and in counter-attack their conduct was admirable.

The ground was still very wet and the conditions deplorable, but the advance must be continued at all costs if the preparations were not to be thrown away and winter to find us still within the old pent-house of Ypres. By the end of the second week in August the higher ground was beginning to dry, though the bogs in between were already hardly passable. One more fortnight would be invaluable, but Sir Douglas could not afford to waste another day. Upon August 16 the advance was renewed.

As the original attack had been from a concavity which was almost a semicircle, and as it had encroached upon the German area round the whole circumference, the result was that the front was now too large for simultaneous attack, and the whole of the units of Plumer's Army which had formerly taken part in the battle were now to the south of the storm-area. The line of battle extended from the French positions in the north down to the north-west corner of Inverness Wood. Along this line the four corps of Cavan (Fourteenth), Maxse (Eighteenth), Watts (Nineteenth), and Jacob (Second), were extended in their former order. In each case the divisions which had borne the brunt of July 31 were now in support, while the old supporting divisions were in the line. As before,

THE THIRD BATTLE OF YPRES 163

we will take the corps in their order from the north, premising that after the usual heavy bombardment the attack began at 4.45 in the morning.

Of the French upon the extreme left of the line it can only be said that they did all and more than they were asked to do. With the grand, swift dash which is the characteristic of their infantry they stormed the various fortified farms along the line of the Steenbeek, though some of them held out long after the main lines of our Allies had passed them. The two ends of the Bridge which crosses the stream at the village of Drie-Grachten were secured, and the whole of the peninsula made good.

The front of Cavan's Fourteenth Corps was formed by the grand old Twenty-ninth Division upon the left, and the Twentieth Light Division, the heroes of many fights, upon the right. Both divisions lived up to their highest that day, which means that many a brave man died at his highest to carry on the record. On the whole, the Mebus or pill-boxes, the new German concrete forts, were less effective in the north than in the south, which may have depended upon the general lie of the country which gave them a shorter area of fire. Small bodies of brave men—sometimes a single brave man—managed to get up to them and to silence them by hurling a sudden bomb through the porthole from which the gun protruded.

The advance of the Twenty-ninth Division was begun by crossing in the early dawn the bridges thrown over the Steenbeek. Starting from the line of the stream, the advanced mud-beplastered lines, extending as they crossed country, coalescing as they concentrated upon any obstacle, moved swiftly for-

CHAPTER VII.

The third Battle of Ypres. Aug. 1 to Sept. 6.

wards to their objectives, which were taken in their entirety. Passerelle Farm was carried by the veterans of the Twenty-ninth, and so was Martin's Mill upon the right, many prisoners being sent to the rear. Another heave took them across the grass-grown lines of the abandoned railway and on into the hamlet of Wijdendrift, the line being established well to the north-east of that place.

Whilst the Twenty-ninth Division had made this fine advance upon the left, the Twentieth had done equally well upon the right, and had ended their brilliant attack by storming after a short but sharp contest the village of Langemarck, that old battle centre of 1914.

The start of the attack was as fine as its execution, for the two brigades were marshalled into their positions in pitch darkness upon ground which was bewildering in its badness, close under the untaken redoubt of Au Bon Gite, whose garrison at any moment might give the alarm. So silent was the operation that the enemy was utterly ignorant of it, though they kept up a continual machine-gun fire all night which made the assemblage even more difficult. In the early dawn the German fort was rushed by two companies of the 11th Rifle Brigade under Captain Slade.

Then keeping within thirty yards of the barrage the attack moved forward as best it might through the swamps. The 60th Brigade was on the right and the 61st upon the left. The latter had never yet failed to carry its objective, and now it surged through the village or Langemarck and out at the farther side. The 12th King's Liverpool with the 7th Battalion of the Sussex, Durham, and

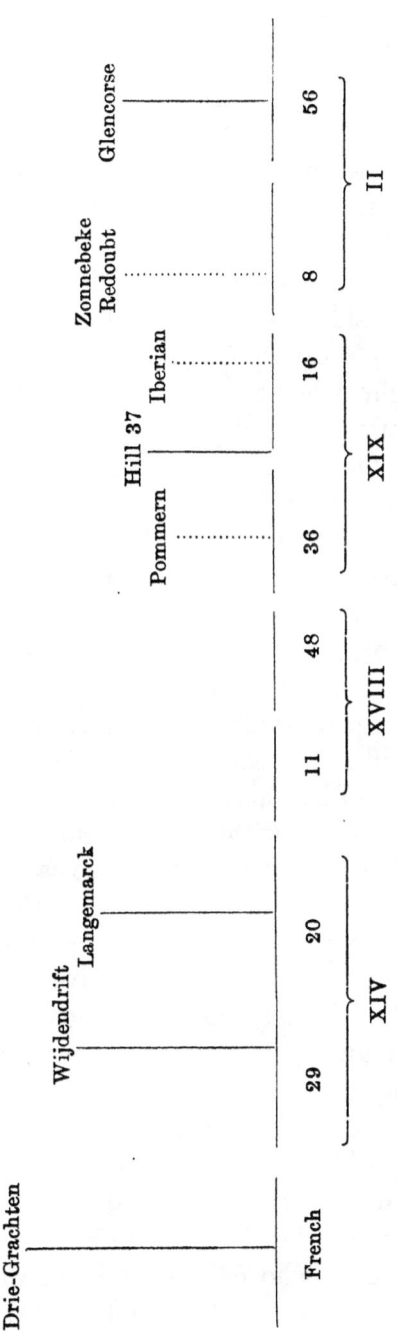

LINE OF BATTLE
August 16, 1917

166   THE BRITISH CAMPAIGN, 1917

CHAPTER VII.
The third Battle of Ypres.
Aug. 1 to Sept. 6.

Yorkshire Light Infantry were the heroes of this exploit. The German colonel commanding the 3rd Battalion 261st Regiment, and a crowd of very shaken prisoners from the 79th Prussian Reserve Division were picked out of the ruins. On the right the 60th Brigade had made an equally fine advance, the King's Royal Rifles being on the flank in touch with the 12th King's Liverpool, with the 6th Shropshires on their right, while the 6th Oxford and Bucks cleared up the numerous pill-boxes at Au Bon Gite on the banks of the Steenbeek. There were many casualties in the advance, including Colonel Prioleau of the Rifle Brigade, caused chiefly by the fire of the murderous Mebus which studded the ground. These were engaged by small groups of men, specially trained for the work, who frequently, by their cool, purposeful courage, succeeded in silencing what would seem to be an impenetrable stronghold. Sergeant Cooper of the Rifles attacked one of these places with twelve men, and had his whole party shot down. None the less, he closed with it, and firing through the loop-hole with a borrowed revolver, he caused the surrender of the garrison of forty men with seven guns, winning his V.C. Such deeds were done all along the line, and without them the advance must have been held up. Finally the 60th Brigade established themselves upon the line of Langemarck, in touch with the captors of the village, but in the late afternoon a heavy German attack broke in between the King's Liverpools and the Rifles, annihilating the left flank Company of the latter battalion, which fought desperately to the end under Captain Dove, who was among those who fell. So critical was the situation at one time that a defensive flank 200 yards

THE THIRD BATTLE OF YPRES 167

in length was held by an officer and fifteen men, with hardly any cartridges in their pouches. Touch was kept, however, between the two Brigades, and before evening they had dug in and consolidated the new position. There had been victory along all this front, and by sunset the whole of the objectives of the Fourteenth Corps, with the exception of a small length of trench to the north-east of Langemarck, were in the hands of Cavan's infantry.

Maxse's Eighteenth Corps was formed by the Eleventh Division upon the left, and the Forty-eighth South Midland Territorials upon the right. The advance was over the Langemarck — Zonnebeke Road, and on over broken Mebus-studded country with no village nor even any farm-house to give a name and dignity to the considerable gain of ground. The advance was, though not complete, of great tactical importance, as it screened the flank of the successful corps in the North.

Brilliant success had marked the operations of the Fourteenth Corps, and modified success those of the Eighteenth. In the case of the four gallant divisions which formed the front of the Nineteenth and Second Corps, it can hardly be said that they had any gains, while their losses were always heavy, and in some cases simply disastrous. Yet, conditions of weather, and ground and position being what they were, it was impossible to impute a shadow of blame to officers or men, who faced a difficult and often an impossible task with the spirit of heroes. To show how desperate that task was, and the extraordinary punishment which was endured by the infantry, the narrative of the Sixteenth and Thirty-sixth Divisions which formed Watts' Corps may be told at greater length.

Chapter VII.

The third Battle of Ypres.

Aug. 1 to Sept. 6.

168 THE BRITISH CAMPAIGN, 1917

CHAPTER VII.

The third Battle of Ypres.
Aug. 1 to Sept. 6.

The Sixteenth which is treated first was on the right of the Corps in the Frezenberg sector of the attack.

This division, which had occupied under torrential rain and heavy fire the Frezenberg Ridge since August 4, was much exhausted before the advance began. The losses had fallen mainly upon the 47th Brigade, which had held the line, but the attacking brigades which now took its place were by no means immune. On the day before the battle, Brigadier-General Leveson-Gower of the 49th Brigade and practically all his staff became casualties from gas poisoning, and the command had to be taken over by the C.O. of the Irish Fusiliers. So heavy was the pressure upon the division that 107 officers and 1900 men were on the casualty lists before the advance had begun. None the less, the spirit of the troops was high, and all were eager for the clash. On August 16 the attack was made at 4·45 in the morning, the Thirty-sixth North of Ireland Division being on the left and the Eighth upon the right of the Sixteenth Division. It was upon a two-brigade front, the 48th being on the right and the 49th upon the left. So difficult were the conditions that it was only a quarter of an hour before zero that the concentration was complete, most of the troops being more fit for a rest than for a battle.

The line of advance was formed by the 7th Irish Rifles and 9th Dublin Fusiliers upon the right, while the 7th and 8th Inniskilling Fusiliers were on the left. At the signal they went forward over very heavy ground, the barrage slowing down to five minutes per hundred yards. We shall first follow the right attack.

Both the Irish Rifles and the Dublin Fusiliers

THE THIRD BATTLE OF YPRES 169

found themselves at once within the sweep of numerous machine-guns which caused very heavy casualties. The Rifles for a time were in touch with the 2nd Middlesex of the Eighth Division upon their right, but the latter got caught in their own barrage with the result that it had to fall back. The Rifles, who had lost practically every officer, moved down the railway and across the Hannebeek, but were so reduced in number that it was not possible for the few survivors to hold the German counter-attack advancing about 4 P.M. from Zonnebeke. The Dublin Fusiliers, who had wilted under a heavy enfilade fire from Vampire Farm and Bremen Redoubt, were in equally bad case, and all officers and orderlies who tried to get forward to the assaulting companies were killed or wounded. Two companies of the 2nd Dublin Fusiliers which came up in support shared in the catastrophe and were practically annihilated. Of one company two officers and three men survived unscathed. Of another one non-commissioned officer and ten men. Such figures will show the absolute devotion with which the Irishmen stuck to their work and are not, so far as can be known, exceeded by any losses endured by considerable units during the war. Some of these scattered remains lay out until the evening of August 17, endeavouring to hold a new line, until after dusk they fell back to the trenches from which they had started.

On the left the Inniskilling Fusiliers got away in fine style with the 7/8th Irish Fusiliers in close support moving so swiftly that they avoided the German barrage. Beck House and other strong points were rapidly taken. A fort named Borry Farm upon the right could not be reduced, however,

CHAPTER VII.

The third Battle of Ypres.

Aug. 1 to Sept. 6.

and its five machine-guns raked the advancing lines. Three separate attacks upon the concrete emplacements of this position all ended in failure. Part of the attacking force remained in front of the untaken position, while another portion passed it on the north side working on to the neighbourhood of Zevenkote. At this side there had been more success as the 7th Inniskillings had taken Iberian Trench and consolidated it. Thence they moved forward to the eminence called Hill 37, but met with heavy blasts of fire from that position and from Zonnebeke. The enemy now counter-attacked from Hill 37, and as the left flank of the Inniskillings was entirely exposed, since they had outrun the Ulster men upon their left, they were forced to retire to a position at Delva Farm. This was untenable, however, since both flanks were now exposed, so the whole line fell back to Iberian Trench. This, however, proved to be also impossible to hold on account of the truly terrible losses. In the whole force in that quarter of the field only one officer seems to have been left standing. Both the 8th Fusiliers upon the right and the Ulster men upon the left had retired, and by 9.30 A.M. there was no alternative for the shattered remnants of the 49th Brigade but to seek the shelter of their own line, while the 6th Connaughts and 7th Leinsters were brought up to support them. Of the 7th Inniskillings there were left one wounded officer and no formed body of men at all, while no other battalion of the brigade was of greater strength than half a company. It was indeed a dreadful day in all this Southern section of the line. The losses had been so heavy that no further attack could be organised, and in spite of the fact that scattered men were still lying

THE THIRD BATTLE OF YPRES 171

out, it was impossible to form a new line. Upon the night of August 17 the Fifteenth Division came forward again to relieve the exhausted but heroic infantry, who had done all that men could do, and more than men could be expected to do, but all in vain.

Chapter VII.
The third Battle of Ypres.
Aug. 1 to Sept. 6.

Nor had their brother Irishmen of the Thirty-sixth Division upon their left any better fortune. The failure of one division may always be due to some inherent weakness of its own, but when four divisions in line, of the calibre of the Thirty-sixth, Sixteenth, Eighth, and Fifty-sixth all fail, then it can clearly be said, as on the first day of the Somme Battle, that they were faced by the impossible. This impossible obstacle took the immediate form of many concrete gun emplacements arranged chequer-wise across the front, each holding five guns. But the contributory causes in the case of all the divisions except the Fifty-sixth was their long exposure in dreadful weather to a sustained bombardment which would have shaken the nerves of any troops in the world, apart from thinning their ranks. In the Sixteenth Division alone 1200 men were under treatment for trench fever and swollen feet, besides the heavy losses from shell fire.

The fortunes of the Thirty-sixth Ulster Division were in all ways similar to those of the Sixteenth. There was the same initial advance, the same experience of devastating fire from concrete strong points, the same slaughter, and the same retreat of a few survivors over ground which was dotted with the bodies of their comrades. Upon the right the attack was urged by the 108th Brigade with the 9th Irish Fusiliers upon the right and the Irish Rifles upon the left, with two other battalions of the same regiment in support. The attack starting from the line of Pommern Castle got forward as far as Gallipoli Farm, but there it was faced by a machine-gun fire, coming chiefly from Hill 35, which was simply annihilating in its effect. Only the remains of the 9th Irish Fusiliers ever got back to their original line. For many hours the Irish Rifles held on to the rising ground to the north-east of Pommern Castle, but by four in the afternoon the shattered 108th Brigade was back in its own trenches.

The attack of Jacob's Second Corps was carried out upon August 16 by two divisions, the Eighth (which had relieved the Twenty-fifth) in the Ypres—Roulers Railway—Westhoek line, and the Fifty-sixth London Territorials which had relieved the Eighteenth Division in the Glencorse Wood—Stirling Castle line.

The Eighth Division advanced with the 23rd Brigade upon the left and the 25th upon the right. The barrage was excellent, the infantry were on the top of their form, and all went well. Starting at 4.45 A.M., within an hour they had taken Zonnebeke Redoubt, Iron Cross Redoubt, and Anzac. This marked their limit, however, for heavy machine-gun fire was sweeping across from machine-gun emplacements of concrete in Nonneboschen Wood in the south. The right flank of the 25th Brigade fell back therefore to the line of the Hannebeek, and the stormers of Zonnebeke Redoubt, men of the 2nd West Yorkshire, were compelled to fall back also to the same line. The Germans were now in an aggressive mood, and were seen several times advancing in large numbers down the wooded slopes in front of the British positions, but were always stopped by the heavy barrage.

Chapter VII.
The third Battle of Ypres.
Aug. 1 to Sept. 6.

THE THIRD BATTLE OF YPRES 173

About 2.30 P.M. their pressure caused a short retirement, and the situation was made more difficult by the failure of the 23rd Brigade to find touch with the division upon their left. The pressure of the counter-attacks still continued, and the German losses were heavy, but the machine-gun fire was so deadly in the exposed Hannebeek Valley that a further withdrawal was ordered until the troops were almost in the line from which they had started.

The advance of the Fifty-sixth Division upon the right could not be said to be more successful. The 167th Brigade were on the left, the 169th in the centre with the desperate task of carrying Nonnebosch and Glencorse, while the hard-worked 53rd Brigade of the Eighteenth Division was detailed to form a defensive flank upon the south. It was really the failure of this attack which contributed greatly to the failure of the whole, for there was a strong point at the north-west corner of Inverness Copse with strong machine-gun emplacements which could sweep the area to the north over a wide arc. Thus all the troops north of this point were faced from the start by a devastating fire. The 167th Brigade got well forward to Nonne Boschen, but was stopped by bogs and so fell behind the barrage. On the left they reached Albert Redoubt, but were driven in by a strong counter-attack. The 169th reached the east end of Glencorse Wood where they killed many Germans and captured sixty gunners, but the counter-attacks gradually drove the line back to whence it started. A German officer captured a few days later has described how he saw the London men, mostly without officers, walking slowly back in front of his advance. It was a day of hard slogging upon this sector with very

CHAPTER VII.

The third Battle of Ypres.
Aug. 1 to Sept. 6.

little to show for it. So serious were the losses of the Fifty-sixth Division that the Fourteenth Division took its place next day, while the other London Territorial unit, the Forty-seventh Division (Gorringe) took over the line of the hard-worked Eighth.

Thus we have passed down the whole line upon August 16, and have noted the victory of the north, the stalemate of the centre, and the failure on the south. There can be no doubt that the losses of the British were very much in excess of those of the Germans, for the line of the latter could be held cheaply owing to the Mebus system which presented a new and formidable problem for the British generals. On the other hand the actual trophies of victory lay with the attack, since in the north they had possessed themselves of the German third line, and had captured 30 guns with more than 2000 prisoners.

During the wet and miserable fortnight which followed this engagement the British line was advanced at many points by local operations, each small in itself but yielding in the aggregate some hundreds of prisoners, and representing a gain of ground of about 800 yards for two miles upon the St. Julien front. The Eleventh and Forty-eighth Divisions which still held this sector were responsible for the greater part of this advance which was carried out by three efforts, upon August 19, 22, and 27. Upon the earlier date the advance of the South Midlanders was particularly fine, when the 145th Brigade was heavily engaged, the Gloucesters and Buckinghams leading a fine assault which gained an appreciable section of ground. The bombing parties of the 4th Berkshires, a battalion recruited from Reading, did particularly good service,

THE THIRD BATTLE OF YPRES 175

following up the first line and reducing a number of strong points which had been left untaken. The losses among the stormers were heavy, but the results were substantial and there were some hundreds of prisoners. Especially fine during this and subsequent actions was the conduct of the field-gunners, British, Canadian, and Australian, who habitually worked their guns in the open with their horses in attendance, changing positions, advancing and unlimbering in the good old fashion with no attempt at camouflage, and defiant of the German shells or aeroplanes. The team-drivers had little to do in the war up to now, but when their chance came they and their gallant horses went through the barrage and the poison clouds as if they were no more than London fogs. The admiration of the gunners for each other was mutual. Mr. Bean, the Australian chronicler, narrates how a British artillery Major complimented the neighbouring Australian battery saying: "We could not believe you could carry on in such a fire": to which the Australian Major replied: "Well, do you know, we were thinking exactly the same thing about you." Of such are the ties of Empire.

On August 22 the Fourteenth Division carried out an attack upon Glencorse and Inverness Woods, going over the top at 7 A.M. The 42nd Brigade was on the left facing Glencorse, the 43rd upon the right facing Inverness. The light infantry battalions went forward in fine style, the 5th Shropshires and 6th Cornwalls upon the left carrying all before them and attaining their full objective, which was strictly limited in its extent. This was held and consolidated. The 6th Somersets and 10th Durhams went forward on the right, but the fighting was severe and the progress slow. None the less it was sure, and before evening the greater part of Inverness Copse was in the hands of these four battalions, together with nearly 200 prisoners. An attempt next morning, August 23, to capture Fitz-Clarence Farm, just north of Inverness Copse, though supported by three tanks, was not a success, two of the tanks being hit by gun-fire and the third reaching the Farm without any infantry at its heels. At the same time a counter-attack upon the 5th Shropshires was beaten back by rifle fire. On the next day there was still heavy fighting in this sector, for the Germans could not bear to give up this wood, and made many attempts to regain it. The 42nd Brigade held every inch of their line in Glencorse, but the 43rd were pushed back to the western edge of Inverness where they held on.

There had been a slight forward movement upon each side of the Fourteenth Division during these three days of battle, the Forty-seventh Division taking an advanced line in the north, while the steadfast Twenty-fourth, still in the line of battle, came forward in the south. The 17th Brigade upon the right of the Fourteenth Division guarded its flank during the advance, and a dashing exploit was performed by one of its officers, Lieutenant Stonebanks of the 1st Royal Fusiliers, who took a strong point with its garrison by a sudden attack, so gaining his cross.

Among the other operations which were carried out between the larger engagements in the hope of improving the local position were a series which covered the ground from Fortuin in the north to the south of the Roulers Railway. This point, which was still occupied by the Nineteenth Corps, was

THE THIRD BATTLE OF YPRES

covered upon the left by the Sixty-first Division, a second line English Territorial unit, which faced Hill 35, while on the right the Fifteenth Division had come back into the battle once more. These two divisions made two advances upon August 22 and upon August 27 in an endeavour to enlarge their front, but neither was successful. Early in September the Forty-second Division, which had returned with a considerable reputation from Gallipoli, took the place of the hard-worked Fifteenth. Upon September 6 they again endeavoured to get forward, but the fact that Hill 37 on their left flank had not been taken proved fatal to their advance. The ground was swept from this position of vantage so that when the Forty-second Division went forward upon September 6 to try and storm the line of farms, Iberian, Beck, and Borry, which lay in front of them, they were smitten on their left flank by this deadly fire and suffered heavy losses—the more heavy because with heroic tenacity they held to their task long after its failure was inevitable. The 125th Brigade showed an intrepidity in this attack which in any former war would have been historical, but in this prolonged exhibition of human and military virtue does but take its place among many as good. The 5th and 6th Lancashire Fusiliers who led the stormers had practically ceased to exist after the action, while the 7th and 8th in support had heavy losses. The general lesson of such attacks would seem to be here, as on the Somme, that it is better to wait for a general advance in order to rectify inequalities of the line, rather than to approach them by local attacks—also that an untaken strong point upon the flank is absolutely fatal to any isolated

CHAPTER VII.

The third Battle of Ypres.
Aug. 1 to Sept. 6.

effort. From this time onwards the line was quiet, making preparation for the great coming attack.

On the rest of the Allied battle-line the principal event of August was a successful Italian attack upon the Isonzo Front beginning upon August 19, which not only gained ground but brought in no less than 20,000 prisoners. On the Verdun Front upon August 20 the French had a fine little victory, winning back the last remains of what they had lost in the great struggle, and taking over 5000 prisoners. Since April 9 the Allied gains in prisoners had been British 45,000, French 43,000, Italians 40,000, Russians 33,000. The British at this date held 102,000 Germans as against 43,000 British prisoners held by the Germans.

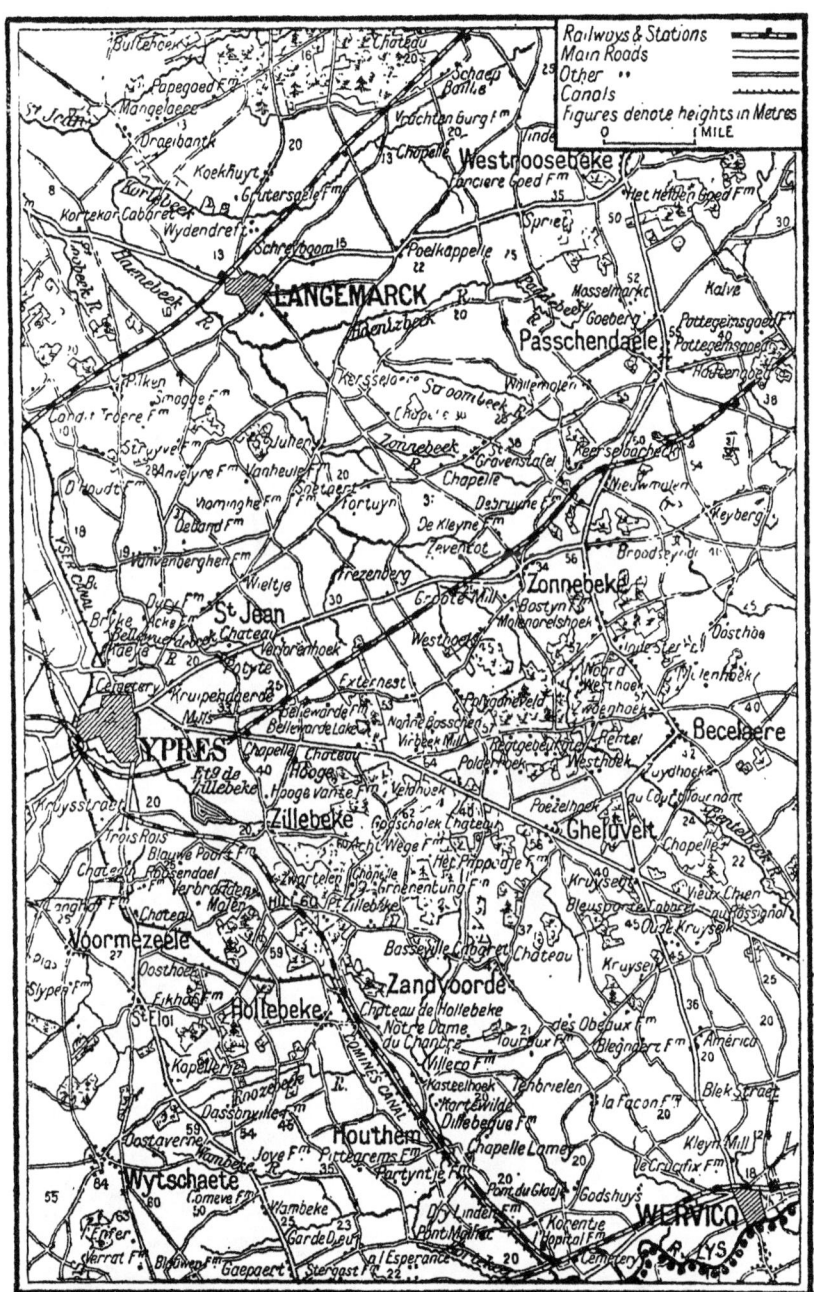

THE YPRES FRONT

CHAPTER VIII

THE THIRD BATTLE OF YPRES

September 6 to October 3, 1917

Engagement of Plumer's Second Army—Attack of September 20—Fine advance of Fifty-fifth Division—Advance of the Ninth Division—Of the Australians—Strong counter-attack upon the Thirty-third Division—Renewed advance on September 26—Continued rain—Desperate fighting.]

THE attack of August 16, with its varying and not wholly satisfactory results, had been carried out entirely by the armies of Antoine and of Gough. It was clear now to Sir Douglas Haig that the resistance of the Germans was most formidable along the line of the Menin Road, where the long upward slope and the shattered groves which crowned it made an ideal position for defence. To overcome this obstacle a new force was needed, and accordingly the Second Army was closed up to the north, and the command in this portion of the field was handed over to General Plumer. This little white-haired leader with his silky manner, his eye-glass, and his grim, inflexible resolution, had always won the confidence of his soldiers, but the complete victory of Messines, with the restraint which had prevented any aftermath of loss, had confirmed the whole army in its high appreciation of his powers.

These changes in the line, together with the

continued rain, which went from bad to worse, had the effect of suspending operations during the remainder of the month save for the smaller actions already recorded. Fresh dispositions had to be made also in order to meet the new German method of defence, which had abandoned the old trench system, and depended now upon scattered strong points, lightly held front lines, and heavy reserves with which to make immediate counter-attacks upon the exhausted stormers. The concrete works called also for a different artillery treatment, since they were so strong that an eighteen-pounder or even a 5·9 gun made little impression. These new problems all pressed for solution, and the time, like the days, was growing shorter.

The front of the new attack upon September 20 was about eight miles in length, and corresponded closely with the front attacked upon July 31, save that it was contracted in the north so that Langemarck was its limit upon this side. Upon the south the flank was still fixed by the Ypres—Comines Canal, just north of Hollebeek. The scheme of the limited objective was closely adhered to, so that no advance of more than a mile was contemplated at any point, while a thousand yards represented the average depth of penetration which was intended. The weather, which had given a treacherous promise of amendment, broke again upon the very night of the assembly, and the troops were drenched as they lay waiting for the signal to advance. Towards morning the rain stopped, but drifting clouds and a dank mist from the saturated soil deprived the attackers of the help of their aircraft —so serious a handicap to the guns. But the spirits of the men rose with the difficulties, after the good

THE THIRD BATTLE OF YPRES 181

old British fashion, and at 5.40 on this most inclement morning, wet and stiff and cold, they went forward with cheerful alacrity into the battle.

The field of operations was now covered by two British armies, that of Gough in the north extending from beyond Langemarck to the Zonnebeke front, while Plumer's Army covered the rest of the line down to Hollebeke. It may be said generally that the task of the men in the south was the more difficult, since they had farther to advance over country which had seemed to be almost impregnable. None the less the advance in the north was admirably executed and reached its full objectives. Cavan's Fourteenth Corps still held the extreme north of the British line, but neither they nor the French upon their left were really engaged in the advance. They covered the front as far south as Schreiboom, where the right of the Twentieth Division joined on to the left of the Fifty-first Highlanders. This latter division formed the left flank of the main advance, though the 59th Brigade, the 60th Brigade, and the 2nd Brigade of Guards did push their line some short distance to the front, on either side of the Ypres—Staden Railway, the 59th Brigade capturing Eagle Trench and the 60th Eagle House. This was a very formidable position, crammed with machine-guns, and it took four days for its conquest, which was a brilliant feat of arms carried out by men who would be discouraged by no obstacle. The garrison were picked troops, who fought desperately, and everything was against the attack, but their pertinacity wore down the defence and eventually, upon Sept. 23, the 10th Rifle Brigade and the 12th Royal Rifles cleared up the last corner of the widespread stronghold.

CHAPTER VIII.

The third Battle of Ypres.
Sept. 6 to Oct. 3.

CHAPTER VIII.

The third Battle of Ypres.

Sept. 6 to Oct. 3.

The hard-worked Highland Territorials of the Fifty-first Division were worn with service but still full of fire. Their advance was also an admirable one, and by nine o'clock they had overcome all obstacles and dug in upon their extreme objective. Quebec Farm was a special stronghold which held the Highlanders up for a time, but finally fell to their determined assault. Rose Farm, Delva Farm, and Pheasant Farm were also strongly defended. About 10 A.M. many strong counter-attacks were made in this area, one of which for a time drove back the line of the Highlanders, but only for a short period. This particular attack was a very gallant one effected by Poles and Prussians of the Thirty-sixth and Two hundred and eighth Divisions. It was noted upon this day that the Prussians fought markedly better than the Bavarians, which has not always been the case. The method adopted both by the Highland Division and in some other parts of the line in order to overcome strong points, such as farms, was a concentration of portable trench-mortars firing heavy charges with a shattering effect. Pheasant Farm was a particularly difficult proposition, and yet it was so smothered by a cloud of these missiles that the distracted garrison was compelled to surrender. This use of what may be called a miniature and mobile heavy artillery became a feature of the last year of the War.

Next to the Fifty-first Division, and covering the ground to the north and east of St. Julien was the Fifty-eighth Division, a new unit of second line London Territorials which had done a good deal of rough service in the line, but had not yet been engaged in an important advance. Upon this occa-

THE THIRD BATTLE OF YPRES 183

sion it bore out the old saying that British troops are often on their top form in a first engagement. Their advance was a brilliant one and attained its full objective, taking upon the way the strongly-fortified position of Wurst Farm. Nowhere in the line was the ground more sodden and more intersected with water jumps. The 173rd Brigade was on the right, the 174th upon the left, the former being led by the young hero of the Ancre Battle and the youngest Brigadier, save perhaps one, in the whole army. It was a magnificent battle *début* for the Londoners and their coolness under fire was particularly remarkable, for in facing the difficult proposition of Wurst Farm they avoided making a frontal attack upon it by swinging first left and then right with all the workmanlike precision of veterans. The capture of Hubner Farm by the 2/6th and 2/8th London was also a particularly fine performance, as was the whole work of Higgins' 174th Brigade.

The two divisions last mentioned, the Fifty-first and the Fifty-eighth, formed the fighting line of Maxse's Eighteenth Corps upon this day. On their right was Fanshawe's Fifth Corps, which had taken the place of the Nineteenth Corps. The most northern division was that sterling West Lancashire Territorial Division, the Fifty-fifth, which had now been in and out of the fighting line but never out of shell fire since the evening of July 31, or seven weeks in all. In spite of its long ordeal, and of the vile ground which lay at its front, it advanced with all its usual determination, the 164th Brigade upon the left, and the 165th upon the right, each of them being stiffened by one battalion from the Reserve Brigade. The 8th Liverpool Irish were

CHAPTER VIII.

The third Battle of Ypres.
Sept. 6 to Oct. 3.

upon the extreme left, which moved down the left bank of the Hannebeek and struck up against the difficult obstacle of Schuber Farm, which they succeeded, with the co-operation of the 2/4th London and of two Tanks, in carrying by assault. Farther south a second farm-house, strongly held, called the Green House, was carried by the 2/5th Lancashire Fusiliers, while the 4th North Lancashire took Fokker Farm upon the right. When one considers that each of these was a veritable fortress, stuffed with machine-guns and defended by 2nd Guards Reserve regiment, one cannot but marvel at the efficiency to which these Territorial soldiers had attained. The 4th Royal Lancasters kept pace upon the right. The advance of the 165th Brigade was equally successful in gaining ground, and there also were formidable obstacles in their path. After crossing the Steenbeek they had to pass a very heavy barrage of high explosives and shrapnel which, however, burst upon percussion and was neutralised to some extent by the softness of the ground. The line of advance was down the Gravenstafel Road. A formidable line of trenches were carried and Kavnorth Post was captured, as were Iberian and Gallipoli, strong points upon the right. A counter-attack in the afternoon which moved down against the two brigades, was broken by their rifle-fire, aided by the advent of the two supporting battalions, the 5th South Lancashires and 5th North Lancashires. The ground thus taken was strongly held until next evening, September 21, when under cover of a very heavy fire the enemy penetrated once more into the positions in the area of the 164th Brigade. Just as darkness fell, however, there was a fine advance to regain the ground, in which the whole

THE THIRD BATTLE OF YPRES 185

of the headquarters staff, with bearers, signallers, runners, and men-servants, swept up to the position which was captured once more. Among other positions taken upon September 20 was Hill 37, which had been so formidable a stronghold for the Germans in the murderous fighting of August 16. This commanding point was taken and held by the 5th, 6th, and 9th King's Liverpools, with part of the 5th South Lancashires, all under the same officer who led the 36th Brigade in their fine attack upon Ovillers. The position was strongly organised, and upon the next day it beat back a very determined German counter-attack.

CHAPTER VIII.

The third Battle of Ypres. Sept. 6 to Oct. 3.

The Ninth Division was on the right of the Fifty-fifth with the South Africans upon the left flank. At the opening of the attack the 3rd (Transvaal) and 4th (Scottish) South African regiments advanced upon the German line. Within an hour the latter had carried Borry Farm, which had defied several previous assaults. At eight o'clock both these regiments had reached their full objectives and the supporting units, the 1st (Cape) and 2nd (Natal) regiments went through their ranks, the men of the Transvaal cheering the men of Natal and the Cape as they passed. By 9.30 the second objectives, including Beck House, had also fallen. There was a considerable concentration of Germans beyond, and the 5th Camerons came up in support, as an attack appeared to be imminent. The artillery fire dispersed the gathering, however, and the 2nd Regiment spreading out on the left to Waterend House established touch with the Lancashire men to their north. Bremen Redoubt had been captured, and this was made a nodal point against any counter-attack, as was Vampire Redoubt. By mid-day the 1st Regiment on the right had lost heavily and was forced to dig in and act upon the defensive as German concentrations were visible in the Hannebeke Woods. A second battalion of the 26th Brigade, the 7th Seaforths, were at this time sent up in support. The left flank was also checked and a defensive post organised at Mitchell's Farm. The shelling from the direction of Hill 37 was very heavy, the more so as the Africans were ahead of the 165th Brigade upon their left. A number of German aeroplanes flying low and using their machine-guns complicated a situation which was already sufficiently serious, for the small-arm ammunition was running low and only a few hundred exhausted men with a thin sprinkling of officers remained in the fighting line. The artillery played up splendidly, however, and though the enemy massed together at Bostin Farm he could never get a sufficient head of troops to carry him through the pelting British barrage. Thus the day drew to a close with heavy losses cheerfully borne, and also with a fine gain of ground which included several of the most sinister strong points upon the whole line. The South Africans have been few in number, but it cannot be disputed that their record in the field has been a superb one.

In the meantime the 27th Brigade, upon the right of the South Africans, had also done a splendid day's work. In the first dash the battalion upon the left front, the 12th Royal Scots, had taken Potsdam Redoubt with its garrison. Thence the line rolled on, the Scots Fusiliers and Highland Light Infantry joining in turn in the advance, until evening found them with the same difficulties and also with

THE THIRD BATTLE OF YPRES 187

the same success as their African comrades. As night fell this right wing was in touch with the Australians near Anzac, and thence passed through the wood and along the railway bank to the junction with the left brigade, which in turn stretched across to Gallipoli and to Hill 37, which was now in the hands of their Lancashire neighbours and bristling with their machine-guns. That night the Ninth Division lay upon the ground that they had won, but the men had been without sleep or warm food for three days and nights under continual fire, so that, hardy as they were, they had nearly reached the limit of human endurance. It is worthy of remark that the wounded in this part of the field were attended to in many cases by captured German surgeons, and that one of these had an experience of Prussian amenities, for his brains were scattered by a sniper's bullet.

The First and Second Australian Divisions joined the left unit of Plumer's Army, but worked in close co-operation with the Ninth Division upon their right. In a day of brilliant exploits and unqualified successes there was nothing to beat their performance, for they were faced by that which tries the nerves of the stoutest troops—an area which has already been tested and found to be impregnable. With all the greater fire did the brave Australian infantry throw itself into the fray, and they had the advantage over their predecessors in that the line was well up on either side of them, and that enemy guns upon their flanks were too busy upon their own front to have a thought of enfilading. The result of the Australian advance was instant and complete, for the remainder of Glencorse Wood and Nonne Boschen were over-run and by ten o'clock the

Chapter VIII.

The third Battle of Ypres.

Sept. 6 to Oct. 3.

"Diggers" were through the hamlet of Polygonveld and into the original German third line beyond it. The western part of Polygon Wood was also cleared, and so, after a sharp fight, was the strong point called "Black Watch Corner," which is at the south-western extremity of the wood. At this point the advance of the Australians was not less than a mile in depth over ground which presented every possible obstacle. Over at least one of their captured redoubts their own Australian flag with the Southern Cross upon it was floating proudly in the evening. The losses of the division were serious, the greater part being due to an enfilade fire from the right, coming probably from the high ground in the south near Tower Hamlets, which struck their flank as they approached the south of Polygon Wood. Anzac upon the left marked their northern limit. Nothing could have been finer than the whole Australian attack. "They went into battle," says their scribe, "not singing and laughing like many British regiments, but very grim, very silent, with their officers marching quietly at the head of each small string of men." They are dour, determined fighters, flame-like in attack, iron in defence, and they have woven a fresh and brilliant strand into the traditions of the Imperial armies. It should be mentioned that it was the 2nd, 3rd, 5th, and 7th Brigades which carried forward the line to victory.

Good as the Australian advance had been it could not be said to have been better than Babington's Twenty-third Division upon their right. They, too, had to cross ground which had been littered by the bodies of their comrades, and to pass points which brave men had found impassable. But all went well

THE THIRD BATTLE OF YPRES 189

upon this day, and every objective was seized and held. Inverness Copse, of evil memory, was occupied at the first rush, and the advance went forward without a check to Dumbarton Lakes and on past them until the Veldhoek Ridge had fallen. A counter-attack which broke upon them was driven back in ruin. The advance was across the marshy Basseville Beek and through the dangerous woods beyond, but from first to last there was never a serious check. It was on the Yorkshires, the West Yorkshires, and the Northumberland Fusiliers of the 68th and 69th Brigades that the brunt of the early fighting fell, and as usual the North-country grit proved equal to the hardest task which could be set before it. The final stage which carried the Veldheek Ridge was also a North-country exploit in this section of the line, as it was the 10th West Ridings and the 12th Durhams, who with fixed bayonets cleared the ultimate positions, reaching the western slopes of the upper Steenbeek Valley where they dug in the new temporary lines.

On the extreme south of the line the advance had been as successful as elsewhere, and at nearly every point the full objective was reached. Upon the right of the Twenty-third Division was the Forty-first, a sound English Division which had distinguished itself at the Somme by the capture of Flers. The leading brigades, the 122nd and 124th, with Royal Fusiliers, King's Royal Rifles, and Hampshires in the lead, lost heavily in the advance. The snipers and machine-guns were very active upon this front, but each obstacle was in turn surmounted, and about 8.30 the Reserve Brigade, the 123rd, came through and completed the morning's work, crossing

CHAPTER VIII.

The third Battle of Ypres.

Sept. 6 to Oct. 3.

190   THE BRITISH CAMPAIGN, 1917

CHAPTER VIII.

The third Battle of Ypres.

Sept. 6 to Oct. 3.

the valley of the Basseville Beek and storming up the slope of the Tower Hamlets, a strong position just south of the Menin Road. Among the points which gave them trouble was the Papooje Farm, which was found to be a hard nut to crack—but cracked it was, all the same. This same brigade suffered much from machine-guns east of Bodmin Copse, both it and the 124th Brigade being held up at the Tower Hamlet Plateau, which exposed the wing of the 122nd who had reached all their objectives. So great was the pressure that the Brigadier of the 124th Brigade came up personally to reorganise the attack. The 11th West Kent, the southern unit of the 122nd, had their right flank entirely exposed to German fire. Two young subalterns, Freeman and Woolley, held this dangerous position for some time with their men, but Freeman was shot by a sniper, the losses were heavy, and the line had to be drawn in. Colonel Corfe of the 11th West Kent and Colonel Jarvis of the 21st K.R.R. were among the casualties. In spite of all counter-attacks the evening found the left of the Forty-first Division well established in its new line, and only short of its full objective in this difficult region of the Tower Hamlets, where for the following two days it had to fight hard to hold a line. The losses were heavy in all three brigades.

On the right of the 41st and joining the flank unit of Morland's Tenth Corps was the Thirty-ninth Division. This Division attacked upon a single brigade front, the 117th having the post of honour. The 16th and 17th Sherwood Foresters, the 17th Rifles, and the 16th Rifle Brigade were each in turn engaged in a long morning's conflict in which

THE THIRD BATTLE OF YPRES 191

they attained their line, which was a more limited one than that of the divisions to the north.

South of this point, and forming the flank of the whole attack, was the Nineteenth Division, which advanced with the West-countrymen of the 57th Brigade upon the right, and the Welshmen of the 58th Brigade upon the left. Their course was down the spur east of Zillebeke and then into the small woods north of the Ypres—Comines Canal. The 8th Gloucesters, 10th Worcesters, 8th North Staffords, 6th Wiltshires, 9th Welsh, and 9th Cheshires each bore their share of a heavy burden and carried it on to its ultimate goal. The objectives were shorter than at other points, but had special difficulties of their own, as every flank attack is sure to find. By nine o'clock the work was thoroughly done, and the advance secured upon the south, the whole Klein Zillebeke sector having been made good. The captors of La Boisselle had shown that they had not lost their power of thrust.

This first day of the renewed advance represented as clean-cut a victory upon a limited objective as could be conceived. The logical answer to the German determination to re-arrange his defences by depth was to refuse to follow to depth, but to cut off his whole front which was thinly held, and then by subsequent advances take successive slices off his line. The plan worked admirably, for every point aimed at was gained, the general position was greatly improved, the losses were moderate, and some three thousand more prisoners were taken. The Germans have been ingenious in their various methods of defence, but history will record that the Allies showed equal skill in their quick modifications of attack,

CHAPTER VIII.

The third Battle of Ypres. Sept. 6 to Oct. 3.

and that the British during this year's campaign had a most remarkable record in never being once held by any position which they attacked, save only at Cambrai. It is true that on some sections, as in the south of the line on August 16, there might be a complete check, but in every action one or other part of the attack had a success. In this instance it was universal along the line.

The Germans did not sit down quietly under their defeat, but the reserve counter-attack troops came forward at once. Instead, however, of finding the assailants blown and exhausted, as they would have been had they attempted a deep advance, they found them in excellent fettle, and endured all the losses which an unsuccessful advance must bring. There were no less than eleven of these attempts upon the afternoon and evening of September 20, some of them serious and some perfunctory, but making among them a great total of loss. They extended over into September 21, but still with no substantial success. As has already been recorded, the front of the 55th Division, at Schuler Farm, east of St. Julien, was for a time driven in, but soon straightened itself out again. In this advance, which embraced the whole front near St. Julien, the German columns came with the fall of evening driving down from Gravenstafel and following the line of the Roulers Railway. They deployed under cover of a good barrage, but the British guns got their exact range and covered them with shrapnel. They were new unshaken troops and came on with great steadiness, but the losses were too heavy and the British line too stiff. Their total lodgment was not more than 300 yards, and that they soon lost again. By nine o'clock all was clear.

THE THIRD BATTLE OF YPRES 193

Among the British defences the ex-German pill-boxes were used with great effect as a safe depository for men and munitions. This considerable German attack in the north was succeeded next day by an even larger and more concentrated effort which surged forward on the line of the Menin Road, the fresh Sixteenth Bavarian Division beating up against the Thirty-third and the Australian Divisions. There was some fierce give-and-take fighting with profuse shelling upon either side, but save for some local indentations the positions were all held. The Victorians upon the right flank of the Australians' position at Polygon Wood were very strongly attacked and held their ground all day. Pinney's Thirty-third Division had come into line, and the German attack upon the morning of September 25 broke with especial fury upon the front of the 98th Brigade, which fought with a splendid valour which marks the incident as one of the outstanding feats of arms in this great battle. Small groups of men from the two regular battalions, the 1st Middlesex and the 2nd Argyll and Sutherlands, were left embedded within the German lines after their first successful rush, but they held out with the greatest determination, and either fought their way back or held on in little desperate groups until they were borne forward again next day upon the wave of the advancing army.

The weight of the attack was so great, however, that the front of the 98th Brigade was pushed back, and there might have been a serious set-back had it not been for the iron resistance of the 100th Brigade, who stretched south to the Menin Road, joining hands with the 11th Sussex of the Thirty-ninth

Chapter VIII.

The third Battle of Ypres.

Sept. 6 to Oct. 3.

o

Chapter VIII.
The third Battle of Ypres.
Sept. 6 to Oct. 3.

Division upon the farther side. The 100th Brigade was exposed to a severe assault all day most gallantly urged by the German Fiftieth Reserve Division and supported by a terrific bombardment. It was a terrible ordeal, but the staunch battalions who met it, the 4th Liverpools who linked up with their comrades of the 98th Brigade, the 2nd Worcesters, 9th Highland Light Infantry, and 1st Queens, were storm-proof that day. On the Menin Road side the two latter battalions were pushed in for a time by the weight of the blow, and lost touch with the Thirty-Ninth Division, but the Colonel of the Queens, reinforced by some of the 16th K.R.R., pushed forward again with great determination, and by 9 A.M. had fully re-occupied the support line, as had the 9th Highland Light Infantry upon their left. So the situation remained upon the night of the 25th, and the further development of the British counter-attack became part of the general attack of September 26. It had been a hard tussle all day, in the course of which some hundreds in the advanced line had fallen into the hands of the enemy. It should be mentioned that the troops in the firing-line were occasionally short of ammunition during the prolonged contest, and that this might well have caused disaster had it not been for the devoted work of the 18th Middlesex Pioneer Battalion who, under heavy fire and across impossible ground, brought up the much-needed boxes and bandoliers. The resistance of the Thirty-third Division was greatly helped by the strong support of the Australians on their flank. It was a remarkable fact, and one typical of the inflexibility of Sir Douglas Haig's leadership and the competence of his various staffs, that the fact that this severe action

THE THIRD BATTLE OF YPRES 195

was raging did not make the least difference in his plans for the general attack upon September 26.

At 5.50 in the morning of that date, in darkness and mist, the wonderful infantry was going forward as doggedly as ever over a front of six miles, extending from the north-east of St. Julien to the Tower Hamlets south of the Menin Road. The latter advance was planned to be a short one, and the real object of the whole day's fighting was to establish a good jumping-off place for an advance upon the important Broodseinde Ridge. Some of the war-worn divisions had been drawn out and fresh troops were in the battle line. The Northern Corps was not engaged, and the flank of the advance was formed by the Eleventh Division (Ritchie) with the 58th Londoners upon their right, the two forming the fighting front of Maxse's Eighteenth Corps. Their advance, which was entirely successful and rapidly gained its full objectives, was along the line of St. Julien—Poelcapelle Road. The total gain here, and in most other points of the line, was about 1000 yards.

Upon the right of Maxse's Corps was the Fifty-eighth Division, which also secured its full objective. The German line upon this front was held by the Twenty-third Saxon Division (Reserve), which yielded a number of prisoners. The Londoners fought their way down the line of the Wieltje—Gravenstafel Road, overcoming a series of obstacles and reaching the greater portion of their objectives. There were no notable geographical points to be captured, but the advance was a fine performance which showed that the Fifty-eighth was a worthy compeer of those other fine London territorial divisions which had placed the reputation of the mother city at the very front of all

CHAPTER VIII.

The third Battle of Ypres Sept. 6 to Oct. 3.

CHAPTER VIII.

The third Battle of Ypres.

Sept. 6 to Oct. 3.

the Imperial Armies. The Forty-seventh, the Fifty-sixth, the Fifty-eighth, and the Sixtieth in Palestine had all shown how the citizen-soldier of the Metropolis could fight.

Fanshawe's Corps consisted upon this date of the Fifty-ninth Division upon the left, and the Third upon the right. The Fifty-ninth Division, which consisted of second-line battalions of North Midland Territorials, made a fine advance upon the right of the Gravenstafel Road, keeping touch with the Londoners upon the left. Here also almost the whole objective was reached. The German positions, though free from fortified villages, were very thick with every sort of mechanical obstruction, in spite of which the attack went smoothly from start to finish. It is clear that the British advance was fully expected at the south end of the line, but that for some reason, probably the wretched state of the ground, it was not looked for in the north.

The Third Division had kept pace with the Australians to the south and with the Midlanders to the north, and had captured the village and church of Zonnebeke, which formed their objective. Very strong counter-attacks upon all the part of the land to the immediate north of Polygon Wood were beaten down by the masterful fire of the British artillery.

To the right of the Fifth Corps the Australians pursued their victorious career, going to their full limit, which entailed the possession of the whole of Polygon Wood. The Fourth and Fifth Divisions were now in the battle line. Pushing onwards they crossed the road which connects Bacelaer with Zonnebeke, and established themselves

THE THIRD BATTLE OF YPRES 197

firmly on the farther side south of Zonnebeke. Some 300 prisoners with a number of machine-guns were taken in this fine advance. The pressure upon the Australians was especially heavy upon the right flank of the Fifth Australian Division, since the left of the Thirty-third Division had been driven in, as already described, by the very heavy German attacks upon September 25, so that the Victorians of the 15th Australian Brigade at the south end of the line started with their flank exposed. They were in close touch throughout with the 19th Brigade of the British Division, and the 2nd Welsh Fusiliers found themselves intermingled with the Victorians in the advance, with whom they co-operated in the capture of Jut Farm. It was a fine feat for the Victorians to advance at all under such circumstances, for as they went forward they had continually to throw out a defensive flank, since the Germans had re-occupied many of the trenches and Mebus, from which they had been ejected upon the 20th. This strip of ground remained for a time with the Germans, but the Thirty-third Division had also advanced upon the right of it, so that it was left as a wedge protruding into the British position. Cameron House was taken at the joining point of the two divisions, and gradually the whole of the lost ground was re-absorbed.

To the right of the Australians the Thirty-third Division went forward also to its extreme objective, gathering up as it went those scattered groups of brave men who had held out against the German assault of the preceding day. This gallant division had a particularly hard time, as its struggle against the German attack upon the day before had been a very severe one, which entailed heavy losses.

Chapter VIII.

The third Battle of Ypres. Sept. 6 to Oct. 3.

CHAPTER VIII.
The third Battle of Ypres.
Sept. 6 to Oct. 3.

Some ground had been lost at the Veldhoek Trench north of the Menin Road, where the 100th Brigade was holding the line, but this had been partially regained, as already described, by an immediate attack by the 1st Queen's West Surrey and 9th Highland Light Infantry. The 2nd Argyll and Sutherlands were still in the front line, but for the second time this year this splendid battalion was rescued from the desperate situation which only such tried and veteran soldiers could have carried through without disaster. Immediately before the attack of September 26, just after the assembly of the troops, the barrage which the Germans had laid down in order to cover their own advance beat full upon the left of the divisional line, near Glencorse Wood, and inflicted such losses that it could not get forward at zero, thus exposing the Victorians, as already recorded. Hence, although the 100th Brigade succeeded in regaining the whole of the Veldhoek Trench upon the right, there was an unavoidable gap upon the left between Northampton Farm and Black Watch Corner. The division was not to be denied, however, and by a splendid effort before noon the weak spot had been cleared up by the Scottish Rifles, the 4th King's Liverpools, and the 4th Suffolks, so that the line was drawn firm between Veldhoek Trench in the south and Cameron House in the north. A counter-attack by the Fourth Guards Division was crushed by artillery fire, and a comic sight was presented, if anything can be comic in such a tragedy, by a large party of the Guards endeavouring to pack themselves into a pill-box which was much too small to receive them. Many of them were left lying outside the entrance.

THE THIRD BATTLE OF YPRES 199

Farther still to the right, and joining the flank of the advance, the Thirty-ninth Division, like its comrades upon the left, found a hard task in front of it, the country both north and south of the Menin Road being thickly studded with strong points and fortified farms. It was not until the evening of September 27, after incurring heavy losses, that they attained their allotted line. This included the whole of the Tower Hamlets spur with the German works upon the farther side of it. The extreme right flank was held up owing to German strong points on the east of Bitter Wood, but with this exception all the objectives were taken and held by the 116th and 118th, the two brigades in the line. The fighting fell with special severity upon the 4th Black Watch and the 1st Cambridge of the latter brigade, and upon the 14th Hants and the Sussex battalions of the former, who moved up to the immediate south of the Menin Road. The losses of all the battalions engaged were very heavy, and the 111th Brigade of the Thirty-seventh Division had to be sent up at once in order to aid the survivors to form a connected line.

The total result of the action of September 26 was a gain of over half a mile along the whole front, the capture of 1600 prisoners with 48 officers, and one more proof that the method of the broad, shallow objective was an effective answer to the new German system of defence by depth. It was part of that system to have shock troops in immediate reserve to counter-attack the assailants before they could get their roots down, and therefore it was not unexpected that a series of violent assaults should immediately break upon the British positions along the whole newly-won line. These raged during the

CHAPTER VIII.

The third Battle of Ypres.

Sept. 6 to Oct. 3.

evening of September 26, but they only served to add greatly to the German losses, showing them that their ingenious conception had been countered by a deeper ingenuity which conferred upon them all the disadvantages of the attack. For four days there was a comparative quiet upon the line, and then again the attacks carried out by the Nineteenth Reserve Division came driving down to the south of Polygon Wood, but save for ephemeral and temporary gains they had no success. The Londoners of the Fifty-eighth Division had also a severe attack to face upon September 28 and lost two posts, one of which they recovered the same evening.

Up to now the weather had held, and the bad fortune which had attended the British for so long after August 1 seemed to have turned. But the most fickle of all the gods once more averted her face, and upon October 3 the rain began once more to fall heavily in a way which announced the final coming of winter. None the less the work was but half done, and the Army could not be left under the menace of the commanding ridge of Paschendaale. At all costs the advance must proceed.

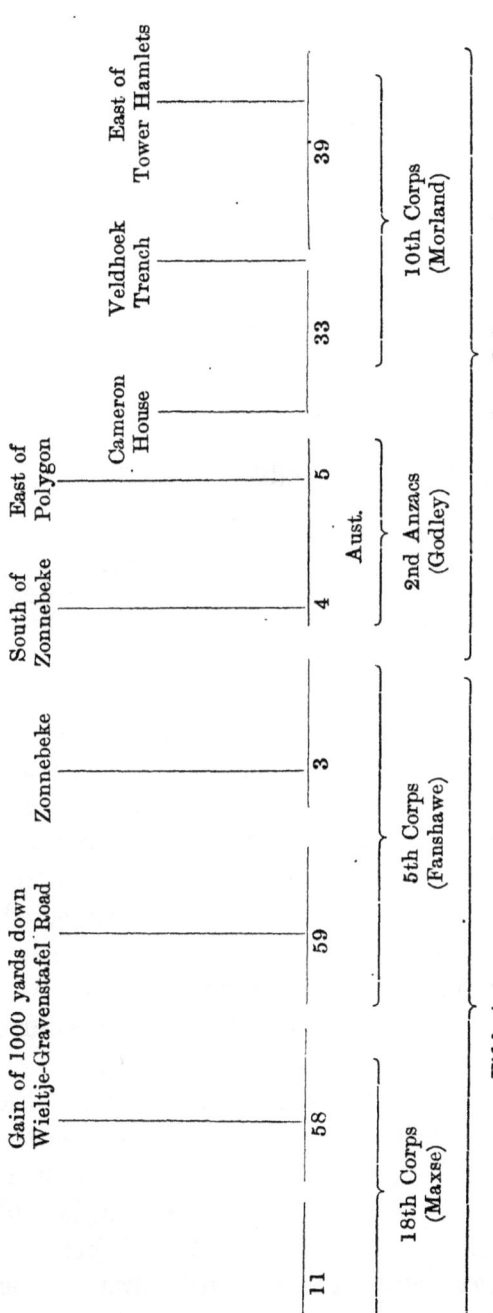

THIRD YPRES BATTLE
September 26

CHAPTER IX

THE THIRD BATTLE OF YPRES

October 4 to November 10, 1917

Attack of October 4—Further advance of the British line—Splendid advance of second-line Territorials—Good work of H.A.C. at Reutel—Abortive action of October 12—Action of October 26—Heavy losses at the south end of the line—Fine fighting by the Canadian Corps—Capture of Paschendaale—General results of third Battle of Ypres.

CHAPTER IX.

The third Battle of Ypres.

Oct. 4 to Nov. 10.

AT early dawn upon October 4, under every possible disadvantage of ground and weather, the attack was renewed, the infantry advancing against the main line of the ridge east of Zonnebeke. The front of the movement measured about seven miles, as the sector south of the Menin Road was hardly affected. The Ypres—Staden railway in the north was the left flank of the Army, so that the Fourteenth Corps was once more upon the move. We will trace the course of the attack from this northern end of the line.

Cavan's Corps had two divisions in front—the Twenty-ninth upon the left and the Fourth upon the right, two fine old regular units which had seen as much fighting as any in the Army. The Guards held a defensive flank together with the French between Houthulst Forest and the Staden railway. The advance of the Twenty-ninth was along the line of the railway, and it covered its moderate objectives without great loss or difficulty. Vesten Farm represented the limit of the advance.

The Fourth Division (Matheson) started from a point east of Langemarck and ended from 1000 to 1500 yards farther on. They advanced upon a two-brigade front with the 11th Brigade upon the right, with the northern edge of Poelcapelle as its objective, while the 10th Brigade upon the left moved upon the line of 19-Metre Hill. The fire from this strong point was very severe, and it drove back the 2nd Seaforths, who were the right battalion of the 10th Brigade, thus exposing the flank of the 1st Hants, who were on the left of the 11th. The veteran Highlanders soon rallied, however, and the line was strengthened at the gap by the advance into it of the 1st East Lancashires. Both the Seaforths and the Lancashire men lost very heavily, however, by a devastating fire from machine-guns. The 1st Somersets upon the right had a misadventure through coming under the fire of British artillery, which caused them for a time to fall back. They came on again, however, and established touch with the 33rd Brigade, who had occupied Poelcapelle. There the Fourth Division lay on their appointed line, strung out over a wide front, crouching in heavy rain amid the mud of the shell-holes, each group of men unable during the day to see or hold intercourse with the other, and always under fire from the enemy. It was an experience which, extended from day to day in this and other parts of the line, makes one marvel at the powers of endurance latent in the human frame. An officer who sallied forth to explore has described the strange effect of that desolate, shell-ploughed landscape, half-liquid in consistence, brown as a fresh-turned field, with no movement upon its hideous expanse, although every crevice and pit was swarming with life, and the constant snap of the sniper's bullet told of watchful, unseen eyes. Such a chaos was it that for three days there was no connection between the left of the Fourth and the right of the Twenty-ninth, and it was not until October 8 that Captain Harston of the 11th Brigade, afterwards slain, together with another officer ran the gauntlet of the sharpshooters, and after much searching and shouting saw a rifle waved from a pit, which gave him the position of the right flank of the 16th Middlesex. It was fortunate he did so, as the barrage of the succeeding morning would either have overwhelmed the Fourth Division or been too far forward for the Twenty-ninth.

Upon the right of the Fourth Division was the Eleventh. Led by several tanks, the 33rd Brigade upon the left broke down all obstacles and captured the whole of the western half of the long straggling street which forms the village of Poelcapelle. Their comrades upon the right had no such definite mark before them, but they made their way successfully to their objective.

Upon the right of the Eleventh Division, the 48th South Midland Territorials had a most difficult advance over the marshy valley of the Stroombeek, but the water-sodden morasses of Flanders were as unsuccessful as the chalk uplands of Pozières in stopping these determined troops. Warwicks, Gloucesters, and Worcesters, they found their way to the allotted line. Winchester Farm was the chief centre of resistance conquered in this advance.

To the right of the Midland men the New Zealanders

THE THIRD BATTLE OF YPRES 205

—that splendid division which had never yet found its master, either on battlefield or football ground—advanced upon the Gravenstafel spur. Once more the record of success was unbroken and the full objective gained. The two front brigades, drawn equally from the North and South Islands, men of Canterbury, Wellington, Otago, and Auckland, splashed across the morass of the Hannebeek and stormed their way forward through Aviatik Farm and Boetleer, their left co-operating with the Midlanders in the fall of the Winzic strong point. The ground was thick with pill-boxes, here as elsewhere, but the soldiers showed great resource and individuality in their methods of stalking them, getting from shell-hole to shell-hole until they were past the possible traverse of the gun, and then dashing, bomb in hand, for the back door, whence the garrison, if they were lucky, soon issued in a dejected line. On the right, the low ridge magniloquently called "Abraham's Heights" was carried without a check, and many prisoners taken. Evening found the whole of the Gravenstafel Ridge in the strong hands of the New Zealanders, with the high ruin of Paschendaale Church right ahead of them as the final goal of the Army.

These New Zealanders formed the left unit of Godley's Second Anzac Corps, the right unit of which was the Third Australian Division. Thus October 4 was a most notable day in the young, but glorious, military annals of the Antipodean Britons, for, with the First Anzac Corps fighting upon the right, the whole phalanx made up a splendid assemblage of manhood, whether judged by its quality or its quantity. Some 40,000 infantry drawn from the islands of the

CHAPTER IX.

The third Battle of Ypres.

Oct. 4 to Nov. 10.

CHAPTER IX.
The third Battle of Ypres.
Oct. 4 to Nov. 10.

Pacific fronted the German and advanced the British line upon October 4. Of the Third Australians it can only be said that they showed themselves to be as good as their comrades upon either flank, and that they attained the full objective which had been marked as their day's work. By 1.15 the final positions had been occupied and held.

Gravenstafel represents one end of a low eminence which stretches for some distance. The First and Second Australian Divisions, attacking upon the immediate right of the Second Anzac Corps, fought their way step by step up the slope alongside of them and established themselves along a wide stretch of the crest, occupying the hamlet of Broodseinde. This advance took them across the road which leads from Bacelaer to Paschendaale, and it did not cease until they had made good their grip by throwing out posts upon the far side of the crest. The fighting was in places very sharp, and the Germans stood to it like men. The official record says: " A small party would not surrender. It consisted entirely of officers and N.C.O.'s with one medical private. Finally grenades drove them out to the surface, when the Captain was bayoneted and the rest killed, wounded, or captured. One machine-gunner was bayoneted with his finger still pressing his trigger." Against such determined fighters and on such ground it was indeed a glory to have advanced 2000 yards and taken as many prisoners. In one of the captured Mebus a wounded British officer was found who had been there for three days. His captors had treated him with humanity, and he was released by the Australians, none the worse for his adventure. There is no doubt that in all this portion of the line the Germans were themselves in the very

Vesten Farm	19-Metre Hill	Poel-capelle	Winchester F.	Kron-prinz F.	Berlin W.	Tyne Cottage	Celtic F.	Noordhemhoek Reutel	Polderhoek	Hampshire Farm
29	4	11	48	N.Z.	Aust. 3	Aust. 2	Aust. 1	7 — 21	5	37
Cavan's XIV.		Maxse's XVIII.		Anzac II.		Anzac I.		Morland's X.		IX. (Hamilton Gordon)
Fifth Army (GOUGH)				Second Army (PLUMER)						

ORDER OF BATTLE
October 4, 1917

act of advancing for an assault when the storm broke loose, and the British lines trampled down and passed over the storm troops as they made for their allotted objectives.

On the immediate right of the Australians was Morland's Tenth Corps, with the Seventh, Twenty-first, and Fifth Divisions in the battle line. The Seventh Division had stormed their way past a number of strongholds up the incline and had topped the ridge, seizing the hamlet of Noordhemhoek upon the other side of it. This entirely successful advance, which maintained the highest traditions of this great division, was carried out by the Devons, Borderers, and Gordons of the 20th Brigade upon the left, and by the South Staffords and West Surreys of the 91st Brigade upon the right. The full objectives were reached, but it was found towards evening that the fierce counter-attacks to the south had contracted the British line in that quarter, so that the right flank of the 91st Brigade was in the air. Instead of falling back the brigade threw out a defensive line, but none the less the salient was so marked that it was clear that it could not be permanent, and that there must either be a retirement or that some future operation would be needed to bring up the division on the right.

To the right of Noordhemhoek the Twenty-first Division had cleared the difficult enclosed country to the east of Polygon Wood, and had occupied the village of Reutel, but encountered such resolute opposition and such fierce counter-attacks that both the advancing brigades, the 62nd and the 64th, wound up the day to the westward of their full objectives, which had the effect already described

THE THIRD BATTLE OF YPRES 209

upon the right wing of the Seventh Division. Both front brigades had lost heavily, and they were relieved in the front line by the 110th Leicester Brigade of their own division. During the severe fighting of the day the losses in the first advance, which gained its full objectives, fell chiefly upon the 9th Yorkshire Light Infantry. In the second phase of the fight, which brought them into Reutel, the battalions engaged were the 8th East Yorks and 12th Northumberland Fusiliers, which had to meet a strong resistance in difficult country, and were hard put to it to hold their own. The German counter-attacks stormed all day against the left of the line at this point around Reutel, making the flanks of the Fifth and Seventh Divisions more and more difficult, as the defenders between them were compelled to draw in their positions. A strong push by the Germans in the late afternoon got possession of Judge Copse, Reutel, and Polderhoek Château. The two former places were recovered in a subsequent operation.

On the flank of the main attack the old Fifth Division, going as strongly as ever after its clear three years of uninterrupted service, fought its way against heavy opposition up Polderhoek Château. The Germans were massed thickly in this quarter and the fighting was very severe. The advance was carried out by those warlike twins, the comrades of many battles, the 1st West Kents and 2nd Scots Borderers upon the right, while the 1st Devons and 1st Cornwalls of the 95th Brigade were on the left, the latter coinciding with the edge of Polygon Wood and the former resting upon the Menin Road. The 13th actually occupied Polderhoek Château, but lost it again. The 95th was much incommoded by finding

P

that the Reutelbeek was now an impassable swamp, but they swarmed round it and captured their objectives, while its left got beyond Reutel, and had to throw back a defensive flank on its left, and withdraw its front to the west of the village. The chief counter-attacks of the day were on the front of the Fifth and Twenty-first Divisions, and they were both numerous and violent, seven in succession coming in front of Polderhoek Château and Reutel. This fierce resistance restricted the advance of Morland's Tenth Corps and limited their gains, but enabled them to wear out more of the enemy than any of the divisions to the north.

Upon the flank of the attack, the advance of the Thirty-seventh Division had been a limited one, and had not been attended with complete success, as two of the German strongholds—Berry Cottages and Lewis House—still held out and spread a zone of destruction round them. The 8th Somersets, 8th Lincolns, and a Middlesex battalion of the 63rd Brigade all suffered heavily upon this flank. On the northern wing the 13th Rifles, 13th Rifle Brigade, and Royal Fusiliers of the 111th Brigade drove straight ahead, and keeping well up to the barrage were led safely by that stern guide to their ultimate positions, into which they settled with a comparative immunity from loss, but the battalions were already greatly exhausted by long service and scanty drafts, so that the 13th Rifles emerged from the fight with a total strength of little over a hundred. It must be admitted that all these successive fights at the south of the Menin Road vindicated the new German systems of defence and caused exceedingly heavy losses which were only repaid by scanty

THE THIRD BATTLE OF YPRES 211

and unimportant gains of desolate, shell-ploughed land.

The total result of this Broodseinde action was a victory gained under conditions of position and weather which made it a most notable accomplishment. Apart from the very important gain of ground, which took the Army a long way towards its final objective, the Paschendaale Ridge, no less than 138 officers and 5200 men were taken as prisoners. The reason for this considerable increase in captures, as compared to recent similar advances, seems to have been that the Germans had themselves contemplated a strong attack upon the British line, especially the right sector, so that no less than five of their divisions had been brought well up to the front line at the moment when the storm burst. According to the account of prisoners, only ten minutes intervened between the zero times allotted for the two attacks. The result was not only the increase in prisoners, but also a very high mortality among the Germans, who met the full force of the barrage as well as the bayonets of the infantry. In spite of the heavy punishment already received, the Germans made several strong counter-attacks in the evening, chiefly, as stated, against the lines of the Fifth and Twenty-first Divisions north of the Menin Road, but with limited results. An attack upon the New Zealanders north of the Ypres—Roulers railway had even less success. Victorious, and yet in the last extremity of human misery and discomfort, the troops held firmly to their advanced line amid the continued pelting of the relentless rain.

The bravery and the losses of the British artillery were among the outstanding incidents of this and subsequent fighting. It was not possible on that water-sodden soil to push forward the great guns. Therefore it became necessary to make the very most of the smaller ones, and for this object the 18-pounder batteries were galloped up all along the line and then unlimbered and went into action in the open within a mile of the enemy. By this spirited action the infantry secured a barrage which could not otherwise have been accurately laid down. It should be emphasised that in this and other advances the numbers of the German were very little inferior to those of the British, which makes the success of the attacks the more surprising. Thus, in this instance, Plumer had eight divisions in line in the southern area of the battle, while opposed to him he had the Tenth Ersatz, Twentieth Division, Fourth Guards, part of Forty-fifth, part of Sixteenth, the Nineteenth Reserve, and the Eighth Division.

In Sir Douglas Haig's long and yet concise despatch, which will always serve the historian as the one firm causeway across a quagmire of possibilities and suppositions, we are told frankly the considerations which weighed with the British Higher Command in not bringing the Flanders Campaign to an end for the year with the capture of the Gravenstafel-Broodseinde Ridge. The season was advanced, the troops were tired, the weather was vile, and, worst of all, the ground was hardly passable. All these were weighty reasons why the campaign should cease now that a good defensible position had been secured. There were however some excellent reasons to the contrary. The operations had been successful, but they had not attained full success, and the position, especially in the north, was by no means favourable for the passing of the winter, since the low-lying ground

THE THIRD BATTLE OF YPRES 213

at Poelcapelle and around it was exposed to fire both from the Paschendaale Ridge and from the great forest upon the left flank and rear. If our troops were weary, there was good evidence that the Germans were not less so; and their minds and morale could not be unaffected by the fact that every British attack had been attended by loss of ground and of prisoners. Then again, it was known that the French meditated a fresh attack in the Malmaison quarter, and good team play called for a sustained effort upon the left wing to help the success of the right centre. Again, the rainfall had already been abnormally high, so that on a balance of averages there was reason to hope for better weather, though at the best it could hardly be hoped that the watery October sunshine would ever dry the fearsome bogs which lay between the armies. Of two courses it has always been Sir Douglas Haig's custom to choose the more spirited, as his whole career would show, and therefore his decision was now given for the continuance of the advance. In the result the weather failed him badly, and his losses were heavy, and yet the verdict of posterity may say that he was right. Looking back with the wisdom that comes after the event, one can clearly see that had the whole operation stopped when the rains fell after the first day, it would have been the wisest course, but when once such a movement is well under way it is difficult to compromise.

Since the line had already been established upon high ground to the south, it was evidently in the north that the new effort must be made, as the front of advance was contracted to six miles from the extreme left wing, where the French were still posted, to a point east of Zonnebeke. The wind was high, the rain intermittent, and the night cloudy and dark; but in spite of all these hindrances the storming troops were by some miracle of disciplined organisation ready in their assembly trenches, and the advance went forward at 5.20 on the morning of October 9.

Chapter IX.
The third Battle of Ypres.
Oct. 4 to Nov. 10.

Upon the left an extremely successful advance was carried out by the French and by the Guards. Of our gallant Allies it need only be said that on this day as on all others they carried out to the full what was given them to do, and established their advanced posts a mile or so to the eastward on the skirts of Houthulst Forest, taking St. Janshoek and pushing on, up to their waists sometimes in water, to the swamps of Corverbeck.

Cavan's Corps consisted of the Guards upon the left, the Twenty-ninth in the centre, and the Fourth Division upon the right. The advance of the Guards was as usual a magnificent one, and the 1st Brigade upon the right, the 2nd on the left, pushed forward the line on their sector for more than a mile, beginning by the difficult fording of the deep flooded Brombeek and then taking in their stride a number of farmhouses and strong points, as well as the villages of Koekuit and Veldhoek—the second hamlet of that name which had the ill-fortune to figure upon the war-map. Four hundred prisoners were left in their hands, mostly of the 417th Regiment, who had only taken over the line at four that morning. The 2nd Brigade of Guards worked all day in close touch with the French, amid the dangerous swamps in the north, while the 1st Brigade kept their alignment with the 4th Worcesters, who formed the left unit of the 88th Brigade upon their right. Even under the awful

THE THIRD BATTLE OF YPRES 215

conditions of ground and weather the work of the Guards was as clean and precise as ever.

The ground in front of the Guards was sown very thickly with the German concrete forts, but it was the general opinion of experienced soldiers that, formidable as were these defences, they were less so than the old trench systems, which in some cases could not be passed by any wit or valour of man. At this stage of its development the Mebus could usually be overcome by good infantry, for if its loopholes were kept buzzing with the rifle bullets of the stormers, and if under cover of such fire other parties crawled round and girt it in, its garrison had little chance. The infantry attained considerable proficiency in these operations, and "to do in a pill-box" became one of the recognised exercises of minor tactics. The losses of the Guards in this brilliant affair were not very heavy, though towards the latter stage the 1st Irish upon the right got ahead of the Newfoundlanders and were exposed to a severe flank fire in the neighbourhood of Egypt House. The 1st Coldstreams upon the extreme left flank were also held up by a strong point near Louvois Farm. It was eventually taken with its forty inmates. The gallant German officer absolutely refused to surrender, and it was necessary to bayonet him. Altogether the two brigades lost 53 officers and 1300 men. In connection with their advance and with the subsequent operations it should be mentioned that the Guards artillery was worthy of the infantry, and that the way they followed up in order to give protective barrages, slithering anywhere over the wet ground so long as they could only keep within good slating distance of the counter-attacks, was a fine bit of work. The pioneer battalion, the 4th Coldstreams,

CHAPTER IX.

The third Battle of Ypres. Oct. 4 to Nov. 10.

and the three R.E. Companies, 55, 75, and 76, put in a great deal of thankless and unostentatious work in the elaborate and difficult preparations for the advance.

The Twenty-ninth Division upon the right of the Guards had the 88th Brigade in front, with the Newfoundlanders behind the Worcesters on the left flank. Their task was to push along the Langemarck—Staden railway and reach the forest. They carried the line forward to Cinq Chemins Farm, where they established their new line. The 1st Essex and 2nd Hants were also heavily engaged, and all four battalions lived up to their high reputation.

To the right of the Twenty-ninth was the 12th Brigade of the Fourth Division, who had taken over the front line from their comrades in that fearsome wilderness already described. The line of advance was along the Ypres—Staden railway, and the front was kept level with that of the Guards. Reinforced by the 1st Rifle Brigade, the advance went swiftly forward over dreadful ground until it reached its limits at Landing Farm, about half a mile north-east of Poelcapelle.

Maxse's Corps upon the right still consisted of the Eleventh and Forty-eighth Divisions. The Eleventh Division had already captured the half of the long village of Poelcapelle, and now after some very hard fighting the second half up to the Eastern skirts fell into the hands of the 32nd Brigade. As they advanced, the Forty-sixth Midland men kept pace with them upon the right. These troops had the very worst of the low-lying ground, though they had the advantage of being in position and not having to assemble in the dark and rain, as was the fate of the more southern troops. The gallant Yorkshire battalions of the 32nd Brigade made several attempts to carry the strong point at the Brewery, east of the village, and the Midlanders had the same difficulties at a machine-gun centre called Adler Farm and Burn's House. These two points, both still untaken, marked the furthest limits of the advance in either case, and in the evening the ground gained was contracted not so much on account of German action as because it was impossible to get supplies up to the extreme line under the observation from the ridge.

Upon the right of Maxse's Corps and forming the left of the Second Anzac Corps was another Territorial Division, the Forty-ninth, drawn from the County of Broad Acres. This division, although it has seldom appeared up to now in the central limelight of battle, had done a great amount of solid work near the Ancre during the Somme battle, and on other occasions. All that will be said about the difficulties of the Sixty-sixth Division apply also to the Forty-ninth, and it may be added that in the case of both units the barrage was too fast, so that it was impossible for the infantry to keep up with it. None the less, they struggled forward with splendid courage, and if they did not win their utmost objective, at least they gained a broad belt of new ground. A limit was put to their advance by Bellevue, a stronghold on one of the spurs under Paschendaale, which was so tough a nut to crack that the weary fighting line was brought at last to a halt. The Sixteenth Rhineland Division, who held this part of the line, won the respect of their adversaries by their tenacity. The West Yorkshires of the 146th Brigade and the York and Lancasters and Yorkshire Light Infantry of the 148th bore the brunt of the battle.

CHAPTER IX.
The third Battle of Ypres.
Oct. 4 to Nov. 10.

On the immediate right of the Yorkshire men was the Sixty-sixth Division, a second-line unit of East Lancashire Territorials only recently arrived upon the seat of war, and destined, like many other new arrivals, to do conspicuously good work on their first venture. The General who commanded the Division would be the first to admit his obligations to the officers who had sent over these battalions in so battle-worthy a condition. Indeed the country owes more than it ever knows to these retired officers, veterans of the Old Imperial wars, who, far from the honours and excitements of the line, devoted their time and strength to the training of the raw material at home. They lead no charges and capture no villages, and their names are read in few gazettes : and yet it is their solid work, based upon their own great experience, which has really led many a charge to victory and proved the downfall of many a village. " If there be a procession through London, the ' dug-outs ' should lead the van," said a soldier who had that broader vision which sees both the cause and the effect.

In the case of all these divisions the conditions before the attack were almost inconceivable. For four days and nights the men were in shell-holes without shelter from the rain and the biting cold winds, and without protection from the German fire. At 6 P.M. on the evening of October 13 the Sixty-sixth and also the Forty-ninth fell in to move up the line and make the attack at dawn. So dark was the night and so heavy the rain that it took them eleven hours of groping and wading to reach the tapes which marked the lines of assembly. Then, worn out with

THE THIRD BATTLE OF YPRES 219

fatigue, wet to the skin, terribly cold, hungry, and with weapons which were often choked with mud, they went with hardly a pause into the open to face infantry who were supposed to be second to none in Europe, with every form of defence to help them which their capable sappers could devise. And yet these men of Yorkshire and Lancashire drove the Prussians before them and attained the full limit which had been given them to win.

CHAPTER IX.

The third Battle of Ypres.

Oct. 4 to Nov. 10.

The Sixty-sixth Division advanced with the 197th Brigade on the right of the Ypres—Roulers railway. It consisted entirely of battalions of the Lancashire Fusiliers, a regiment which from Minden onwards has been in the van of England's battles. Upon their left was the 198th Brigade, consisting half of East Lancs and half of Manchester battalions. So covered with mud were the troops after their long night march that the enemy may well have wondered whether our native soldiers were not once more in the line. Savagely they stuck to their task with that dour spirit which adverse conditions bring out in our soldiers; every obstacle went down before them; they reached their utmost limit, and then, half buried in the mud and stiff with cold, their blue and cramped fingers still held steady to their triggers and blew back every counter-attack which the Germans could launch. It was a fine performance, and the conditions of the attack cannot be defined better than by the following extract from the account of an officer engaged : " After advancing through the mud for a further three hours, I halted the Company in shell-holes to enable me to discover our exact whereabouts; this was a bad mistake, because when I found the direction we had to go in

CHAPTER IX.
The third Battle of Ypres.
Oct. 4 to Nov. 10.

I could not awake the poor fellows, who had fallen asleep as soon as they had sat down. I had to slave-drive, and somehow got them a little further forward before getting blown up myself." It should be added that at a later date some Australians who got up close to Paschendaale reported that they found "not far from the village some of the dead of the second-line Lancashire Territorials, who had fought beside us in an earlier battle."

Upon the south of the Second Anzac Corps were the Australian divisions, who carried forward the movement they had so splendidly initiated. The advance set before them on this day was not a deep one, but such as it was it was carried 600 yards over the ground north of Broodseinde. Owing to the difficult lie of the ground, the attacking troops were particularly exposed to machine-gun fire, especially at the cutting of the Roulers railway which at this point comes through the low ridge. The result was a considerable loss of men. The Australians had been a week in the line without rest in continual fighting, and they were very weary, but still full of dash and zeal and sympathy for others. "We met one British officer," says Mr. Bean, "stumbling back with both his puttees long since lost in the mud. 'Bitterly disappointed we were late,' he said. 'Hard luck, too, upon the Australians.' One thought to oneself when one heard of the conditions, that it was only due to their undiluted heroism that they ever got there at all." It was the Second Australian Division which was chiefly engaged in this difficult battle, and it was they who carried Daisy Wood, the chief obstacle in that area. The First Australian Division were hardly included in the

THE THIRD BATTLE OF YPRES 221

original scheme, being too far to the right; but being unable to witness a fight without joining in it they advanced upon Celtic Wood, passed through it, and had some excellent fighting with a strong German trench upon the further side of it. The operation was a raid rather than an advance, but it was very useful, none the less, as a distraction to the Germans.

On the extreme south of the line Reutel, which had been left in German hands upon October 4, was now carried by storm in a very brilliant operation which removed the salient of the Seventh Division to which allusion has already been made. This advance was carried out by two battalions, the 2nd Warwicks upon the left and the 2nd Honourable Artillery Company upon the right. The former took, after hard fighting, the outlying woods and trenches to the north of the village, but the Londoners achieved the more difficult task of carrying the village itself. It was a desperate enterprise, carried out under heavy fire, which was so deadly that when the depleted ranks reached their further objective not an officer was left standing. The high quality of the rank and file is shown in the prompt way in which they took the necessary steps upon their own initiative, by which the new line should be held. As to their losses, they can be best indicated by the dry official comment: "The remnants of A, C and D Companies were withdrawn to Jolting Trench and organised into two platoons under Sergeant Jenkinson." The Colonel might well be proud of his men, and London of her sons.

The extreme right of the British attacking line upon October 9 was formed by the 15th Brigade of the Fifth Division. Once again they got into the

CHAPTER IX.

The third Battle of Ypres.
Oct. 4 to Nov. 10.

Polderhoek Château, and once again they had to retire from it and resume the position in front of it. There have been few single points in the War which have been the object of such fierce and fluctuating strife.

The net effect of this battle in the mud was to fling the whole line forward, the advance being much more shallow in the south than in the north. The line had rolled down from the Broodseinde Ridge, crossed the shallow valley, and now established itself upon the slope of Paschendaale. Two thousand one hundred prisoners had been taken in this advance. It was clear, however, that matters could not remain so, and that, be the weather what it might (and worse it could not be!) Sir Douglas was bound to plant his men upon the higher ground of Paschendaale before he called his halt for the winter.

Upon October 12, under conditions which tended to grow worse rather than better, Sir Douglas Haig made a fresh attempt to get forward. As the Paschendaale Height became more clearly the final objective, the attack narrowed at the base, so that instead of extending from the Menin Road in the south, it was now flanked by the Ypres—Roulers railway, and so had a front of not more than five miles. The new attack was carried out largely by the same troops as before in the north, save that the 51st Brigade of the Seventeenth Division was pushed in between the Guards upon the left and the 12th Brigade of the Fourth Division upon the right. Advancing along the line of the Ypres—Sladen railway, the 3rd Brigade of Guards and their comrades of the Fourteenth Corps got forward to their limited objectives, where they sank once more into the sea of

THE THIRD BATTLE OF YPRES 223

mud through which they had waded. On both sides the making of trenches had entirely ceased, as it had been found that a few shell-holes united by a small cutting were sufficient for every purpose as long as the head of the soldier could be kept out of the water. So useful were these holes as shelters and rifle-pits that it became a question with the British artillery whether they should not confine their fire entirely to shrapnel, rather than run the risk of digging a line of entrenchments for the enemy.

In this advance the 51st Brigade did remarkably well, advancing 1200 yards and securing two objectives. It is amongst the curiosities of the campaign that Major Peddie of the 7th Lincolns, with another officer and four men, took 148 prisoners from a farm—a feat for which he received the D.S.O.

On Maxse's front the Eighteenth and Ninth Divisions had taken over the front line. The Eighteenth made some progress, but the Ninth, of which it can truly be said that they never leave a front as they found it, took the village of Wallemolen, making a good advance.

The New Zealanders were on the right of the Ninth Division, covering a front of 1600 yards from Adler House on the left to the Ravebeek upon the right, where they joined the Australian Division. They were faced partly by uncut wire in the Bellevue position and partly by marsh. The conditions for the Australians upon their right were no better. The matter was made worse by the impossibility of getting the heavier guns forward, while the light ones slid their trails about in the mud after every discharge in a manner which made accurate shooting well-nigh impossible. The losses were heavy in the attack,

CHAPTER IX.

The third Battle of Ypres.
Oct. 4 to Nov. 10,

224 THE BRITISH CAMPAIGN, 1917

CHAPTER IX.
The third Battle of Ypres.
Oct. 4 to Nov. 10.

two Colonels of New Zealand battalions being among the dead. The New Zealand Rifle Brigade were particularly hard hit. It was found that progress was impossible under such conditions, and the attack was called off. So far as the Germans went, 1000 more were added to the occupants of the cages—so far as the mud and weather went, they gained a clear victory over the British Army, for the losses were heavy, and there was very little gain of ground in exchange.

Upon October 22, the ground having dried a little, there was some movement at the northern end of the line, the position being improved and 200 prisoners taken. The two operations which effected these results were carried out in the north by Franks' Thirty-fifth Division co-operating with the French, and in the Poelcapelle region by the 53rd Brigade of the Eighteenth Division, which carried the point known as Meunier Hill, the Essex, Suffolks, and Norfolks of this splendid unit covering themselves once more with glory. The Thirty-fourth Division, which had taken the place of the Fourth upon the right of Cavan's corps, also moved forward in correspondence with the flanking units, the Northumberland Fusiliers of the 103rd Brigade keeping touch with the 8th Norfolks of the 53rd.

Some hard fighting was associated with the attack of the Thirty-fifth Division in the north. It may be remarked that the Bantam idea had not proved to be a successful one. It had been abandoned, and the Thirty-fifth was now undistinguishable from any division either in its physique or in its spirit. Upon this occasion both the 105th Brigade upon the left and the 104th upon the right fought with magnificent courage. The advance of

THE THIRD BATTLE OF YPRES 225

the former Brigade was particularly fine in the region of Panama House. The 14th Glosters and 16th Cheshires attained their fullest objective, and though the latter were finally bent back by the strong German attacks in the afternoon, the Glosters' fighting line, reinforced by some of the 16th Sherwood Foresters, held fast under the most desperate circumstances. Their Colonel might well be proud of the fact that in an attack carried out by one French and two British divisions his battalion of Glosters was the only one which remained rooted and unshaken upon the ultimate line. The Lancashire Fusiliers shone greatly also in the attack, though they were unable to maintain their most advanced positions. The German shell-fire, and especially the German snipers from the wood on the left, and from a covered road, were the cause of heavy losses, but the troops were in excellent fettle, and the 104th Brigade actually executed a little raid on its own during the night, bringing back a machine-gun and five more prisoners.

On October 26, the rain still pouring down as heavily as ever, and the earth about as liquid as the heavens, the advance was once again renewed upon a narrow front which was mostly on the slope of the hill and therefore offered some foothold for the struggling infantry. Paschendaale was but a few hundreds of yards away, and it was imperative that it should be held before the season ended. Haig's troops were weary, and several fresh divisions which he could have called upon were already earmarked for the surprise attack which he was planning in the south. It was imperative, however, to have some fresh thrusting force which could be trusted to break down the remaining obstacles and not only seize the

Q

CHAPTER IX.

The third Battle of Ypres.
Oct. 4 to Nov. 10.

dominant village, but hold it after seizure. For this object the close Canadian beleaguerment of Lens, which was to have ended in an assault, was abandoned, and the Canadian Corps was brought round to the Ypres front, taking the place of the Anzac Corps. In the new advance it occupied, therefore, the central position of the line.

There had been several divisional changes in the north. The front of General Cavan's line consisted now of the Fiftieth Division next the French, the Thirty-fifth Division, and the Fifty-seventh Division. Maxse's battle line was the Fifty-eighth London Division and the Sixty-third Naval. In spite of every possible disadvantage, fresh ground was gained by these units, and Varlet Farm, Bray Farm, and Banff House were added to the British area.

The conditions of these low-lying valleys to the north, which had long been difficult, had now become really impossible, and this was the last attempt to advance in the Houlthulst Forest area. It takes personal and detailed narrative to enable the reader to realise the situation which the troops had to face. An officer of the 170th Brigade, a Lancashire unit which displayed great valour and lost half its numbers upon this date, writes: "I have never seen such a sight as that country was in the valley of the Broombeek and Watervlietbeek just south of Houthulst Forest. Nothing on earth but the wonderful courage of the Lancashire lads enabled them to get so far as they did. We went over with our rifles and Lewis guns bound up with flannel so as to keep the mud out, and with special cleaning apparatus in our pockets, but you can't clean a rifle when your own hands are covered an inch thick! We killed a great

THE THIRD BATTLE OF YPRES

number—one of the Sergeants in the 'Loyals' laid out 13 with his bayonet; altogether we actually killed over 600 with the bayonet; but, as I say, the ground was too heavy to allow us to out-manœuvre the pill-boxes, and though we took three or four, the rest did us in. In one box we got 38 Boche, killed them all with a Lewis gun through the porthole." After that day no more advance was tried in the low-lying valleys named. The impossibility was seen.

CHAPTER IX.

The third Battle of Ypres. Oct. 4 to Nov. 10.

The Canadian Corps went forward with one brigade of the Fourth Division upon the right and two brigades of the Third Division upon the left. A brigade of the First Australian Division supported their left upon the Ypres—Roulers railway, and the Sixty-third Naval Division continued the attack. Each of these units gained ground under the most desperate conditions. The Australians captured Decline Wood, so securing the flank of the attack. The Canadians pushed forward on each side of the Revebeek, one of the innumerable streams which meander through this country. The Third Canadian Division advanced finely, but their right-hand brigade was held up by the machine-gun fire from Bellevue Spur, which had wrought such damage in the former attack, and was compelled to fall back upon its original line. The Canadians rallied for a second spring, and in the afternoon by a splendid effort, when all their Northern grit and energy were needed, they flooded over the obstacle and lined up with their comrades. They were now right astride of the main ridge and close up to the edge of the village. To the north, the Sixty-third Naval Division, which formed the right unit of Maxse's Corps, pushed forward to the line of the

Chapter IX.
The third Battle of Ypres.
Oct. 4 to Nov. 10.

Paddebeek, while the Londoners of the Fifty-eighth Division kept their place upon the left. The German artillery had greatly increased in strength, thanks to the Russian collapse, and every fresh idiocy of Petrograd was transmuted into showers of steel and iron in the plains of Flanders. Their infantry also became more aggressive with this stronger support, and two heavy counters broke upon the Canadians in the afternoon of October 26. In spite of every obstacle, it was an important day in this section of the line for Paschendaale was almost reached, and the Germans must have viewed with despair the ever-advancing line, which neither they nor Nature had been able to stop.

In the south the operations during the day were not so successful, and the subsidiary aims were not attained. In the morning, the Fifth Division attacked and once again captured the Wood and Château of Polderhoek. The 1st West Kents and 13th Warwicks of the 13th Brigade carried out this dashing and arduous operation, and took some 200 men, who formed the garrison. The Seventh Division meanwhile had advanced upon Gheluvelt, the 2nd West Surrey, 1st South Staffords and Manchesters of the 91st Brigade advancing to the south of the Menin Road in order to guard the flank of their comrades who followed the line of the road which would lead them to this famous village. The flanking brigade was held up, however, at the old stumbling-block near Lewis House and Berry Cotts, where the German fire was very deadly. This failure enabled the enemy to bring a very heavy cross-fire upon the 2nd Borderers and 2nd Gordons of the 20th Brigade, forming the column of attack. In spite of this fire,

THE THIRD BATTLE OF YPRES   229

the stormers forced their way into Gheluvelt, but found themselves involved in very hard fighting, while their guns were choked with mud, and useless save as pikes or clubs. Under these circumstances they were forced back to their own line.. Encouraged by this success, the Germans then advanced in very heavy masses and attacked the new positions of the Fifth Division with such fury that they also had to loose their grip of the precious twice-conquered Château and fall back on the line whence they started. It cannot be denied, therefore, that though the British gained ground in the north upon October 26, they sustained nothing but losses after their great exertions in the south upon that date. The two outstanding features of the fighting seem to have been the extreme difficulty of keeping the weapons in a serviceable condition, a factor which naturally told in favour of the stationary defence, and also the innocuousness of percussion shells, since in such a swamp they bury themselves so deeply that their explosion does little harm. Some 500 prisoners were made in the southern area, but many more in the north.

Upon October 30, in cold and windy weather, the attack was renewed upon a comparatively narrow front, with the First Australian Division upon the extreme right, then the Fourth Canadians, then the Third Canadians, and finally the Sixty-third Division upon the left. The Canadians advancing along the ridge towards the doomed village were faced by a terrific concentration of German guns upon that limited space and by strong infantry attacks, none of which turned them from their purpose. The direction of the attack was from west and south-west.

CHAPTER IX.

The third Battle of Ypres.

Oct. 4 to Nov. 10.

The Fourth Canadians soon had all their objectives and held them firmly, taking Crest Farm on the edge of the village. The Third Canadians had heavy resistance to overcome, but captured the spur in front of them and joined up with their comrades at Graf. The Sixty-third Division found it very difficult to get forward, however, and this held back the left wing of the Canadians. Five severe attacks were made upon the Canadians, but were all beaten off by their steady fire. In some cases, notably at Crest Farm, the machine-guns captured from the Germans were turned upon their late owners as they debouched from the village. There was considerable evidence of demoralisation among the German infantry upon this occasion whenever the British could get to grips with it, and some sections actually ran away at the outbreak of the fight, which is a very unusual occurrence in so disciplined and brave an army. The latter part of the action was fought in driving rain, which hardly allowed vision of more than a couple of hundred yards.

All these heroic exertions were consummated at six on the morning of November 6, when the Canadian infantry, advancing with heroic dash, flung themselves upon the village and carried the British line right through it, emerging upon the naked ridge beyond. The advance on the left was made by the 1st Brigade, while the 5th Brigade took the village. Many strong points lay just north of the hamlet, but each of them was rushed in turn. It was a splendid success, and wrought by splendid men. The chronicler cannot easily forget how by a wayside Kentish station he saw the wounded from this attack lying silent and patient after their weary journey,

THE THIRD BATTLE OF YPRES 231

and how their motionless, clay-spattered figures, their set, firm faces and their undaunted eyes, gave him an impression of military efficiency and virtue such as none of the glitter and pride and pomp of war have ever conveyed. So fell Paschendaale, and so, save for some minor readjustments upon the Ridge, ended the great battle which can only be all included in the title "The Third Battle of Ypres."

CHAPTER IX.

The third Battle of Ypres.

Oct. 4 to Nov. 10.

Several attempts were made to clear the whole of the ridge but the rain was still continuous, the ground a nightmare, and the fire of the German guns was concentrated upon so limited a space that the advance was hardly possible. Jacob's Second Corps had come back into the line, and one of its units, the First Division, came up upon November 9 on the left of the Canadians, and endeavoured in co-operation with them to extend the position. The Germans had cleverly removed their heavy guns to such a position that they could reach the ridge, while the British guns, immobile in the mud, could not attempt any counter-battery work. In this way a very intense fire, against which no reply could be made, was kept up on the ridge. On November 10 the 2nd Canadian Brigade upon the right and the 3rd British Brigade upon the left endeavoured to work forward; but the losses were heavy and the gains slight. The two leading British battalions, the 1st South Wales Borderers and the 2nd Munsters, were the chief sufferers. It was clear that the season was too far advanced to attempt any useful work. On November 12 the Thirty-second Division relieved the First, and the line was again slightly advanced; but no more could be done and the troops settled down into the quagmire to spend the winter as best they might. The Eighth Corps took over the lines of the Canadians, who returned, after their splendid and arduous work, to their old sector at Lens.

On the other sectors of the northern front there had been a lull while this last stage of the Paschendaale fighting was in progress. It was broken only by a sharp, sudden attack by the Fifth Division upon its old enemy, the Poldershoek Château, upon November 6. After some severe fighting the attack failed and the British line remained as before.

Thus, after a continuance of three months, the long struggle came to an end. Only the titanic Battle of the Somme had exceeded it in length and severity. The three great Battles of Ypres are destined to become classical in British history, and it will be a nice question for the judgment of posterity which of the three was the most remarkable military performance. Though the scene was the same, the drama was of a very different quality in each act, but always equally intense. In the first, inferior numbers of British troops with a vastly inferior artillery held up the German Army in its first rush for the coast, and, by virtue of the high training and close cohesion of the old regulars, barred their path even at the cost of their own practical annihilation. In the second, a less homogeneous and less trained British force, still with a very inferior artillery, held back a German line which was formidable, less for its numbers than for the sudden use of new methods of warfare against which their opponents could neither guard nor reply. The line receded under the pressure, but the way was still barred. In the third, the British advanced and steadily pushed back a German Army

THE THIRD BATTLE OF YPRES 233

which was probably inferior in numbers—and certainly was so in gun power—but which held a series of predominating positions stiffened by every method which experience could suggest or ingenuity devise. Their resistance was helped by the most adverse weather conditions which could be conceived. The net result of the fighting was not only the capture of the crest of the final ridge, but the taking of 24,000 prisoners and 72 guns. When one remembers that the Germans in the days of their ascendancy could not in the two battles of Ypres put together have taken more than 5000 men, one can measure the comparative success of each army in this conflict of giants. It would be vain to pretend that we did not hope for a greater gain of ground in this great autumn movement, but the reach of a General must often exceed his grasp, and here it was no small prize which still remained with the victor.

CHAPTER IX.

The third Battle of Ypres.

Oct. 4 to Nov. 10.

One can only sum up the matter by quoting the measured words of the Field-Marshal in Command : " This offensive, maintained for three-and-a-half months under the most adverse conditions of weather, had entailed almost superhuman exertions on the part of the troops of all arms and services. The enemy had done his utmost to hold his ground, and in his endeavours to do so had used up no less than seventy-eight divisions, of which eighteen had been engaged a second or third time in the battle, after being withdrawn to rest and refit. Despite the magnitude of his efforts, it was the immense natural difficulties, accentuated manifold by the abnormally wet weather, rather than the enemy's resistance, which limited our progress and prevented the complete capture of the ridge."

Whilst this long and arduous struggle had been

CHAPTER IX.

The third Battle of Ypres.

Oct. 4 to Nov. 10.

raging the chief events upon the other seats of war had been a fine French victory on the Aisne which yielded nearly 10,000 prisoners. This was upon September 23, but the rejoicings of the Allies were turned to sorrow by the news next day of the set back of the second Italian army at Caporetto, where the soldiers, demoralised by insidious propaganda, offered at the most critical sector hardly any resistance to the enemy who had been reinforced by some German divisions. The result was that the other Italian armies upon right and left were compelled to fall back and could find no standing ground until they had crossed the Piave. Udine and the whole Friulian Plain were lost and all the results of so many heroic months were undone. It was one of the saddest tragedies of the war, though destined in the future to be most gloriously avenged.

CHAPTER X

THE BATTLE OF CAMBRAI

First phase, November 20—Tanks *en masse*—Attack on the Tunnel Trench—Byng's great advance—Fine work of Braithwaite's Sixty-second Division—Hard fighting of Pulteney's Third Corps—Exploit of Fort Garry Horse—Second day of battle—Rally of Germans—Capture of Bourlon Wood by Fortieth Division—Attack by the Guards on La Fontaine.

THE year 1917 had begun with high hopes for the Allies since they had planned a common offensive which could hardly have failed to break the German resistance. Both France and England had honourably carried out their share in the common contract. It was the sudden and absolute break down of Russia which caused the year to set in gloom rather than in glory. The phenomenon of that great fermenting putrefying country was more like some huge cataclysm of nature, some monstrous convulsion of the elements, than any ordinary political movement, so that anger and contempt were softened into pure amazement as the gradual dissolution of the vast organism took place from week to week before a wondering world. It was as though a robust man had suddenly softened into liquid putrescence before one's eyes. But from a military standpoint it was a disaster of the first order for the Allies and checked their victorious career in the West, where the failing

CHAPTER X.

The Battle of Cambrai. First Phase. Nov. 20.

German line could always be buttressed up by fresh guns and fresh divisions from the East. Now on the top of this misfortune another unforeseen and almost incredible occurrence placed them at a further disadvantage. The Italian army had done so splendidly well and had won such unfailing ascendancy over the Austrians that their stability seemed as firm as the mountains amid which they fought. It seems, however, that insidious and treasonable propaganda of the familiar type had spread disaffection in the ranks, and the Second Army, which held the very centre of the Gorizian line, collapsed suddenly. The result was a very great success for the Austrian and German forces, who pushed through the breach, and with little loss to themselves captured more than 200,000 prisoners and nearly 2000 guns. It was a very severe blow for the Allies, and never was their fine spirit better shown than by the instant steps which they took to hold Italy up in the moment of her extreme need. By road and by rail reinforcements poured through the passes of the Alps and along the shores of the Mediterranean. Whilst the flanking armies of the Italians fell back upon new lines French and British divisions were hastening forward to share their pressing danger. The Isonzo and the Tagliamento had been in succession abandoned, for a severe flanking attack from the north threatened to break through the passes and debouch upon the Friulian Plain. Finally the line of the Piave was reached which still covered Venice. Here the steadier troops were halted. In the First Army upon the right there had been little disorganisation, and their retreat along the coast under constant pressure was a fine bit of work. Ten batteries of British heavies were

THE BATTLE OF CAMBRAI 237

among the artillery of this army, and every one of them was man-handled to the new positions. By mid-winter two French and two British Corps, veterans of many battles, were lined up on or near the Piave, waiting eagerly to try conclusions with these new adversaries. This detached British army was commanded by General Plumer, with Generals Lord Cavan and Haking as his Corps commanders. The two Corps, the Thirteenth and Fourteenth, were made up of the Fifth, Seventh, Twenty-third, Forty-first, and Forty-eighth Divisions, grand units all. It was a sore loss to the battle-line of Flanders—a loss which in the case of two of them was but temporary.

Chapter X.
The Battle of Cambrai.
First Phase.
Nov. 20.

We shall now descend the line to the section which extends from Bullecourt in the north to Villers-Ghislain in the south, opposite to the important town of Cambrai, some seven miles behind the Hindenburg Line. It was here that the Field-Marshal had determined to strike his surprise blow, an enterprise which he has described in so lucid and detailed a despatch that the weary chronicler has the rare experience of finding history adequately recorded by the same brain which planned it. The plan was a very daring one, for the spot attacked was barred by the full unbroken strength of the Hindenburg main and support lines, a work so huge and solid that it seems to take us back from these superficial days to the era of the Cyclopean builder or the founder of the great monuments of antiquity. These enormous excavations of prodigious length, depth, and finish are object lessons both of the strength of the Germans, the skill of their engineers, and the ruthlessness with which they exploited the slave and captive labour with which so much of it was built. Besides this

CHAPTER X.

The Battle of Cambrai. First Phase. Nov. 20.

terrific barricade there was the further difficulty that the whole method of attack was experimental, and that to advance without artillery fire against such a position would appear to be a most desperate venture. On the other hand it was known that the German line was thin and that their man-power had been attracted northwards by the long epic of the Paschendaale attack. There was a well-founded belief that the tanks would prove equal to the task of breaking the front, and sufficient infantry had been assembled to take advantage of any opening which might be made. The prize, too, was worth a risk, for apart from the possibility of capturing the important centre of Cambrai, the possession of the high ground at Bourlon would be of great strategic value. The enterprise was placed in the hands of General Byng, the famous leader of the Third Cavalry Division and afterwards of the Canadian Corps, who had taken Allenby's place at the head of the Third Army. Under him were from the north, the Sixth, Fourth, Third, and Seventh Corps under Haldane, Woolcombe, Pulteney, and Snow, containing some of the most seasoned fighting material in the army. The troops were brought up stealthily by night, and the tanks which were crawling from every direction towards the trysting-place were carefully camouflaged. The French had been apprised of the attack, and had made arrangements by which, if there were an opening made to the south some of their divisions should be available to take advantage of it.

The tanks were about four hundred in number and were under the separate command of General Elles, a dashing soldier who inspired the utmost enthusiasm in his command. It had always been

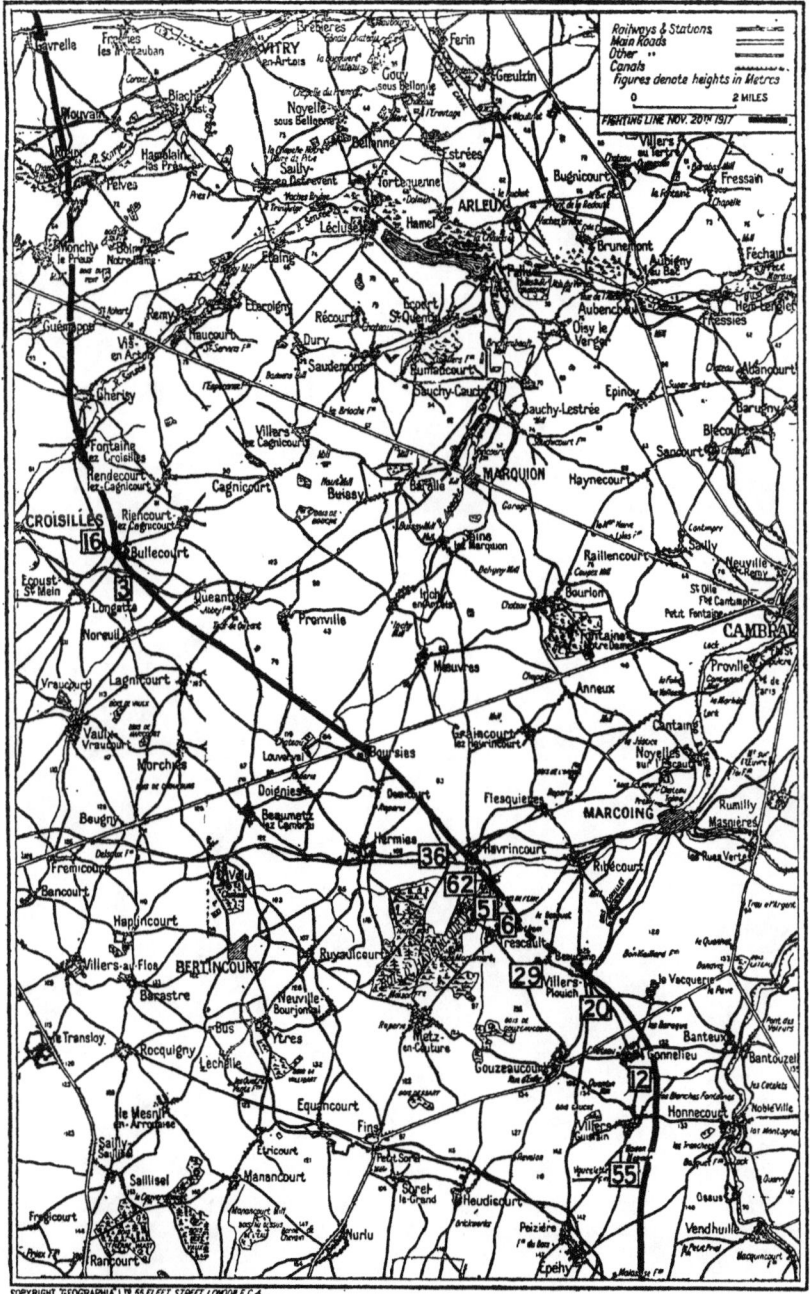

To face page 230.

THE BATTLE OF CAMBRAI 239

the contention of the tank designers in England that their special weapon needed, what it had never yet found, virgin ground which was neither a morass nor a wilderness of shell-holes. The leading lines of tanks had been furnished with enormous faggots of wood which they carried across their bows and which would be released so as to fall forward into any ditch or trench and to form a rude bridge. These ready-made weight-bearers were found to act admirably.

CHAPTER X.

The Battle of Cambrai. First Phase. Nov. 20.

One difficulty with which the operations were confronted was that it was impossible for the guns to register properly without arousing suspicion. It was left to the gunners, therefore, to pick up their range as best they might after the action began, and this they did with a speed and accuracy which showed their high technical efficiency.

Taking the description of the operations upon November 20th from the north end of the line we shall first deal with the subsidiary but very important and successful attacks carried out by Haldane's Sixth Corps in the neighbourhood of Bullecourt. The Hindenburg Line at this point consisted of a front trench with a second or support trench 300 yards behind it, and many scattered Mebus or concrete machine-gun forts. The British had already a lodgement in part of the front trench, and the main objective now was the support trench which was called " Tunnel Trench " because it had a tunnel 30 or 40 feet down along its whole length with staircase entrances every 25 yards. The units to whom the attack was entrusted were the Third Division upon the right, and the Sixteenth Irish Division upon the left.

The morning of November 20 was overcast but not actually raining, with low visibility, which may

240 THE BRITISH CAMPAIGN, 1917

CHAPTER X.

The Battle of Cambrai. First Phase. Nov. 20.

account for the fact that the German barrage was feeble, slow, and inaccurate.

The advance of the Sixteenth Division was by three brigades, the 47th on the right, the 48th in the centre, and the 49th upon the left. Every up-to-date infantry-saving device, the artillery barrage, the machine-gun barrage, and the Stokes-mortar smoke-screen was used to the full. The guns had been reinforced by a portion of the artillery of the Thirty-fourth Division, and the support which they gave was admirably effective. We will trace the attack from the right.

The flank battalion was the 6th Connaughts with the 1st Munsters upon their left. Their objective was taken with a spring. The Munsters were able to consolidate at once. The Connaughts had more trouble as a rush of German bombers came down upon their right, driving the flank company in and forcing it back down the sap. For several hours there was hard fighting at this point, which was often hand-to-hand when the Irish bayonet men rushed at the German bomb-throwers. Finally a block and a defensive flank were formed, and two big Mebus, Mars and Jove, were left in the hands of the stormers.

In the centre the advance of the 10th Dublin Fusiliers and of the 2nd Dublin Fusiliers was entirely successful. So sudden was the attack that many of the enemy were found wearing their gas masks. Two large Mebus, Juno and Minerva, with a good stretch of tunnel trench remained, together with many prisoners, in the hands of the stormers. The position was rapidly wired with concertina wire and new trenches dug for defence and communication by the

THE BATTLE OF CAMBRAI 241

155th Field Co. R.E. and the 11th Hants Pioneer battalion.

On the left the storming battalions were the 2nd Royal Irish and the 7/8th Irish Fusiliers. The Royal Irish carried both tunnel and support trenches with the Flora Mebus, taking 200 prisoners. Many Germans retreated into the tunnel, but were pelted out again by Mills grenades. The Fusiliers were equally successful, but had one short hold-up owing to the determined resistance of a single officer and ten men. This little party made a brave fight, and were so situated that they commanded two lines of trench. Eventually they were all killed. The support trench was occupied, the tunnel cleared by the 174th Tunnelling Company, and the whole position made good in a most workmanlike way. A series of counter-attacks were stamped out by the barrage before they could get properly going.

The tunnel, as explained, was a continuous gallery opening into the trench and extending eastwards. It had numerous chambers leading off, fitted with wire bunks, tables, etc. This section was elaborately mined, but the position of the leads had been accurately disclosed by a deserter, and they were soon cut by the sappers.

In this swift and successful operation some 635 prisoners of the 470th and 471st Regiments were taken, with many minor trophies. Many Germans had been killed, 330 bodies being counted in the trenches alone. Altogether it was a remarkably smooth-running operation, and the model of an attack with limited objective, upon which General Haldane and all concerned might be congratulated. It was the more remarkable as it was carried out without

CHAPTER X.

The Battle of Cambrai. First Phase. Nov. 20.

R

242 THE BRITISH CAMPAIGN, 1917

CHAPTER X.

The Battle of Cambrai. First Phase. Nov. 20.

preliminary bombardment, and no help from the tanks.

While the Irish had attacked upon the left a single brigade of the Third Division, the 9th, advanced upon their right, and keeping pace with their comrades carried out a most successful attack, securing a further length of the tunnel trench. There was no further fighting of consequence in this area of the battle, save for some movement forward on the part of the Irish division and one short counter-attack by the Germans.

It will be understood that this attack was some miles to the north of the main battle, and that a long section of unbroken Hindenburg Line intervened between the two. Along this line the Fifty-sixth Division kept up a spirited Chinese attack all day. The real advance was upon a frontage of six miles which covered the front from Hermies in the north to Gonnelieu in the south. Every company of the advancing units had been instructed to fall in behind its own marked tank. At 6.20, just after dawn, in a favouring haze, General Elles gave the signal, his iron-clad fleet flowed forward, the field of wire went down with a long splintering rending crash, the huge faggots were rolled forward into the gaping ditches, and the eager infantry crowded forward down the clear swathes which the monsters had cut. At the same moment the guns roared out, and an effective smoke-barrage screened the whole strange spectacle from the German observers.

The long line of tanks, magnified to monstrous size in the dim light of early dawn, the columns of infantry with fixed bayonets who followed them, all advancing in silent order, formed a spectacle which none who took part in it could ever forget. Everything went

THE BATTLE OF CAMBRAI 243

without a hitch, and in a few minutes the whole Hindenburg Line with its amazed occupants was in the hands of the assailants. Still following their iron guides they pushed on to their further objectives. As these differed, and as the fortunes of the units varied, it will be well to take them in turn, always working from the left of the line.

CHAPTER X.

The Battle of Cambrai. First Phase. Nov. 20.

The British front was cut across diagonally by a considerable canal with deep sides, the Canal du Nord. Upon the north side of this was one division. This flank unit was the famous Thirty-sixth Ulsters, who behaved this day with their usual magnificent gallantry. Advancing with deliberate determination, they carried all before them, though exposed to that extra strain to which a flank unit must always submit. Their left was always enfiladed by the enemy and they had continually to build up a defensive line, which naturally subtracted from their numbers and made a long advance impossible. None the less, after rushing a high bank bristling with machine-guns they secured the second Hindenburg Line, where they were firmly established by 10.30 after a sharp contest with the garrison. They then swept forward, keeping the canal upon their right, until by evening they had established themselves upon the Bapaume — Cambrai Road. It was the brigade moving parallel to the Sixty-second Division upon which the heavier work fell.

Upon the immediate right of the Irishmen was Braithwaite's Sixty-second Division of West Riding Yorkshire Territorials—one of those second line units whose solid excellence has been one of the surprises of the war. Six of them had already come to the front, and not one of the six which had not made its

CHAPTER X.

The Battle of Cambrai. First Phase. Nov. 20.

mark. On this occasion the men of the West Riding made an advance which was the admiration of the army, and which the Field-Marshal, who weighs his words carefully, described as "a brilliant achievement." The first obstacle in front of the 185th West Yorkshire Brigade upon the right was the village of Havrincourt, which, with the aid of the tanks, they carried in dashing style, though the resistance from the Château was very fierce. Behind it lay the reserve German line, which also was taken at the point of the bayonet. Upon the left the 187th Brigade, containing two Yorks and Lancaster and two Yorkshire Light Infantry battalions, swept gloriously forward and got every objective, including the northern half of Havrincourt. The 2/5th Yorkshire Light Infantry was particularly fine, as it charged without tanks and yet kept up with the line. The 186th Brigade, consisting of four battalions of the West Riding Regiment, then passed through in a splendid rush which carried them up to and through the village of Graincourt, regardless of the fact that Flesquières on the right was untaken. Surging on the 188th Reserve Brigade reached and captured the important village of Graincourt, much aided by two audacious tanks. With an energy which was still unabated they pushed on to Anneux, where they reached the fringe of the houses. It was a truly splendid day's work, in which four and a half miles of every devilry which German sappers could build or German infantry defend was inexorably beaten down. In all these operations they were aided and supported, not only by the tanks, but by the 11th Hussars, and also by a body of King Edward's Horse. Thirty-seven guns and 2000 prisoners were the fine trophies of this one division.

THE BATTLE OF CAMBRAI 245

Upon the right of Braithwaite's Yorkshiremen was the Fifty-first Highland Territorial Division. They also made a fine advance, but were held up by the strongly organised village of Flesquières. The approach to it was a long slope swept by machine-gun fire, and the co-operation of the tanks was made difficult by a number of advanced field-guns which destroyed the slow-moving machines as they approached up the hill. If the passage of the Hindenburg Line showed the strength of these machines, the check at Flesquières showed their weakness, for in their present state of development they were helpless before a well-served field-gun, and a shell striking them meant the destruction of the tank, and often the death of the crew. It is said that a single Prussian artillery officer, who stood by his gun to the death and is chivalrously immortalised in the British bulletin, destroyed no less than sixteen tanks by direct hits. At the same time the long and solid wall of the Château formed an obstacle to the infantry, as did the tangle of wire which surrounded the village. The fighting was very severe and the losses considerable, but before evening the Highlanders had secured the ground round the village and were close up to the village itself. The delay had, however, a sinister effect upon the British plans, as the defiant village, spitting out flames and lead from every cranny and window, swept the ground around and created a broad zone on either side, across which progress was difficult and dangerous. It was the resistance of this village, and the subsequent breaking of the bridges upon the canal, which prevented the cavalry from fulfilling their full role upon this first day of battle.

CHAPTER X.

The Battle of Cambrai. First Phase. Nov. 20.

None the less as dismounted units they did sterling work, and one small mounted body of Canadian Cavalry, the Fort Garry Horse from Winnipeg, particularly distinguished itself, getting over every obstacle, taking a German battery, dispersing a considerable body of infantry, and returning after a day of desperate adventure without their horses, but with a sample of the forces which they had encountered. It was a splendid deed of arms, for which Lieutenant Henry Strachan, who led the charge after the early fall of the squadron leader, received the coveted Cross.

Upon the right of the Fifty-first Division was the Sixth, which was faced by the village of Ribecourt. Into this it stormed, and after some heavy street and house fighting it cleared it of its German garrison. The advance was carried out with the 71st Brigade upon the right and the 18th upon the left. The village was carried by storm by the 9th Norfolks of the 71st Brigade passing through the 1st Leicesters, who, together with the 2nd Sherwood Foresters, had stormed the Hindenburg Line, following close upon the tanks, upon whose iron flanks they could hear the rifle bullets patter like hailstones. The losses of the division were light, as their instructions were to dig in upon the further side of the village and act as a connecting link. The Foresters, however, had at least one sharp tussle before they gained their full objective. A shock battalion charged them, and there was a period of desperate fighting during which the Germans displayed a valour which sometimes was almost that of fanatics. " One of their companies was cut off. We offered them quarter, but they would not hear of

THE BATTLE OF CAMBRAI 247

it. The last to go was a young sub. When he saw that all was up he drew his revolver and shot himself. As he fell I ran forward in the hope to save him, for he was a brave lad. When I got to his side he looked at me with a look of intense hate and tried to take aim with his pistol. It fell from his hand and he fell dead with that look of hate still on his face."

In connection with this advance of the Sixth Division it should be stated that the 2nd Durham Light Infantry upon the left charged a battery and captured the guns, a fine feat of arms.

Upon the right of the Sixth Division was the Twenty-ninth Regular Division which was held back from the advance until its flank was secured upon the right. When this had been accomplished by the Twelfth Division it dashed swiftly forward upon a three-brigade front, the 87th and 86th Brigades seizing respectively Marcoing and Neuf Wood which is immediately beyond it. Here they found themselves in very close collaboration with the Sixth Division, through whom they passed in their advance. On the right the 88th Brigade, after hard fighting in the Hindenburg support line, captured Les Rues Vertes and part of Mesnières. The taking of these two villages was really of great importance in the general scheme of operations, and the advances of the divisions upon either flank may be looked upon as simply a screen to cover the Twenty-ninth while it sped forward upon its venture. The reason of this was that the Canal de l'Escaut, a very formidable obstacle, covered the whole German front south of Cambrai, and that unless it were taken all advance in this direction was impossible. There were bridges at Mesnières and Marcoing, and these were the nearest

Chapter X.
The Battle of Cambrai.
First Phase.
Nov. 20.

CHAPTER X.

The Battle of Cambrai. First Phase. Nov. 20.

points to the British line. Hence it was that the flanks of the Twenty-ninth were carefully covered and a clear opening made for it, that with one tiger-spring it might seize this vital position. The bridge at Marcoing was captured intact, the leading tank shooting down the party who were engaged in its demolition. At Mesnières, which is the more important point, the advancing troops were less fortunate, as the bridge had already been injured and an attempt by a tank to cross it led to both bridge and tank crashing down into the canal. This proved to be a serious misfortune, and coupled with the hold-up at Flesquières, was the one untoward event in a grand day's work. Both the tanks and the cavalry were stopped by the broken bridge, and though the infantry still pushed on their advance was slower, as it was necessary to clear that part of the village which lay north of the canal and then to go forward without support over open country. Thus the Germans had time to organise resistance upon the low hills from Rumilly to Crevecœur and to prevent the advance reaching its full limits. A footbridge was secured by the Newfoundlanders at Mesnières, and it may be mentioned as a curious example of the wide sweep of the British Empire that the first man to get across it, and to lose his life in the gallant deed, was an Esquimaux from Labrador. The centre brigade got about 1500 yards beyond Marcoing, but there the Germans from Cambrai had formed a new line which could not be forced. The enemy recognised this advance as being for the moment the most menacing part of the British line, and at once adopted the very strongest measures to push it back and secure the bridgeheads of the canal. Several times upon November 21 they raged against this point of the line and made desperate attempts to gain the two villages. Noyelle, which was held by the 1st Lancashire Fusiliers, was also strongly attacked upon that day, but with the aid of the 2nd Royal Fusiliers and 16th Middlesex the village was held against a series of onslaughts, one position changing hands seven times. Some of these counter-attacks were delivered by Prussian Guards, hastily brought from Lens, and the fighting was as severe as it usually is when the Kaiser's own men put in an appearance. These events, however, were on the 21st, and we must return to the first day of the battle.

<small>CHAPTER X.

The Battle of Cambrai. First Phase. Nov. 20.</small>

On the right of the Twenty-ninth was the Twentieth Division. In front of them, upon the farther side of the line, had lain the powerfully fortified farm of La Vacquerie, and this they had taken with their first rush. Beyond lay a long slope, strongly held by the Germans, called the Welsh Ridge. This also was stormed by the Twentieth, who kept pace with the right flank of the Twenty-ninth, and pushed their advance forward as far as the canal. At the same time the 59th Brigade was thrown out upon the right to make a prolongation of the defensive flank built up by the Twelfth Division and so screen the main attack. All went well with the right of this advance, but the left, consisting of the 10th K.R.R., was held for a time by a strong point which eventually surrendered and yielded 200 prisoners. Some of this battalion saw the enemy running towards Mesnières and pursued them to the main bridge. The troops received a most affectionate welcome from the inhabitants of the houses along the Cambrai Road. The attack upon the left was carried out by the 12th K.R.R. and 6th Oxfords of the 60th Brigade, which swept with little resistance over the Hindenburg Line, but had some trouble with strong points beyond. One of these points of resistance which was carried by the 12th K.R.R. accounted for all the officers of the party and 62 out of 96 men, before it was put out of action by the survivors. Captain Hoare, a veteran Rifleman who had risen from the ranks, was killed at this point, and his orderly, a lad of twenty named Shepherd, took over the direction of the party and carried the operation through with such dash and valour that he was awarded the Victoria Cross.

We now come to the Twelfth Division upon the flank, the first English division of the New Army, a unit which had greatly distinguished itself at Ovillers and elsewhere. Its task was in some ways the most difficult of any, as it had not only to advance upon important objectives but to build up a flank line of resistance as it went, since the whole attack might have been checked and brought to ruin by an enemy assault from the south. The 36th Brigade upon the left advanced with the 9th Royal Fusiliers and 7th Sussex in their front line, while two companies of the 8th Fusiliers were thrown out upon the left to aid in the attack upon La Vacquerie. On the right by the Banteaux Spur was the 35th Brigade with the 9th Essex and 5th Berkshires in the front. The latter battalion lost heavily from the fire of guns on their right. When on the line of Bleak House the supporting battalions, two companies of Fusiliers and the 11th Middlesex upon the left, the 7th Suffolks and part of the 7th Norfolks upon the right, passed

THE BATTLE OF CAMBRAI 251

on to the objective. The 37th Brigade then passed through upon the right and settled in an echelon of battalions along the flank, the 7th East Surreys and 6th Buffs starting the line, while the 6th West Kent and 6th West Surrey prolonged it. While executing this delicate and complicated movement the battalions were under heavy fire and had to clear Lateau Wood of the enemy, so that it was a fine bit of work on the part both of the leaders and of the men. The two chief points of German resistance outside the wood were the forts of Pam-Pam and Bonavis, both of which were attacked by tanks and then carried by storm by the Kentish infantry. By 11 o'clock the whole advance, covering a front of 2000 with a depth of 5500 yards, had reached its full objectives at every point. The total losses of the division were about 1300 men. Major Alderman, commanding the West Kents, was among those who fell. It may be added that from this day until the fateful 30th the division was out of the battle and made no move, save that on November 24 the 35th and 36th Brigades pushed a short way down the slope eastwards to the St. Quentin Canal.

Some allusion has already been made to the dispositions of the cavalry. The original plan was that the First and Fifth Cavalry Divisions, closely supported by the Second, should, the instant that the way was clear, push forward to surround and isolate Cambrai, and also to isolate and threaten Bourlon Wood from the north and east. The situation was never such, however, as to allow any large body of cavalry to get through. At dawn on the morning of the 21st a patrol of 5th Lancers ascertained that the Germans still held the Marcoing—Beaurevoir line in force. On the left, however, the success of the Fifty-first Division had made more open space, and on this side the Bays and the 4th Dragoon Guards penetrated upon the 21st as far as Fontaine and did some useful work.

The Twelfth Division formed the flank of Pulteney's Third Corps. Upon its right was Snow's Seventh Corps, the left-hand unit of which was the Fifty-fifth Division of Lancashire Territorials, which had not been involved in the advance, and indeed was nominally resting after its supreme exertions at Ypres where it had taken a notable part in battle after battle. It had been planned, however, that some demonstration should be made upon this front in order to divert the enemy's forces and to correspond with the attack at Bullecourt upon the north. This was carried out by the 164th Brigade and may have had the desired effect although it gave no permanent gain. A point called the Knoll, with an adjacent farm, was carried by the stormers and was held for most of the day, but they were forced back to their own old lines in the evening, after a long day of battle in which they incurred such heavy losses that the brigade was seriously crippled at a later date when the full strength of the division was urgently needed.

This ended the first day of the battle, which represented a considerable victory, and one which vindicated the enterprise and brain-power of the British inventor and engineer as much as the valour of the soldier. The German line was deeply indented over a front of 6 miles and to a depth of $4\frac{1}{2}$ miles. More than 5000 prisoners with many guns had been taken. The famous Hindenburg Line had been severed. The villages of Havrincourt, Graincourt,

THE BATTLE OF CAMBRAI 253

Ribecourt, Marcoing, Noyelle, and Mesnières were all in British hands. It was a good beginning, so good that it was determined not to suspend the operations, but to try the results of a second day and see what could be attained before the arrival of the full German supports. Even with their excellent rear organisation and their great junction at Cambrai, it was hoped that a clear forty-eight hours must pass from the opening of the battle before they could build up a really formidable line.

CHAPTER X.

The Battle of Cambrai. First Phase. Nov. 21.

There were no operations of any importance during the night of the 20th, but early upon November 21 the British line began to move forward once more, the same divisions being engaged in the advance. In the north the Ulstermen, who had attained the line of the Cambrai—Bapaume Road, crossed that boundary and pushed onwards up the slope for about a mile until they reached the outskirts of the village of Mœuvres which they were unable to retain. It was soon apparent, both here and at other points along the line, that the Germans with their usual military efficiency had brought up their reserves even more rapidly than had been expected, and the resistance at Mœuvres was so determined that the tired division was unable to overcome it. The 169th Brigade of the Fifty-sixth Division pushed up on the left of the Ulstermen and occupied the German outpost line, from which they were able later to attack the main Hindenburg Line.

The Sixty-second Division upon the right of the Ulstermen had got to the edge of Anneux upon the night before, and now the 2/4th West Ridings were able to complete their conquest. The 186th Brigade then drove across the Cambrai Road and reached the edge of the considerable plantation called Bourlon Wood which rises upon a swelling hill, the summit being so marked in that gently undulating country that it becomes a landmark in the distance. Here there was very strong opposition, with so murderous a machine-gun fire that all progress was arrested, though a number of tanks drove their way in among the trees in an effort to break down the resistance. In the meantime the flank of the Yorkshiremen had been protected by the capture of the village of Cantaing with several hundred more prisoners.

Early in the day the Fifty-first had got round the northern edge of Flesquières, the village which had held up the centre of the advance upon the first day. As a consequence it fell and the front was cleared for a further advance. The Scotch infantry was then able to make a rapid advance of nearly three miles, taking Cantaing with 500 prisoners upon the way, and winding up in front of the village of Fontaine-Notre-Dame, which they stormed in a very brilliant fashion with the aid of tanks and of some squadrons of the First Cavalry Division as already noted.

Farther south the Sixth and Twenty-ninth Divisions acting in close co-operation had pushed their way through Mesnières, where they met and defeated a counter-attack from the direction of Rumilly. It was clear that every hour the German line was thickening in this quarter. Whilst the Sixth cleared the ground upon the left, the Twenty-ninth pushed forward and reached Noyelle, where with the aid of those useful allies, the dismounted troopers of the First and Fifth Cavalry Divisions, including the Umballa Brigade of Indians, they made good the village as already described.

THE BATTLE OF CAMBRAI 255

In the meantime the 10th Rifle Brigade of the Twentieth Division upon the right had first taken and then lost Les Rues des Vignes, an important position upon the British side of the canal. In the afternoon the 11th Rifle Brigade managed to cross the canal and endeavoured to push up towards Crevecœur, but at this point the river Scheldt ran on the farther side and offered an impediment which could not be crossed. Orders were issued by General Byng that a fresh attempt should be made next morning, but the troops were weary and the losses heavy so the instructions were cancelled and the line remained unaltered at this point.

CHAPTER X.

The Battle of Cambrai. First Phase. Nov. 21.

The end of the second day of battle found the British Command faced with a difficult problem, and we have the Field-Marshal's own lucid analysis of the alternative courses open, and as to the reasons which prompted his decision. The capture of Cambrai had never been the goal of the operations, though a cavalry raid which would have disorganised the communications through that town had at one time seemed possible. A turning of the line to the south with the co-operation of some French divisions which were ready upon the spot, was part of the original conception, and was baulked by the insufficient hold established upon the farther side of the Canal de l'Escaut. But the central idea had been the capture of the high ground of Bourlon Hill and Wood for with this in British possession a considerable stretch of the defensive German line would lie open to observed artillery fire, and its retention would probably mean a fresh withdrawal to the east. It had been hoped that the goal would have been attained within forty-eight hours, but this time had elapsed and the

CHAPTER X.

The Battle of Cambrai. First Phase. Nov. 22.

assailants were at the bottom instead of the summit of the hill, with a resistance in front which was continually growing more obstinate. What was to be done ? The troops could not remain where they were, for the Bourlon Hill overlooked their position. They must carry it or retire. There was something to be said for the latter policy, as the Flesquières Ridge could be held and the capture of 10,000 prisoners and over 100 guns had already made the victory a notable one, while the casualties in two days were only 9000. On the other hand, while there is a chance of achieving a full decision it is hard to abandon an effort; reinforcements were coming up, and the situation in Italy demanded a supreme effort upon the Western front. With all these considerations in his mind the Field-Marshal determined to carry on.

November 22 was spent in consolidating the ground gained, in bringing up reinforcements, and in resting the battle-weary divisions. There was no advance upon the part of the British during the day, but about one o'clock in the afternoon the Germans, by a sudden impetuous attack, regained the village of Fontaine and pushed back the Fifty-first Division in this quarter. No immediate effort was made to regain it, as this would be part of the general operations when the new line of attack was ready to advance. Earlier in the day the Germans had thrown themselves upon the front of the Sixty-second, driving back its front line, the 2/6th and 2/8th West Yorkshires, to the Bapaume—Cambrai Road, but the Yorkshiremen shook themselves together, advanced once more, and regained the lost ground with the help of the 2/4th York and Lancasters. The Germans spent this day in building up their line, and with their better railway facilities had probably the best of the bargain, although the British air service worked with their usual utter self-abnegation to make the operation difficult.

The new advance began upon the night of November 22, when the 56th Londoners reinforced the Ulsters upon the left of the line on the outskirts of the village of Mœuvres. To the west of the village, between it and the Hindenburg Line, was an important position, Tadpole Copse, which formed a flank for any further advance. This was carried by a surprise attack in splendid style by the 1st Westminsters of the 169th Brigade. During the day both the Londoners and the Ulstermen tried hard, though with limited success, to enlarge the gains in this part of the field.

The attack was now pointing more and more to the north, where the wooded height of Bourlon marked the objective. In the southern part the movements of the troops were rather holding demonstrations than serious attacks. The real front of battle was marked by the reverse side of the Hindenburg Line upon the left, the hill, wood, and village of Bourlon in the centre, and the flanking village of Fontaine upon the right. All of these were more or less interdependent, for if one did not take Bourlon it was impossible to hold Fontaine which lay beneath it, while on the other hand any attack upon Bourlon was difficult while the flanking fire of Fontaine was unquenched. From Mœuvres to Fontaine was a good six miles of most difficult ground, so that it was no easy task which a thin line of divisions was asked to undertake—indeed only four divisions were really engaged, the Thirty-sixth and Fifty-sixth on the left, the Fortieth in the centre, and the Fifty-first on the right.

CHAPTER X.

The Battle of Cambrai. First Phase. Nov. 22.

258   THE BRITISH CAMPAIGN, 1917

CHAPTER X.

The Battle of Cambrai. First Phase. Nov. 23.

The operations of November 23 began by an attack by the enduring Fifty-first Division, who had now been four days in the fighting line against Fontaine Village—an attempt in which they were aided by a squadron of tanks. Defeated in the first effort, they none the less renewed their attack in the afternoon with twelve more tanks, and established themselves close to the village but had not sufficient momentum to break their way through it. There they hung on in most desperate and difficult fighting, screening their comrades in the main Bourlon attack, but at most grievous cost to themselves.

Meanwhile the Thirty-sixth Division had again attacked Mœuvres, and at one time had captured it all, save the north-west corner, but heavy pressure from the enemy prevented them retaining their grasp of it. The two brigades of this division upon the east of the canal were unable, unfortunately, to make progress, and this fact greatly isolated and exposed the Fortieth Division during and after its attack.

This main attack was entrusted to the Fortieth Division, a unit which had never yet found itself in the full lurid light of this great stage, but which played its first part very admirably none the less. It was a terrible obstacle which lay in front of it, for the sloping wood was no less than 600 acres in extent, a thick forest with autumn foliage, hardly touched by shell-fire, while the village upon its north-western flank came also within the area of their attack. The men, however, had been specially exercised in wood fighting, a precaution which all agree to have been of the greatest possible value in the day of battle. When at 10.30 A.M. the signal was given to advance the 121st Brigade went

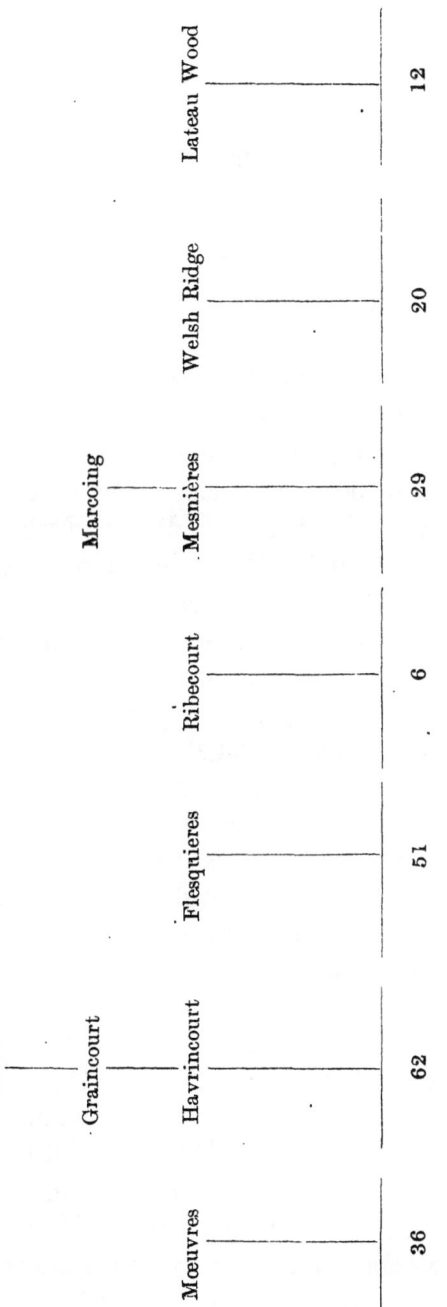

BATTLE LINE OF THIRD ARMY
November 20, 1917

CHAPTER X.

The Battle of Cambrai. First Phase. Nov. 23.

forward with alacrity upon the left, while on the right the 119th Brigade plunged into the wood, the brigadier, a dare-devil little warrior, setting an example to his men which none who followed him will forget. About thirty tanks lumbered forward in front of the advancing lines. The west edge of the wood formed the dividing line between the right and left attack.

It was arranged that the tanks should, so far as possible, go down those rides which are so conspicuous a feature of every French forest, while the infantry should move up between them. The 119th Brigade moved forward with the 19th Welsh Fusiliers upon the right, the 12th South Wales Borderers on the left, while the 17th Welsh were in close reserve. It was the second occasion in the war when a splendid piece of woodland fighting was carried through by the men of the Principality, and even Mametz was not a finer performance than Bourlon. They rapidly broke through the German front line, capturing numerous prisoners and machine-guns. The Colonel of the Fusiliers pushed his way forward to the north edge where he established posts, while the flank of the Welsh Borderers brushed the village of Bourlon and got north of that point. The 17th Welsh meanwhile formed defensive flanks upon either side, while the 18th Welsh came up to reinforce, and pushed ahead of their comrades with the result that they were driven in by a violent counter-attack. The line was re-established, however, and before one o'clock the 119th Brigade were dug in along the whole northern edge of the forest. It was a fine attack and was not marred by excessive losses, though Colonel Kennedy of the 17th Welsh was killed. Among

THE BATTLE OF CAMBRAI 261

many notable deeds of valour was that of Sergeant-Major Davies of the 18th Welsh, who knelt down in the open and allowed his shoulder to be used as the rest for a Lewis gun, until a bullet struck him down.

It was clear that the Germans would make every effort to regain the wood, and immediate steps were taken to strengthen the defence, which was already firmly established. The 14th Argyll and Sutherlands were sent up to thicken the line, as were the 15th Hussars, who were doing great service as a mobile foot battalion. More machine-guns were also pushed to the front. The result of these measures, all taken before nightfall, was that the inevitable counter-attacks, which materialised before dawn, were shot back by a blaze of fire from the fringe of brushwood. Early in the morning of November 24, a resolute endeavour of the German stormers gained a lodgment for them to the right of the British line, where they captured some of the machine-guns. During the whole of this day the enemy pressed hardly upon the weakening line, and at three in the afternoon had pushed them back from the whole of the right half of the wood, but Welshmen, Highlanders, and Hussars gathered themselves for a supreme effort, and dashing at the Germans swept them back once more to their old position. We shall leave the 119th Brigade still holding fast upon the evening of the 24th to their advanced position, while we follow the fortunes of the 121st Brigade from the time of the original attack upon November 23.

This Brigade had, as already stated, advanced upon the village of Bourlon with the 20th Middlesex upon the right and the 13th Yorkshires upon the left, the latter in close touch with the 107th Brigade

CHAPTER X.

The Battle of Cambrai. First Phase. Nov. 24.

of Ulstermen upon the west of their front, the whole line to swing round and attack the western edge of the village. The 21st Middlesex were in close support to give weight to the left of the line, while the 12th Suffolks were in reserve. The Ulstermen had been held up by heavy machine-gun fire which exposed the left flank of the Yorkshires, who in turn could not get forward. This in turn brought the two Middlesex battalions to a halt, who were already well up to the village. Three out of six tanks upon this flank were put out of action by armour-piercing bullets. After a pause both the Yorkshires and some of the Middlesex got into the village, but their flank was always bare, and the best they could do was to hold on to the southern edge. None the less the line was firm and formidable, as was found by a German attack carried out by the 9th Grenadier Regiment in the late afternoon, which was swept back by the British fire. All day the enemy strove hard to clear the village, and all day the 121st Brigade held splendidly to its gains. Where all were fine the non-commissioned officers were particularly splendid. Sergeant-Major Hall of the 21st Middlesex, three times wounded and still rallying his company, was but one of many. Some critic has finely said that if the Day of Judgment were to come a British non-commissioned officer would still be found imploring his neighbours not to get the wind up. It is an interesting fact that the attack by the 121st Brigade had been countermanded, but the wires were broken and the message miscarried, so that the whole fine episode was strictly unofficial.

During the night the hard-pressed line was thickened by the arrival of the 19th Hussars and

Bedford Yeomanry, who took over the left of the position. The 14th H.L.I. were also brought up from the reserve brigade, and twelve more tanks came into line. The 12th Suffolks had formed upon the left of the Highlanders, and these two battalions with the cavalry and tanks made a united attack upon the remaining portion of the village of Bourlon on the morning of the 24th, which was countered by the Germans in the afternoon. In the confusion of house-to-house combat the two battalions were separated, the Suffolks getting penned in at the south corner of the village, while the Highlanders, who had made a splendid advance, were isolated in the north-east. The situation was serious, and two reserve battalions, the 13th Surreys and 12th Royal Lancasters, were brought up after dusk. A body of dismounted cavalry drawn from the 2nd and 5th Dragoon Guards and the 11th Hussars were also pushed into the fight. With these troops the Brigadier made a strong attempt upon the morning of November 25 to force his way through the village, which was now mostly in German hands, but the tanks which he had expected did not arrive, and his infantry were not strong enough for the task. Colonel Battye of the Highlanders had been killed, and Colonel Warden of the East Surreys, who had assumed local command, did all that a man could do, but the losses were too heavy, and the Highlanders were seen no more. Up to the 26th Colonel Warden, with his headquarters in the firing line, was able to send up rations to the survivors of the three isolated companies who had made a wonderful resistance for nearly two days. In the end it was only by great skill that his own battalion, the East Surreys, were rescued from

CHAPTER X.

The Battle of Cambrai. First Phase. Nov. 25.

their dangerous position, for the forces of the Germans were in overwhelming strength, and overlapped the village upon both sides. Some of the East Surreys were cut off for two days in the south-eastern part of the village before the survivors could be got clear. Colonel Warden received the D.S.O. for his splendid work.

In the meantime, from the morning of the 25th, the 119th Brigade had made a splendid fight in the wood against fierce attacks which beat up against their right flank. The Guards had come up to relieve the 51st Highlanders, and on this date three battalions of the 3rd Guards Brigade, the 2nd Scots Guards, 1st and 4th Grenadier Guards, were thrown in to help the Fortieth Division in its heavy task. Two companies of the 11th Royal Lancasters were also brought forward, and succeeded in doing some very brilliant work. The flank was held during the day. Upon that night the weary division was drawn out, being relieved by the Sixty-second Yorkshire Division, which by some miracle after only two days of rest was judged to be battleworthy once more. It was indeed a case of the tired relieving those who were only a little less tired than themselves, but the line had to be held and not another man was available. The artillery of the Fortieth Division, which had shown remarkable efficiency and co-operated very closely with the infantry, remained in action. During its brilliant spell of service the Fortieth Division had taken 750 prisoners, but its casualties were very heavy, amounting to 172 officers and more than 3000 men.

The British position was now a difficult one, for the enemy held the ridge above Fontaine and also the

THE BATTLE OF CAMBRAI 265

high ground between Bourlon and the Hindenburg Line, so that they had commanding observation upon both sides. With great persistence, however, in spite of the continual thickening of the German line the British commanders determined, after a pause for breath, to make one more effort to capture both Fontaine, which had relapsed into enemy hands, and the village of Bourlon with the whole of the Ridge. The Guards, the Forty-seventh London Territorials, and the Second Division had all appeared upon the scene, so that the striking force was stronger than before. Upon November 27 the Guards made a strong effort upon Fontaine, having relieved the Fifty-first Division in that sector. The 3rd Guards Brigade had already become involved, as described in the defence by the Fortieth Division of Bourlon Wood. It was the 2nd Brigade which was now marshalled to attack upon a very wide front from Fontaine village on the right to Bourlon village on the left, this latter advance being in support of the attack by the Sixty-second Division upon the position which had been lost. This attack made at 6.20 in the morning of November 27, after a night of snow and tempest, was carried out by the 186th and 187th Brigades, the object being to get back Bourlon wood and village. The latter brigade got half-way through the village at one time, but could not make good the ground. The 186th, working through the woods to the north-west of Fontaine, gained their objectives, but had both flanks in the air, and were eventually in the evening compelled to fall back, all the West Riding battalions having lost heavily. Meanwhile the 2nd Brigade of Guards had been fighting hard in support of the Sixty-second. This

CHAPTER X.

The Battle of Cambrai. First Phase. Nov. 27.

attack was carried out by the 2nd Irish, while the 3rd Grenadiers, 1st Coldstream, and 1st Scots were respectively upon the left, centre, and right of the advance upon the village, which came down the line of the Cambrai Road.

The attack started at 6.20 in the morning after a night of snow and tempest. The flank battalion of Scots Guards by the use of a sunken road got well up to the village without heavy loss, but a blast of machine-gun fire from a small house about 200 yards away played havoc with the 3rd Grenadiers, who none the less rushed forward, stormed the house, and secured their first objective. The Coldstreams also suffered heavily from machine-gun fire from a post north of the railway, and half their numbers were on the ground before they also reached their objective. The remains of these two gallant battalions cleared the whole village and captured about a thousand prisoners, but were unable to get more than six hundred to the rear. By ten o'clock the whole position had been taken, but the victors had suffered so severely that they were unable to cover so large a perimeter, and about eleven o'clock the Germans, passing through the numerous gaps in the defence, bade fair to cut off the whole British force. The 4th Grenadiers of the 3rd Brigade was sent up under Lord Gort to reinforce, and the remains of the 2nd Brigade was drawn clear of the village and settled into trenches in front of it. The attack was in many ways a very difficult one, for the village was strongly fortified, there was much wire intact south of the Cambrai road, and the machine-gun fire from La Folie Wood swept all the approaches. Eventually the force of the enemy was so strong, and it had

THE BATTLE OF CAMBRAI 267

penetrated so far round the flanks of the battalions that Lord Fielding, who commanded the Guards division, gave orders that they retire to their original line. The brigade lost heavily in the venture.

Meanwhile the gallant Yorkshiremen of the Sixty-second, together with the 2nd Irish Guards, drove their way through Bourlon Wood in spite of a desperate resistance from a German line which included several battalions of the Guards. Many prisoners were taken, but many others escaped in the confused fighting among the brushwood and tree-trunks. Once again the counter-attacks were too strong for the thin ranks who had reached their goal, and the British, after reaching both the village and the north end of the wood, were pushed out once more. At the same time the British held a strong position on the hill and in the wood, so that there were still hopes of a successful issue if the German resistance could be outworn. It should be remarked that through all the fighting the battle line was greatly strengthened by the fact that a dismounted battalion was formed from each brigade of cavalry, or nine in all, who relieved and supported the very weary infantry. The trophies of the battle up to date had been over 100 German guns, 10,500 prisoners, 350 machine-guns, and, above all, the valuable stretch of Hindenburg's Line.

It was in this last phase of the advance, and indeed after the fighting had ended, that General Bradford was killed by a chance shell. This young soldier, who at the age of twenty-five commanded one of the brigades of the Sixty-second Division, was one of the great natural leaders disclosed by the war. It was indeed a cruel fate which took him away between full

CHAPTER X.

The Battle of Cambrai. First Phase. Nov. 27.

promise and full performance. "He had the dash and enthusiasm of youth tempered by the knowledge and experience which comes to most men only with later years." So wrote his immediate commander. England could ill spare such a man at such a time.

All was quiet for the next few days, during which the Fifty-ninth Division relieved the Guards, while the Forty-seventh Division relieved the Sixty-second Yorkshiremen.

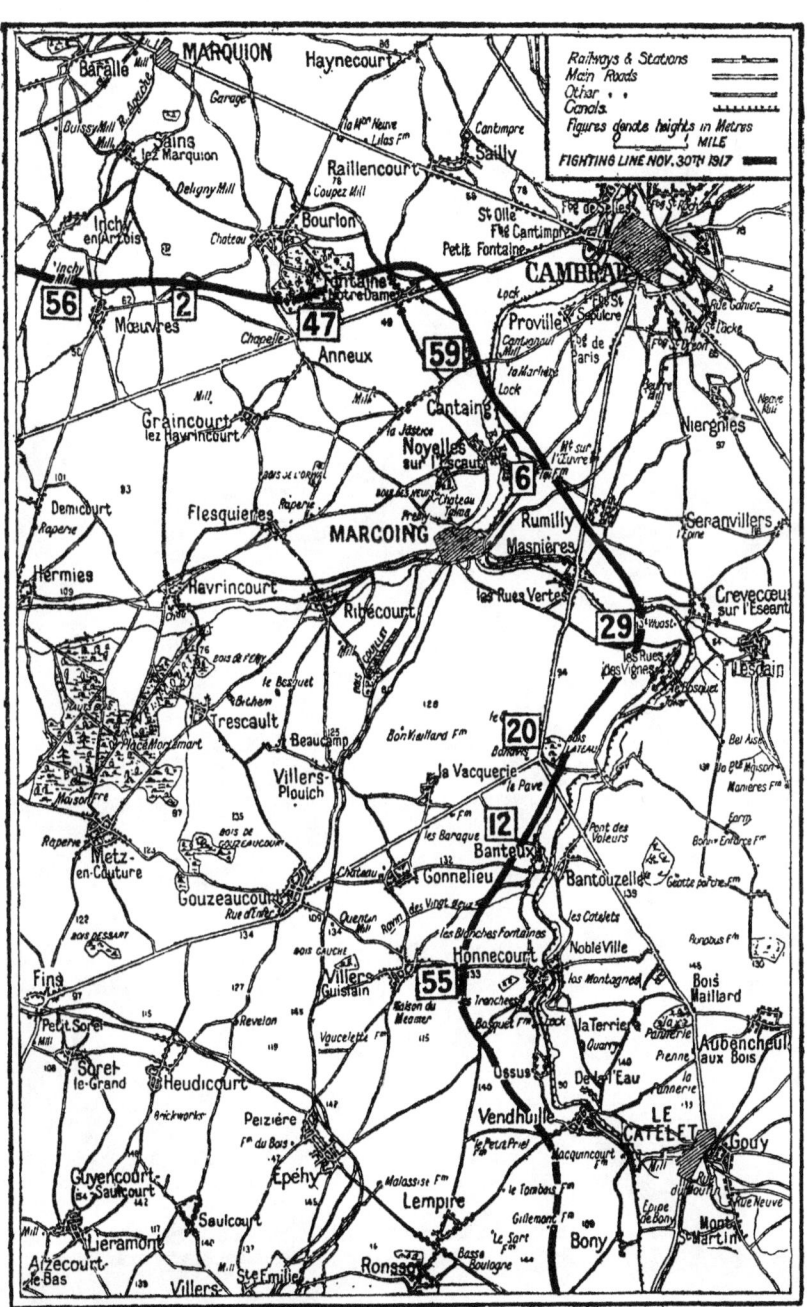

CHAPTER XI

THE BATTLE OF CAMBRAI (*continued*)

Second phase of battle on November 30—Great German attack—Disaster to three divisions—Desperate fight of Twenty-ninth Division—Fine advance by the Guards—Capture and recapture of Gouzeaucourt—Hard battle in the Bourlon Sector—Heavy losses of the Germans—Retraction of the British line.

IT was clear to the British Commanders before the end of November that the enemy had grown so strong that the initiative had passed to him, and that instead of following up attacks it was a question now of defending positions against a determined endeavour to shove back the intruders and splice the broken line. The multifarious signs of activity behind the German lines, the massing of troops, the planting of batteries, and the registration of ranges, all warned the experienced observers that a great counter-offensive was about to begin. There was no question of a surprise at any point of the line, but Bourlon was naturally the place where the enemy might be expected to be at his full strength, since it was vital that he should regain that position. At the same time it was clearly seen that the storm would break also at the south end of the line, and General Snow had given every instruction to General Jeudwine of the Fifty-fifth Division which held the position next to the scene

Chapter XI.
The Battle of Cambrai. Second Phase. Nov. 30.

CHAPTER XI.

The Battle of Cambrai. Second Phase. Nov. 30.

of action. This experienced leader took every step which could be thought of, but he was sadly handicapped by the state of his division which had been so severely hammered at Ypres, and had in the last few days had one brigade knocked to pieces at Knoll. With only two brigades, full of young troops who had taken the place of the casualties incurred in the north, he had to cover at least 10,000 yards of ground. His line was stretched until it was little more than a string of sentries with an occasional strong point dotted up and down. We will begin by endeavouring to follow what occurred in this southern sector, and then turn to the equally important, though less dramatic, doings in the north.

The attack in the south was delivered upon a front of ten miles from Vendhuille in the south to Mesnières in the north. To take a single comprehensive view of it, it hardly affected the Twenty-fourth Division upon the right of Snow's Seventh Corps, it crashed with full force upon the Fifty-fifth Division, especially the left brigade, it swept impetuously upon the Twelfth and Twentieth Divisions, driving in part of the line of each of these units, and finally it raged with equal fury but less success against the Twenty-ninth Division, in the region of Mesnières. The weight and swiftness of the blow, coming with the shortest possible artillery preparation, and strongly supported by low-flying aeroplanes, must add to the reputation of General von Marwitz who planned it. It was a success, and it is difficult to see how it could have been prevented from being a success by any means which the defenders had it in their power to adopt. The undulating country in which troops could assemble, and the morning mist which screened them from

THE BATTLE OF CAMBRAI

observation were two factors which contributed to the result.

Shortly after seven in the morning the tempest suddenly broke loose. The surprise was so well carried out that though the British General was expecting an attack, and though he had his wire patrols pushed up to the German trenches only a hundred yards off, still their reports at dawn gave no warning of any sound to herald the coming rush. It came like a clap of thunder. An experienced officer in the front British trench said: "My first impression was that of an earthquake. Then it seemed to me that an endless procession of aeroplanes were grazing my head with their wheels. On recovering from the first shock of my surprise the Germans were far behind me." There was no question of protective barrage, for the quickest answer to the most urgent S.O.S. would have been too late to help.

This account refers particularly to the 166th Brigade, upon the left of the Fifty-fifth Division, which got the full blast of the storm. It and the guns behind it were overrun in an instant by the weight and speed of the advance. The General in command did all that could be done in such an emergency, but it was impossible to form a fixed line. The alternative was to swing back hingeing upon the right of the division, and this was done so that there was always a flank formed upon the left of the stormers. There was a ravine, called Ravine 22 upon the maps, which ran down between the Fifty-fifth and Twelfth Divisions. With the terrific force of a flood the Germans poured down this natural runway, destroying the British formations upon each side of it. The Fifty-fifth Division was shattered to pieces at this point by

Chapter XI.

The Battle of Cambrai. Second Phase. Nov. 30.

so terrific an impact upon their feeble line, but the small groups into which they were broken put up as good a fight as they could, while the line formed anew between the village of Villers-Guislain and the farm Vaucelette which was a strong pivot of resistance. In this part of the field units of the 165th Brigade of Liverpool battalions, together with the 5th Royal Lancasters and the 10th Liverpool Scottish of the 166th Brigade, stood stoutly to their work, and though the enemy after penetrating the lines were able to get the village of Villers-Guislain, which they had turned and surrounded, they were never able to extend their advance to the south on account of this new line of defence through Vaucelette, though it was composed entirely of infantry with no artillery support. However, even with this limitation the situation was bad enough, since the 166th Brigade was almost cut to pieces, and so complete was the destruction upon the extreme left that one battalion, the 5th South Lancashires, was entirely destroyed, and nothing heard of it until its leader, Colonel James, was reported as a badly wounded prisoner in Germany. Of the division generally it was said by a higher General that " they fought like tigers," as might be expected of men who had left a great name on the battle of Ypres, and who were destined for even greater fame when four months later they held Givenchy at the critical moment of the terrible battle of Armentières. Here, as always, it is constancy in moments of adversity and dour refusal to accept defeat which distinguish both the British soldier and his leaders.

We shall now see what happened to the Twelfth Division upon the left of the Fifty-fifth. When the German stormers poured down Ravine 22 their left-

THE BATTLE OF CAMBRAI 273

handed blow knocked out the 166th Brigade, while their right-handed crushed in the side of the Twelfth Division. From the ravine in the south to Quarry Farm in the north, the German infantry surged round the position like a mountain spate round some rock-hearted islet, where the edges might crumble and be washed out by the torrent, but the solid core would always beat back the waters. The line of the division was a curved one, with the 35th Brigade upon the right, the 36th in the centre, and the 37th upon the left. It was upon the right-hand brigade that the storm burst with its full shattering force. The 7th Suffolks next to the fatal ravine shared the fate of the 5th South Lancashires upon the southern edge of it. By a coincidence the Colonel had been invalided for appendicitis the day before, but Major Henty who was in command was killed. The 5th Berks and 9th Essex, broken up into small parties and enveloped in a smoke cloud through which they could only catch dim glimpses of rushing Germans, were pushed back to the north and west, still keeping some sort of cohesion, until they reached the neighbourhood of Bleak House where they rallied once more and gathered for a counter-attack. Everywhere over this area small parties were holding on, each unconscious of all that was passing outside its own little smoke-girt circle. Close to Villers-Guislain upon the south side of the ravine Sapper Company 70, together with the 5th Northampton Pioneers, held on bravely for many hours, shooting into the flank of the German advance who poured over the British gun positions which were well forward at this point in order to support the troops in Mesnières and Marcoing. Some of the incidents round the guns were epic in character,

CHAPTER XI.

The Battle of Cambrai. Second Phase. Nov. 30.

T

CHAPTER XI.

The Battle of Cambrai.
Second Phase.
Nov. 30.

for the British gunner does not lightly take leave of his piece. Many were fought to the last instant with their crews hacking at them with pickaxes and trenching tools to disable them even while the Germans swarmed in. Lieut. Wallace, of the 363rd Battery, with five men served three guns point-blank, their trails crossing as they covered three separate fields of fire. Each of this band of heroes received a decoration, their leader getting the V.C. The 92nd R.F.A. near La Vacquerie also repulsed four separate attacks, firing with open sights at a range of 200 yards, before they were forced to dismantle their guns and retire.

The 7th Norfolks on the left edge of the 35th Brigade were farthest from the storm-centre, and stoutly beat off all attacks. Only one lieutenant was left upon his feet at the end of the day. Separated from their comrades the Norfolks were rather part of the 36th Brigade upon their left, who were also fiercely attacked, but were more happily situated as regarded their flank. The 9th Royal Fusiliers were pushed back to the Cambrai Road on the north, but with some of the Norfolks built up a solid line of resistance there. Next to them upon the left the two companies of the 8th Royal Fusiliers which were in the line, were practically annihilated in spite of a splendid attempt to rescue them made by the other two companies led by their heroic Colonel Elliott Cooper. In this brave effort the leader gained his Victoria Cross, but also unhappily a wound from which he eventually died. This counter-attack drove the Germans back for the first time in this terrible morning, but their lines were reinforced and they came on once more.

The 37th Brigade upon the left had their own set of troubles to contend with. The Germans had

THE BATTLE OF CAMBRAI

beaten hard upon the neighbouring Twentieth Division, breaking into their line upon the right of their flank 59th Brigade. In this way they got into Lateau Wood and on to the Bonavis Ridge, which placed them upon the left rear of the 37th Brigade. The unit was in imminent danger of being cut off, but held strongly to its line, the pressure falling particularly heavily upon the 7th East Surreys and upon the 6th Buffs. Pam-Pam Farm was the centre of some very desperate fighting on the part of these two units. The Brigade was sorely tried and forced backwards but still held its own, facing upon two and even three different fronts, as the enemy drifted in from the north and east.

In the meantime a train of independent circumstances had built up a reserve line which was destined to be of great importance in limiting the German advance until reinforcements could arrive. Their stormers had within an hour or two reached not only Villers-Guislain and Gonnelieu, but had even entered Gouzeaucourt, three miles deep in the British line. This village, or rather a quarry upon its eastern edge, was the Headquarters of the Twenty-ninth Division, and the Germans were within an ace of capturing General de Lisle, its famous commander. The amazed Commandant of the local hospital found a German sentry at his door instead of a British one, and with the usual British good-humour sent him out a cup of tea. No doubt he did the same to the Irish Guardsman who in turn relieved the German in the afternoon. The C.R.A. of the Twenty-ninth Division was wounded and taken, and Captain Crow of the Staff was killed. General de Lisle with quick decision organised a temporary defence for the south end of the

CHAPTER XI.

The Battle of Cambrai. Second Phase. Nov. 30.

village, and then hurried up to join his hard-pressed men at Marcoing. The General of the Twelfth Division had energetically hurried up the two battalions which he held in reserve. They were the 6th West Surreys and the 11th Middlesex. Some hundred of odds and ends near Headquarters were also formed into a unit and pushed to the front. These went forward towards the firing with the vaguest notion of the situation, meeting broken groups of men and catching occasional glimpses of advancing Germans. The Brigadier of the 35th Brigade had been nearly caught in Gonnelieu, and found the enemy between him and his men. As he came back with his staff, still very lightly clad, pausing occasionally to fire at the advancing Germans, he passed Ganche Wood and there met the advancing battalions, which he helped to marshal along a low ridge, the Revelon Ridge. The Northumberland Hussars lined up on the right of these troops and two brigades of cavalry coming up from the south formed on the left of them at a later hour. The whole held firm against all enemy attacks and made a bulwark until the time when the Guards advanced in the afternoon. As will afterwards be described, when that event occurred this Revelon line formed roughly a prolongation of the new line established by the Guards and Cavalry, so that a long dam was formed. Commanding officers in this critical part of the field gave a sigh of relief in the early afternoon as they realised that the worst was over.

The Twentieth Light Division was on the left of the Twelfth, and its experience was equally trying. It was upon the Riflemen of the 59th Brigade that the main shock fell, and it came with such sudden violence that the Germans were through the right unit and in

THE BATTLE OF CAMBRAI 277

the rear of the rest before the situation was fully realised. The 61st Brigade upon the left had also a most desperate time, their flank being penetrated and turned so that for a time they were cut off from their comrades of the Twenty-ninth Division at Mesnières. By this determined German attack the south bank of the canal was partially cleared for their advance, which put them in the position that they could possibly push along that bank and get hold of Les Rues Vertes and the southern ends of the bridges so as to cut off those British troops who were across the canal. In this dangerous movement they nearly had success, and it was only the desperate fighting of some of the 86th Brigade which saved the situation. The prospects were even worse upon the right of the Division for the Germans broke through Lateau Wood, and so got completely behind the 10th K.R.R., who were the flank battalion. From the desperate struggle which ensued only 4 officers and 16 Riflemen ever emerged, for the battalion was attacked on three sides and was overwhelmed after a long and splendid defence, which twice repulsed heavy frontal attacks before the flank advance rolled up the line. The battalion got separated from its own headquarters in Lateau Wood, and Colonel Sheepshanks with the twenty odd men who composed the Staff fought a little battle of its own against the stormers coming down towards the Bonavis—Mesnières Road. The survivors of the brigade rallied upon the reserve battalion, the 11th R.B. on the Hindenburg Line. The 11th K.R.R. on the left of the brigade front had endured a similar experience but their losses were not so terribly severe. The aeroplane attack worried the troops almost as much as the infantry, so that it is no

Chapter XI.

The Battle of Cambrai. Second Phase. Nov. 30.

Chapter XI.

The Battle of Cambrai. Second Phase. Nov. 30.

exaggeration to say that there were times when they were assailed from four sides, the front, each flank and above at the same instant. These aeroplanes gave the impression of being armour-clad and invulnerable to rifle-fire.

Upon the left of the Twentieth Division, with its centre at the village of Mesnières, was the Twenty-ninth Division, a good unit to have in the heart of such a crisis. The Twenty-ninth and Sixth Divisions held the centre of the British line that day, and were the solid nucleus upon which the whole battle hinged both to left and right of them. Both divisions were seriously compromised by the push-back to the south of them, and their battery positions were taken in reverse, but they held the whole of their ground without giving an inch and completely beat off every German attack. A Guernsey battalion made its mark in the fighting that day and rendered most excellent service, as did the Newfoundlanders; but the main strength of the divisions lay of course in their disciplined British veterans, men whose war-hardened faces, whether in Gallipoli or Flanders, had never been turned from an enemy. It is no light matter to drive such a force, and the four German divisions who drove in from Mesnières to Bauteaux were unable to make even a dint in that formidable line. For two days the villages, both Marcoing and Mesnières, were firmly held, and when at last a readjustment of the line was ordered it was carried out voluntarily and deliberately in accordance with the new plans made necessary by the events in north and south.

In this great fight the 86th Brigade was on the right at Mesnières with the 16th Middlesex upon the

THE BATTLE OF CAMBRAI 279

right, the 1st Lancashire Fusiliers upon the left, and the 2nd Royal Fusiliers by the sugar factory east of the village—details which have been rescued by the industry of Mr. Percival Phillips. The 87th Brigade extended to the left, covering a wide front as far as the Cambrai Road. The 1st Inniskillings were on their right, the 1st Borders on their left, and the 2nd South Wales Borderers in support. The 88th Brigade was in reserve at the time of the attack, but quickly moved up and was in the heart of the subsequent fighting.

Masses of German infantry were reported at Crevecœur, and within a very short time a rush of grey infantry was swirling down past the flank of the Middlesex men, and breaking the connection with the Twentieth Division on the right. Some of the assailants got along the south bank, and actually seized Les Rues Vertes at the same moment that a counter-attack by the Guernsey men swept into the village and drove them out again. This was a really vital point, as the capture and retention of the village would have been most serious. Many soldierly actions were performed in this clash of arms, showing that the mechanical side of modern warfare can never quite eliminate the brave pushing heart and the strong arm. Captain Gee of the Staff, among others, rescued an ammunition dump armed with a revolver and a heavy stick, with which he beat down all opposition at the cost of a serious wound to himself —a fair price to pay for a subsequent V.C. The Germans were foiled for the moment, but they had found the weak spot in the line, and all day they hammered at it with characteristic tenacity, while all day the men of the Twenty-ninth stood up to one

CHAPTER XI.

The Battle of Cambrai. Second Phase.

Nov. 30.

CHAPTER XI.

The Battle of Cambrai. Second Phase. Nov. 30.

attack after another, their dwindling line fraying to the last degree, but never breaking before the enemy. Les Rues Vertes became a Golgotha of Germans, but it was still in the evening safe in the hands of the British defenders. One of the classical examples of British courage and discipline during the war, fit to rank with Colonel Pears and his cancer at Ovillers, was furnished by Colonel Forbes Robertson of the 16th Middlesex, now a V.C., who, stricken in both eyes and temporarily blind, was still led by his orderly up and down the line in order to steady it. Let such a story help our descendants to realise the kind of men who stood between Germany and the conquest of the world.

Next morning saw no surcease of the fighting in this quarter of the field. If anything, the ranks of the assailants were thicker and their rushes more insistent upon the morning of the 21st. But the Twenty-ninth had called up its reserves, and stood with every bristle on end across the German path. The trouble behind the line had greatly weakened the artillery support, but the trench-mortars gave all the help possible to the hard-worked infantry. The villages were knocked to pieces by the enemy guns, but the British stuck like leeches to the ruins. The General of the 86th Brigade was among his men in the front of the battle, encouraging them to dwell upon their aim and steadying their weary ranks. The 87th Brigade in the north, though itself attacked, spared some reinforcements for the hard-pressed men in the south. Once Les Rues Vertes was lost, but a counter-attack led by the Brigade-Major won it back again. This was still the position when on the night of December 1 the orders were given for the

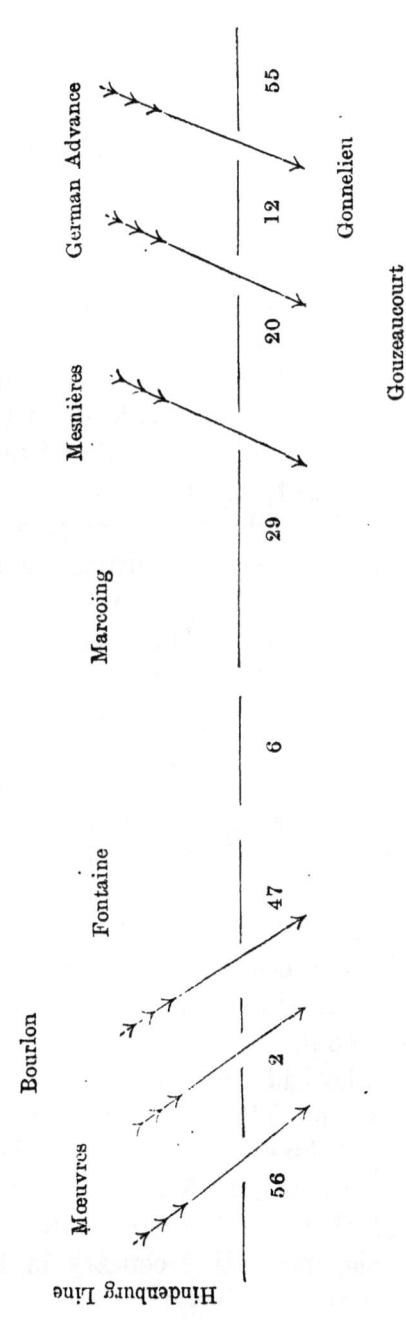

BATTLE ORDER OF THIRD ARMY
November 30, 1917

Chapter XI.
The Battle of Cambrai. Second Phase.
Nov. 30.

general readjustment of the line by the evacuation of the Mesnières salient. Well might Sir Douglas Haig send a special order to General de Lisle thanking him for the magnificent services rendered during two days and a night by the Twenty-ninth Division.

It has been stated that the Mesnières salient was evacuated, but two battalions of the Twenty-ninth Division, the Newfoundlanders and the South Wales Borderers, had been left upon the north bank of the canal—with them was the 16th Brigade of the Sixth Division who had been sent up to aid and relieve the Twenty-ninth. These troops had a cruel experience, as the enemy upon December 3 concentrated so heavy a fire upon them that they were driven back across the canal, the 16th Brigade being partly broken by the severity of the attack. This incident led to a retraction of the line in this quarter.

For the sake of continuity of narrative we shall now, before turning to the very important episodes in the north, show how the Guards came up in the south and how the new line was firmly established in this critical quarter of the field. The reader will therefore carry back his mind to that fateful hour when the left of the Fifty-fifth had been swept away, the Twelfth and Twentieth shattered, and the Twenty-ninth was holding on with all its strength in the first spate of the German flood.

The Guards, who had been drawn out after their hard spell of service in the Bourlon attack, were moving into a rest camp behind the lines when they were stopped by the amazing tidings that the British line was broken and that the Germans were scattered anywhere over the undulating country in front of them. It was 11.15 and they were marching from

THE BATTLE OF CAMBRAI 283

the hamlet of Metz when the first news of disaster reached them—news which was very quickly followed by signs as gunners were met coming back with the sights and sometimes the broken breech-blocks of their abandoned guns in their hands. Over the ridge between Metz and the Gouzeaucourt Wood a number of gunners, sappers, and infantry came in driblets, none of them hurrying, but all with a bewildered air as though uncertain what to do. To these worried and broken people the sight of the taut lines of the Guards must indeed have been a great stay in their trouble. "There were a good many men," says one officer, "coming towards us without arms or equipment, but these I presumed to belong to some unit resting in the vicinity." It is only fair to state that several labour companies had been caught in the sudden storm and that many of the broken formations seem to have been from their ranks, though others behaved with extraordinary valour, and exchanged their spades for rifles with the greatest alacrity. The Guards moved forward in the direction of the turmoil, but their progress was slow, as there were gun-teams upon the narrow road. The 1st Brigade under General de Crespigny was leading, being the unit which had suffered least in the Bourlon fighting. The young Brigadier, a famous sportsman as well as a dashing but cool-headed soldier, galloped ahead in an effort to clear up the situation, and after doing a mile or so across country he suddenly saw the grey coats of German infantry among the trees around him. Riding back he halted his brigade in a hollow by Gouzeaucourt Wood, fixed bayonets, and then, deploying them into the line, advanced them in extended order across the fields. There was no artillery support at

CHAPTER XI.

The Battle of Cambrai. Second Phase. Nov. 30.

all, but from the front there came an occasional shell, with the constant cracking of machine-guns, which increased as they topped the low ridge before them. "We advanced into the blue in perfect lines," says one who was present. Once under fire the brigade went forward in short rushes of alternate companies. "Our fellows were not shouting," says the same witness, "but chatting among themselves, and smiling in a manner that boded ill for the Huns." The 2nd Coldstreams were on the right, the 2nd in the centre, and the 1st Irish upon the left, with the 2nd Grenadiers in close support. As de Crespigny's brigade came upon the fringes of the German advance they swept them up before them, keeping the Metz—Gouzeaucourt Road as their right boundary, while a force of dismounted cavalry moved up upon the farther side. The Irish upon the left passed through the wood and broke with a yell about 2 P.M. into Gouzeaucourt village, which was not strongly held. The Germans bolted from the eastern exits and the Guardsmen passing through made a line beyond, getting in touch upon the left with the 4th Grenadier Guards of the 3rd Brigade, which formed up and advanced upon that side. They were aided in this advance by a small detached body representing the Headquarters' Guard of the Twenty-ninth Division and by a company of North Midland R.E. who held their post inviolate all day, and were now very glad to join in an offensive. As the line advanced beyond the village they came into a very heavy fire, for the St. Quentin Ridge faced them, and it bristled with machine-guns. Field-guns and 5·9's were also playing upon them, but nothing could check that fine advance, which was in time to save a number of heavy guns

THE BATTLE OF CAMBRAI 285

which could by no possibility be removed. It was itself aided in the later stages by the 20th Hussars upon the right and by a brigade of guns of the Forty-seventh London ·Division which swung into action straight from the line of march and did good service in supporting the attack. By nightfall the total ground gained was over two miles in depth, and a definite line of Guardsmen and cavalry of the Second and Fifth Divisions covered all this section of the field, limiting and defining the German advance. General Byng must surely have breathed more freely when the good news reached his Headquarters for, but for this energetic operation, there was nothing to prevent the Germans flooding into the country behind and getting to the rear of the whole northern portion of the Third Army.

The real work of the Guards had been done when once they had dammed the stream, and their strength after their recent labours was hardly sufficient to carry them through a long battle, but in spite of this they were advancing once more upon the morning of December 1. The same two brigades were in·front, but the 2nd Grenadiers and 3rd Coldstreams formed the fighting line of the 1st Brigade, joining up on the left with the Welsh Guards of the 3rd Brigade. Cavalry was moving on the right of them, while on the left they were in touch with the Rifle battalions of the 60th Brigade covering the village of La Vacquerie. The two brigades had different objectives, the left brigade being directed upon Gonnelieu, while the right moved upon Ganche Wood, the divisional tanks supporting the advance. The first brigade advanced with the battalions already named, and they swept in magnificent order up to the

Chapter XI.

The Battle of Cambrai. Second Phase. Nov. 30.

fringe of the wood where they were met by two successive counter-attacks which they repelled. The wood was cleared but there were many snipers in the trees, and the losses of officers and N.C.O.'s were proportionately high. The tanks were held up by the denseness of the forest. Cavalry came up upon the right, and with their assistance the wood was finally secured, together with some guns and several hundred prisoners. It was a fine feat of arms.

The 2nd Brigade had a difficult task at Gonnelieu and the Quentin Ridge. The 1st Welsh on the right and the 4th Grenadiers on the left headed the advance, but they were held up at once by machine-guns on the right until a tank lumbered up and saved the situation. Isolated parties of the 2nd Grenadiers forced their way into the village, but it bristled with machine-guns and could not be held. Finally the line was formed 200 yards from the western edge.

That night the Guards were drawn out after their onerous and splendid service, being relieved by the Ninth Division. In the week they had lost 125 officers and 3000 men, but they had turned the tide of battle upon the critical instant of a critical day, when, amid commencing disorganisation, the presence of the most highly disciplined and steadiest force in the British Army was particularly needed. Few of our units can be fairly said to have added to their laurels in this sector of the second phase of Cambrai, but at least the Twenty-ninth Division and the Guards can look back to it with every satisfaction.

At La Vacquerie village and its environs, to the left of the Guards' advance, some very fierce fighting had broken out upon the morning of December 1.

THE BATTLE OF CAMBRAI 287

The enemy began by endeavouring to out-flank the village upon the right, pressing down from Gonnelieu and attacking the sunken road known as Forster Lane which is north of Gonnelieu. A company of the 9th Essex, somewhat shaken by its previous experience, and the 12th Rifles held this position. The Colonel and the Headquarters Staff of the Rifle battalion found itself engaged in a very lively free fight with the heavy masses of enemy infantry who were pouring down Fusilier Ridge. By trickling forward small parties they managed to capture Forster Lane, but all their attempts to get beyond it were beaten back. Captain Lloyd of the Rifles, who was prominent in the defence, fell mortally wounded, but the line, though heavily shelled and hard pressed, still held its ground. All this occurred to the south of the village which had itself been heavily attacked after a very heavy shell-fall. The German bombers, who came on very bravely, drove their way into the village but were ejected once more, the Riflemen leaving their trenches to pelt them with bombs. A second attack was even more fiercely pressed. "The Germans who attacked La Vacquerie," says one who was present, "were brave and determined men and their bombers were well trained, but our men had been told to hold the village at all costs, and gallantly led by their officers and N.C. officers they carried out their orders." In the evening the Riflemen still held the shattered ruins of the village, but they were utterly exhausted by their splendid exertions, and never was a relief more welcome than when the 183rd Brigade of the Sixty-first South Midland Division came up after nightfall and took over the hazardous charge. In the final readjust-

Chapter XI.
The Battle of Cambrai. Second Phase. Nov. 30.

ment of the British line the village of La Vacquerie remained with the Germans.

The enemy had suffered heavily, and as will be shown gained absolutely nothing in the north, but in the south it must be admitted that he had substantial trophies, including a strip of British line, some thousands of prisoners, and about 100 guns.

It was the first truly successful offensive on a large scale which he had made since the gas attack upon April 22, 1915, nearly two and a half years before, and it would be a sign of a poor spirit if we did not admit it, and applaud the deftness and courage of the attack.

After several days of quiet the Germans tried one other taste of the quality of the Guards by a sudden assault upon their new line on December 5. They advanced bravely in two lines from Gonnelieu, but were beaten off by close rifle-fire. As they turned their flight was greeted with a volley of bombs from their own people behind them. It was observed that the stormers upon this occasion carried their packs as though they meant to stay. A good many of them did so. Next day the Guards were relieved by the Ninth Division.

We shall now turn to Woolcombe's Fourth Corps in the northern sector which extends from Tadpole Copse upon the left to that solid centre of resistance furnished by the two veteran divisions at Marcoing and at Mesnières. It was upon the left of this curve that the German attack broke upon November 30 from the Hindenburg Line to the village of Fontaine, a front of about six miles, the object being to cut off the whole Bourlon salient. The attack, which began about nine o'clock, differed from that on the south,

THE BATTLE OF CAMBRAI 289

because the element of surprise was wanting and because the ground was such that the attacking troops could be plainly seen. The final result was to push back the British line, but this was mainly as a readjustment to correspond to the change in the south. To effect this small result all accounts are agreed in stating that the Germans incurred such murderous losses that it is improbable that any have been more severe since the early days of the war. If, on the balance, the British lost the day in the south, they gained it in the north, for with limited loss to themselves they inflicted most severe punishment upon the enemy.

Chapter XI.
The Battle of Cambrai. Second Phase.
Nov. 30.

The arrangement of the troops upon the northern curve of the battle line was as follows. Forming a defensive flank between the old British line and Tadpole Copse was the 168th Brigade, and to its right, facing Mœuvres, the 169th Brigade, both of them of the Fifty-sixth London Territorial Division, which had been a week in the fighting line and was very worn. Next to them upon the right was the Second Regular Division under General Pereira, from Mœuvres to Bourlon, with elements of the 5th, 6th, and 99th Brigades in front. Upon their right was the Forty-seventh London Territorial Division occupying the line drawn through Bourlon Wood. Upon their right again was the Fifty-ninth South Midland Territorials near Fontaine, who in turn linked up with the left of the Sixth Division, thus completing the semicircle of battle.

After a short but very severe bombardment the German infantry advanced upon the line from Tadpole Copse to Bourlon Wood, a front of about four miles. There were four fresh German divisions, with three

U

others in reserve, and the attack was driven on with the utmost resolution, falling upon the outlying British outposts with a force which often destroyed them, although the furious resistance of these scattered bodies of men took all the edge off the onslaught. It was also beaten into the earth by the British artillery, which had wonderfully fine targets as the stormers in successive lines came pouring over the open ground between Mœuvres and Bourlon. The artillery of the Fortieth Division had been left in the line, and a gunner officer of this unit described how his guns swung round and enfiladed the German attack upon the right as it stormed up to the line of the Forty-seventh Division. "It was one howitzer battery, D 178, that first tumbled to the fact that the Boches were attacking and had driven in some of the Second Division posts. This battery swung its guns round at right angles, getting on to the advancing enemy in enfilade and over open sights. Every other battery in the country opened within five minutes." Every observer agrees that the targets were wonderful, and that it was only in places where the ground gave him protection that the German storm troops could reach the expectant British infantry, who received him with such a murderous fire of rifles and Lewis-guns that his dead were heaped thickly along the whole front. Seven brigades of British artillery were enjoying themselves.

Taking the action from the left the outposts of the 169th Brigade were driven in, but put up a series of desperate fights. From Mœuvres to Tadpole Copse the action raged, and then the enemy poured out from the back of that portion of the Hindenburg Line which ran upon the flank of the 168th Brigade so that both units were involved in heavy fighting with a limited

THE BATTLE OF CAMBRAI 291

field of fire which gave fewer advantages to the defence than were found on the rest of the line. The Westminsters, the London Scottish, the Post Office Rifles, and the 2nd Londons all bore themselves with special bravery in a long day of desperate fighting during which Commanding Officers were in at least one instance compelled to stand, bomb in hand, defending their own headquarters. It was a grim battle, and the losses were heavy, coming upon troops which had already lost enough to shake the morale of any ordinary infantry, but the thin ranks held firm and the positions were retained. At one time the Germans were round the right flank of the 169th Brigade, and so cut off a company of the 13th Essex. There is a wonderfully dour military spirit amongst these East Saxons. It was an anxious situation, and it was saved by the utter self-abnegation of the company in question, who held a hurried council of war in which they swore to fight to the death. This grim gathering, which might furnish a theme for a great artist, consisted of Captain Robinson, Lieut. Corps, Sergeant-Major Edwards, Platoon-Sergeants Phillips, Parsons, Fairbrass, Lodge, and Legg. With a hand-clasp they returned to their work, and during the whole night their rifle-fire could be heard, though no help could reach them. In the morning they lay with their faces to the sky and their men around them, all true to their vow to death. It is a story to remember.

The left flank of the Second Division was held by this same 13th Essex, the 2nd South Stafford, and 17th Middlesex battalions of the 6th Brigade. This brigade was cut into two parts by the Canal du Nord, a huge trough of brick-work without any water, eighty feet across, with steep sloping sides. The

CHAPTER XI.

The Battle of Cambrai. Second Phase. Nov. 30.

bridges across were swept by German fire, and the only transit was by ropes to help the climber. All day the fight raged furiously here, the Germans within bombing distance of the defence, which was never penetrated for an instant. Save for one small isolated trench with about seventy men this whole line held firm against every form of attack. Snipers and bombers fired across from bank to bank, while down in the dried bed of the canal there was constant close-range fighting. All night the difficult post was held, as was the line on the extreme left where the 17th Middlesex were blowing back every attack with their well-sustained fire. There was no more wonderful individual record in the battle than that of Captain MacReady-Diarmid of the 17th Middlesex, who fought like a d'Artagnan of romance, and is said to have killed some eighty of the enemy in two days of fighting before he at last himself met that fate from which he had never shrunk. A V.C. was assigned to his family.

On the right of the 6th Brigade was the 99th Brigade, the victors of Delville Wood, who were also furiously engaged, meeting such waves of German infantry as were able to get past the zone of the British barrage. German field-guns unlimbered suddenly on the crest looking down on the British lines only a few hundred yards off. The crews were shot down so swiftly that only one gun got in three rounds. Then there came a rush of two battalions in full marching order, debouching in fours from Bourlon village, and deploying in the open. These also were shot to bits. The whole front of the brigade was dotted with broken guns and huddled grey figures, while many, despairing of getting back, threw up their

THE BATTLE OF CAMBRAI 293

hands and sought refuge in the British lines. Battalion after battalion was thrown in at this point, until the best part of a division was spread bleeding over some twenty acres of ground. The three battalions chiefly engaged, the 1st Berkshires, 17th Royal Fusiliers, and 1st Rifles from right to left, had such a day as trench warfare could never afford.

CHAPTER XI.

The Battle of Cambrai. Second Phase. Nov. 30.

At the outset the force of the attack pressed back the 1st Berkshires upon the right, together with the left wing of the Forty-seventh Division. For a few moments the situation was alarming. However, after three hours of ding-dong fighting the volume of fire was too much for the stormers and they fell back. At the same time the 17th Royal Fusiliers, who had rallied under cover of their outposts, shot down everything in front of them. The 1st K.R. Rifles had a day of wonderful fighting — snipers, rifle grenadiers, Lewis gunners, and machine-gunners were all equally glutted with slaughter. "The Germans in mass formation came on in waves offering a splendid target at a range from 1500 to point-blank. In addition they were enfiladed by the machine-gunners and subjected to very heavy fire from our guns for two and a half hours. The second attempt never looked like succeeding and was smothered in a very short time."

The 17th Royal Fusiliers have been mentioned as being in the line at this point though they really belonged to the 5th Brigade. The fact was that in a previous operation they had won a long trench advancing at right angles to the British position and leading up to the Germans. This was called the "Rat's Tail" on account of its shape, and it was still occupied by the Royals when the attack broke out, so that they were placed in a most difficult position and were pressed back down this long trench, fighting a desperate rearguard as will be told later. Their presence in the "Rat's Tail" was the more unfortunate as it helped to screen the Germans, and to contract the fire-field of the main line behind them. After clearing the "Rat's Tail" the remains of the battalion found themselves upon the right of the 1st K.R.R.

The remaining brigade of the division, the 5th, had some of its men also in the front line and as busy as its comrades. It is stated in the account already quoted that even the wounded men of the 2nd H.L.I. were propped up, so that they might continue to fire upon the Germans. It was a brigade which had suffered many an evil quarter of an hour in the past, and it is no wonder that the men took a fierce joy in such a fight when at last they could meet their hated enemy face to face. Side by side with the Highlanders were those veterans of 1914, the 2nd Oxford and Bucks, the battalion that broke the Prussian Guard. They also had many an arrear to wipe off, nor were their less experienced comrades of the Royal Fusiliers less intent upon the work in hand. It was a costly experience for the War-lord and his legions.

In the evening, save for the one loss at the Canal lock which has been already recorded, the whole 3500-yard front of the Second Division stood inviolate, and was clearly defined when the British force withdrew by the thick pile of German dead which marked it. Indeed it is claimed that at the end of the day the posts which were thrown forward by the defenders were more advanced than before the attack had broken. Those posts which had been overwhelmed in the morning were found to have perished most gloriously, for in almost every case the British dead were ringed round with the bodies of their assailants. Among the many epics of these isolated posts none is more glorious than that of a platoon of the 17th Fusiliers under the two Company Officers, Captain Stone and Lieut. Benzeery, both mentioned in despatches, who fought absolutely to the last man in order to give time for the main body behind them to get ready for the assault. The official report of the officer commanding says: "The rearguard was seen fighting with bayonet, bullet, and bomb to the last. There was no survivor." The annals of war can give few finer examples of military virtue.

Another splendid epic had been furnished by the posts of the 1st Berkshire battalion upon the right of the Second Division. They were all drawn from one Company under the command of Lieut. Valentin, also mentioned for his gallantry. The Germans surged in upon them in the afternoon, and there was a most grim and terrible fight. Three of the posts were destroyed, but when the ground was regained it was difficult to find the British bodies on account of the piles of German dead which were heaped round and over them. Six other posts remained intact after six hours of close fighting, in which they were continually attacked by superior numbers who fell in heaps before the steady fire of these experienced soldiers. Rapid fire had been brought to perfection by the training system of the Second Division, and General Pereira was justified of his wisdom. The six weary posts which remained intact after the storm had passed are said to have killed not less than five hundred of their assailants.

Gorringe's Forty-seventh London Territorial

Chapter XI.

The Battle of Cambrai. Second Phase. Nov. 30.

Division upon the right had endured a similar experience to that of their comrades of the Second Division, and Kennedy's 140th Brigade upon the left had been particularly strongly engaged. The 6th London Rifles and the 15th Civil Service Rifles held the post of honour, and the conditions were much the same as those already described, save that the field of fire was more restricted. In the afternoon attack, a gap was formed between these two battalions, but was quickly closed by one of those heterogeneous musters of signallers, orderlies, and general utility men who have so often done good and unobtrusive service—silent supers who suddenly spring into the limelight, play the part of the hero, and then fade away to the wings once more. This attack of the afternoon fell with great force upon the right unit of the division, the 141st Brigade who lay in their gas-masks half poisoned with mephitic vapours among the brushwood of Bourlon Forest. These fine troops, the London Irish, Poplar, St. Pancras, and Blackheath battalions, endured all that gun or gas could do, and held their whole line intact until the evening.

In the early morning Woolcombe's Fourth Corps, exhausted in body but triumphant in the knowledge of the terrible losses which they had inflicted upon the enemy, withdrew unmolested and in absolute order to the smaller perimeter which had been marked out for them by General Byng when he had time to realise the exact effect of the German gains upon the south end of his line. Everything portable was carried off by the retiring troops, who made it a point of honour to leave nothing at all to the enemy. Three days later, in conformity with the general plans, the lines were laid down afresh along the Flesquières

THE BATTLE OF CAMBRAI 297

Ridge, so that the whole salient was smoothed out, and yet Byng's troops held all the solid advantages gained upon November 20 in the shape of a long stretch of the Hindenburg Line. This continued to be the permanent position of the Third Army during the winter, and up to the fateful 21st of March 1918, when the great German thunderbolt was hurled. In the movements entailed by this withdrawal there was no molestation from the enemy save that the rearguards of the Forty-seventh Division were strongly engaged. Two companies of the 15th Civil Service Rifles were for a time cut off, but broke their way through all resistance and rejoined the main body.

On the north of that new portion of the line which had been established by the Guards and taken over by the Ninth Division there was a long ridge called Welsh Ridge, running up from La Vacquerie Farm. The enemy was still strong in this quarter where the British artillery was particularly weak—a defect which was partly compensated for by the loyalty of the neighbouring French Commander. The Sixty-first South Midland Territorial Division had taken over from the Twelfth in this area and found themselves involved in several days of hard fighting, in the course of which La Vacquerie Farm was lost to the Badeners, but the general line of the ridge was maintained, consolidated, and turned into the permanent front of the Army.

So ended the swaying fortunes of this hard-fought and dramatic battle, beginning with a surprise attack of the British upon the Germans, and ending by an attack of the Germans upon the British which, if not a surprise to the commanders, at least produced some surprising and untoward results. The balance of these

CHAPTER XI.

The Battle of Cambrai. Second Phase. Dec. 1.

varied actions was greatly in favour of the British, and yet it could not be denied that something of the glory and satisfaction of Byng's splendid original victory were dimmed by this unsatisfactory epilogue which was only made less disastrous to the British cause by the very heavy losses which their enemy incurred upon the northern sector. On the balance in ground gained the British had a solid grip of 11,000 yards of the famous Hindenburg Line, as against an unimportant British section between Vendhuille and Gonnelieu. In prisoners the British had 11,000 as against 6000 claimed by the Germans. In guns the British took or destroyed 145 against 100 taken or destroyed by their enemies. In the larger field of strategy the whole episode was fruitful as it stopped all reinforcement of the Germans in Italy during the critical weeks while the Italians were settling down upon the line of the Piave. One result of the action was a reorganisation of the British machine-gun system which was found to have acted in an unequal fashion during the operations, some formations giving excellent results while others were less satisfactory.

The Battle of Cambrai virtually brought the fighting of 1917 to an end, although there were several sharp local actions at different points along the line —actions which would have filled special editions in former wars, and now can hardly be afforded a paragraph if any just proportion be observed. Chief among them was a spirited German attack upon the Sixty-third Naval Division upon December 29 in the sector of the Canal du Nord, which began by the loss of some trench elements, but ended with little change. There was a sharp fight also early in December at that blood-stained country-house, Polderhoek Chateau,

THE BATTLE OF CAMBRAI 299

where the New Zealanders attacking upon a narrow front made an attempt upon one of the most difficult points in the Flanders line. The men of Otago and of Canterbury proved once more what extraordinarily good military material is bred in the great Pacific island, but after a sharp tussle in which both sides lost heavily, there was no substantial change in the position.

Chapter XI.
The Battle of Cambrai. Second Phase. Dec. 1.

Another local fight which was sufficiently serious to demand mention here was upon December 2, when the 26th Brigade of the Eighth Division with part of the Thirty-second Division stirred up the German line in the Flanders area. After two days of fighting matters remained here much as they started.

The year 1917 had been a very glorious one both to the French and to the British Armies, which, pursuing their system of the limited objective, had hardly met with a single repulse in a long campaign. The victories of Arras, Messines, Langemarck, Paschendaale, and Cambrai were added to the great record of Sir Douglas Haig and his men, while the French, save for the losses incurred in their great April attack, had an unbroken record of success. And yet in spite of these results in the West the year was a disappointing one for the Allies, since the Russian defection which involved Rumania in ruin, greatly weakened their position and clearly showed that the year 1918 would find them confronted with the whole force of Germany aided by contingents of her Allies. Storm clouds piled high in the East. Only from over the far Western rim of the Atlantic came a slowly waxing light.

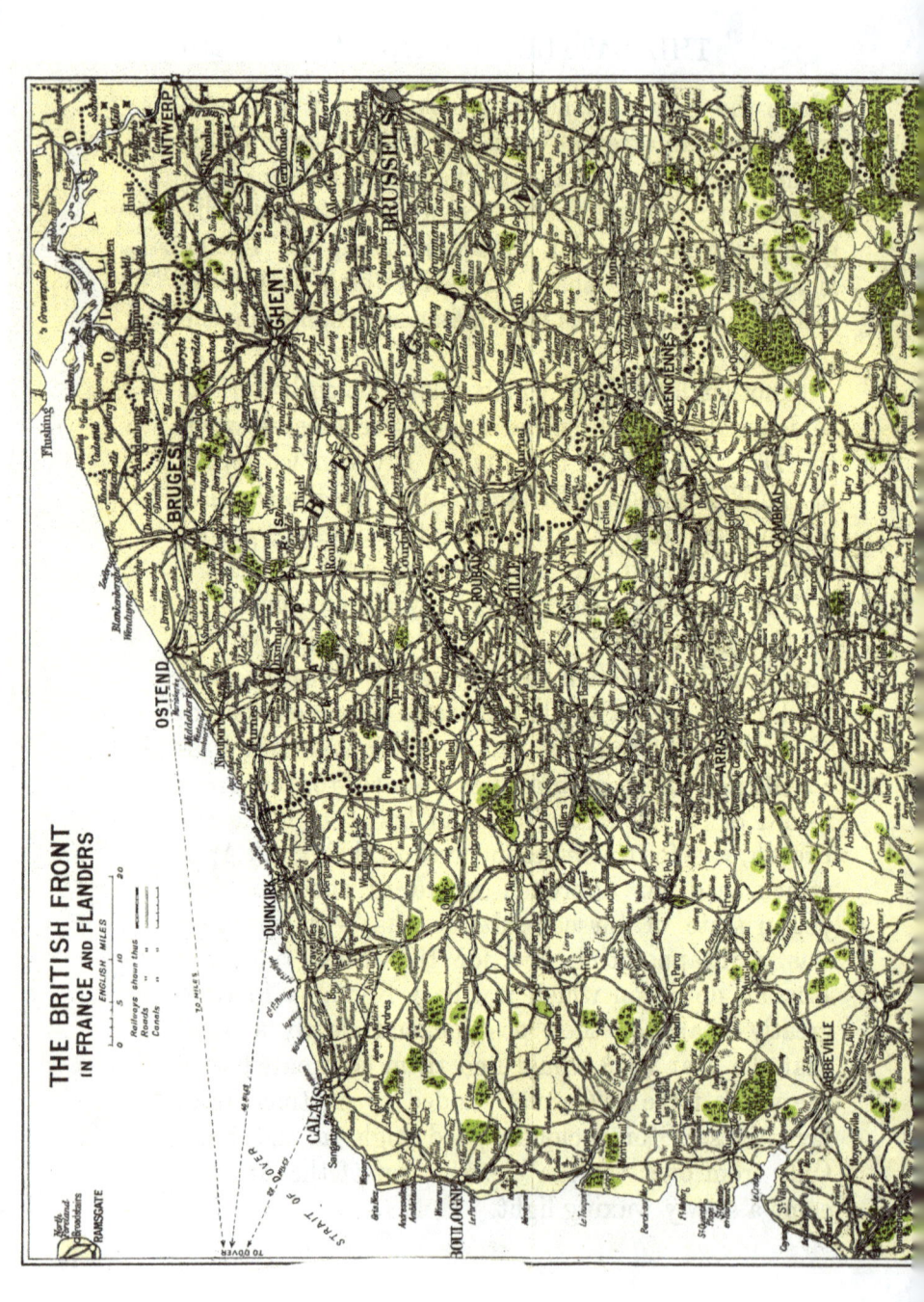

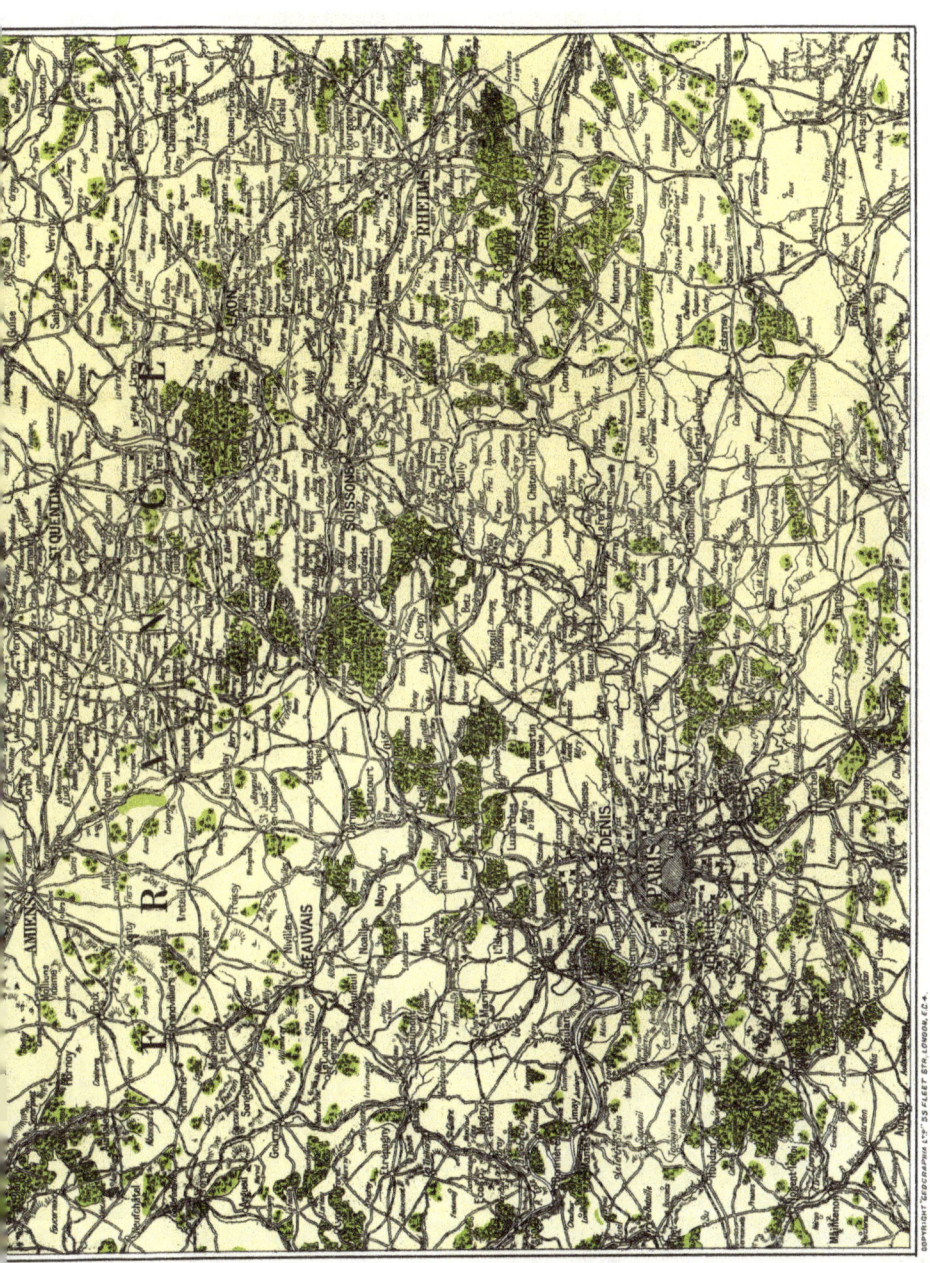

INDEX

Abadie, Colonel, 124, 126, 127
Aisne, French attack upon the, 64; victory, 234
Alderman, Major, 251
Allenby, General Sir Edmund, 2, 16, 20
America breaks off diplomatic relations with Germany, 18
Ancre, British advance on the, 5-8
Antoine, General, 134, 156, 179
Archibald, Lieutenant, 67
Arras, 9, 10, 11, 22, 30
Arras, battle of: preparations preceding the battle, 20-24; attack of the Seventh Corps, 25-30; capture of Neuville Vitasse, 27; and of the Ibex Trench, 28; general advance of the Sixth Corps, 30-36; attack of the Seventeenth Corps, 36-41; Canadian success at Vimy Ridge, 41-43; review of first day's fighting, 43-44; capture of Monchy, 46-48; practical results of battle, 56; work of the airmen, 57; fight of the Australians at Bullecourt and Lagnicourt, 58-61; object of battle attained, 62; stand by the Middlesex and Argylls, 66-67; Fifteenth Division capture Guémappe, 68-69; storming of Gavrelle, 69-70; H.A.C. at Gavrelle, 74-76; loss of Fresnoy, 83-84; capture of Rœux, 84-85; capture of Bullecourt, 90-92 .
Arras-Soissons front, German retreat on, 8-16
Avion, 117, 121

Babington, General Sir J., 108, 188
Bagdad, British enter, 17
Baillescourt Farm, action at, 6
Bainbridge, General Sir E., 99
Ball, Captain Albert, 57
Bapaume occupied, 10
Basset, M. Serge, 117
Battye, Colonel, 263
Bavaria, Prince Rupprecht of, 98
Bean, Mr., Australian chronicler, quoted, 91, 175, 220
Beaumont Hamel, 3, 5, 37
Bellewarde Ridge, 151
Belsham, Captain, 67
Benzeery, Lieutenant, 295
Berners, Brigadier-General, 85
Birdwood, General Sir William, 4
Bixschoote, 137, 156
Bols, General Sir L., 109
Bourlon, 238, 257, 258, 261, 262, 263, 264, 265, 269, 282, 283, 289, 290, 292
Bourlon Wood, 251, 254, 255, 256, 257, 258, 259, 260, 264, 267, 289, 296
Bowell, Lieutenant, D.S.O., 119
Bradford, General, 267
Braithwaite, General, 243, 245
British extend their front in France, 1
British Armies, general disposition of, in beginning of 1917, 2
Broodseinde, 195, 206, 211, 212, 222
Brown, Brigadier-General, 99 .
Brusiloff, General, 132
Bullecourt, 11, 58, 87, 90-92, 237, 239, 252
Burstall, General, 41
Byng, General Sir Julian, 21, 115, 238, 255, 285, 296, 297, 298

Cambrai, 192, 237, 238, 247, 248, 251, 253, 255
Cambrai, battle of: Tanks *en masse*, 238, 242; attack on Tunnel Trench, 239-242; great advance, 242-243; work of Sixty-second Division, 243-244; advance of Fifty-first Division, 245-246; Fort Garry Horse, 246; attack of the Twenty-ninth Division on Marcoing and Mesnières, 247-249; advance of Twentieth and Twelfth Divisions, 249-251; German rally, 253-256; attack on and capture of Bourlon Wood, 257-260; fight for Bourlon village, 261-264; attack on La Fontaine, 265-267; great German attack, 269; the Fifty-fifth, Twelfth, and Twentieth Divisions, 270-275, 276-278; great fight of the Twenty-ninth Division, 275-276, 278-282; advance of the Guards, 282-286; capture of Gouzeaucourt, 284; battle in Bourlon sector, 288-297; retraction of British line, 297; observations on Cambrai battle, 297-298
Campbell, General, 25
Campbell, Major, 101
Canal de l'Escaut, 247, 255
Canal du Nord, 243, 291, 298
Caporetto, Italian disaster at, 234, 236
Cator, General, 92
Cavan, General Lord, 137, 138, 145, 162, 163, 167, 181, 202, 214, 224, 237
Charlton, General, 103
Chemin des Dames, 64
Cherisy, 76, 77
Chidlow-Roberts, Captain, 120
Cojeul River, 25, 45, 50, 52, 66, 80, 85
Cooper, Colonel Elliott, V.C., 274
Cooper, Sergeant, V.C., 166
Corfe, Colonel, 190
Corps, Lieutenant, 291
Cousens, Captain, 28
Crevecourt, 248, 255, 279
Crow, Captain, 275
Currie, General Sir A., 41

Davies, Sergeant-Major, 261
De Crespigny, General, 283, 284
De Lisle, General, 275, 282
Deverell, General, 79
Dove, Captain, 166
Du Cane, General, 61

Edwards, Sergeant-Major, 291
Elles, General, 238, 242
Evans, Private Ellis H., 144

Fairbrass, Sergeant, 291
Fanshawe, General Sir E. A., 4, 5, 183, 196
Fayet, capture of, 15, 62
Fergusson, General Sir Charles, 21, 36, 48, 72
Fielding, General Lord, 267
Flesquières, 244, 245, 248, 254, 256, 296
Fontaine, Colonel de la, 154
Fontaine, 256, 257, 258, 265, 266, 288, 289
France: co-operation with British at third battle of Ypres, 134, 137, 156; attack and victory on the Aisne, 64, 234; victory at Verdun, 178; sends troops to help Italy, 236, 237
Freeman, Lieutenant, 190
Fresnoy, 76, 82, 83-84

Gavrelle, 54, 65, 69, 70, 73, 81, 82
Geddes, Sir Eric, 3
Geddes, Captain, 159
Gee, Captain, V.C., 279
General survey of early months of 1917, 16-19
Germany's declaration of unrestricted submarine warfare, 18
Gheluvelt, 228, 229
Glencorse Wood, 151, 153, 154, 159, 161, 173, 175, 176, 187, 198
Godley, General Sir A., 97, 205
Gonnelieu, 242, 275, 276, 285, 286, 287, 298
Gordon, General Sir Alex. Hamilton, 97
Gorringe, General, 174, 295
Gort, Colonel Lord, 140, 226
Gott, Lieutenant, 125
Gough, General Sir Hubert, 2, 4, 7, 16, 25, 58, 61, 96, 114, 133, 138, 155, 179, 181
Gouzeaucourt, 275, 283, 284

INDEX 303

Graham, Major, 119
Graincourt, 244, 252
Greer, Colonel, 140
Guémappe, 47, 49, 52, 68, 70
Gwynn, Mr. Stephen, M.P., 103

Haig, Field-Marshal Sir Douglas, 4, 16, 20, 56, 62, 64, 92, 133, 134, 135, 155, 162, 179, 194, 212, 213, 222, 225, 233, 237, 244, 255, 256, 282, 299
Haine, Lieutenant, V.C., 74, 75, 76
Haking, General Sir R., 237
Haldane, General Sir J., 21, 30, 36, 40, 238, 239, 241
Hall, Sergeant-Major, 262
Harper, General, 145
Harrison, Lieutenant, V.C., 82
Harston, Captain, 204
Havrincourt, 244, 252
Henderson, Lieutenant, V.C., 67
Henty, Major, 273
Hermies, 242
Hermon, Colonel, 39
Hickie, General Sir W., 102
Higgins, Brigadier-General, 183
Hindenburg, Marshal von, 15
Hindenburg Line, the, 45, 56, 59, 66, 87, 90, 91, 92, 237, 239, 242, 243, 245, 246, 247, 250, 253, 257, 265, 267, 277, 288, 290, 297, 298
Hindenburg Line, the, defined, 11
Hitchings, Lieutenant, 82
Hoare, Captain, 250
Holland, General, 41, 55, 115
Holmes, General, 101
Horne, General Sir H., 2, 20, 115
Houthulst Forest, 134, 137, 202, 214, 226
Hull, General, 27

Inverness Wood, 154, 159, 160, 162, 173, 175, 176, 189
Isonzo front, successful attack on, by the Italians, 178
Italy: successful attack on the Isonzo front, 178; disaster at Caporetto, 234, 236; effect of collapse on Western offensive, 236; French and British send help, 236, 237

Jacob, General Sir C., 4, 8, 137, 150, 151, 162, 172, 231

James, Colonel, 272
Jarvis, Colonel, 190
Jenkinson, Sergeant, 221
Jeudwine, General Sir Hugh, 269
Johnson, General Bulkeley, 48

Kennedy, Brigadier-General, 296
Kennedy, Colonel, 260
Kettle, Professor, 103
Kincaid-Smith, General, 99
Knapp, Father, 140
Korniloff, General, 132
Kut, recapture of, 17

La Basseville, 131, 132, 155
Laffert, General von, 98
Lagnicourt, 58, 60, 90
Lambton, General, 37
Langemarck, 164, 166, 167, 181, 203
La Vacquerie, 249, 250, 274, 285, 286, 287, 288
Leadbeater, Sergeant, 118
Lees, Captain David, 140
Legg, Sergeant, 291
Lens, 20, 54, 56, 89, 226, 232
Lens, operations round, 115-123
Les Rues Vertes, 247, 277, 279, 280
Leveson-Gower, Brigadier-General, 168
Lipsett, General, 41
Lloyd, Captain, 287
Lodge, Sergeant, 291
Lomax, Lieutenant, 13, 14
Lukin, General, 36
Lumsden, Major, V.C., 13, 14

McCracken, General Sir F., 21, 54
Macdowell, Major, V.C., 42
McGowan, Captain, 90
McGrady, Private, 128
MacNamara, Major, 90
MacReady-Diarmid, Captain, V.C., 292
Marcoing, 247, 248, 253, 273, 276, 278, 288
Martin, Captain, 129
Marwitz, General von, 270
Matheson, General, 203
Maude, General Sir F. S., 17
Maxse, General Sir Ivor, 21, 137, 145, 162, 167, 183, 195, 216, 217, 223, 226, 227
Menin Road, 153, 179, 190, 193, 194, 195, 198, 199, 202, 209, 210, 211, 222, 228

Mesnières, 247, 248, 249, 253, 254, 270, 273, 277, 278, 282, 288
Mesopotamia, operations in: recapture of Kut, 17; capture of Bagdad, 17
Messines, 44, 57, 95, 97, 98, 115, 134, 135, 179
Messines, battle of: preparations for the battle, 96; composition of British line, 96-97; advance of Australians and New Zealanders, 97-99; capture of Messines village, 98; Wytschaete captured by the Irish Divisions, 102-104; general advance and capture of Messines Ridge, 106-110; results of battle, 110-112
Monash, General Sir John, 97
Monchy, 35, 44, 46-48, 49, 50, 51, 52
Morland, General Sir T., 96, 107, 138, 155, 190, 208, 210
Mœuvres, 257, 258, 289, 290

Nicholson, General, 37
Nieuport, 123, 130
Norman, Colonel, 144
Nugent, General, 102

O'Brien, Lieutenant, 74
Oppy, 54, 65, 73, 76, 81, 117
Osmond, Major, 74, 76

Page, Colonel, 146
Parsons, Sergeant, 291
Paschendaale, 200, 211, 213, 217, 220, 222, 225, 230, 231, 238
Pears, Colonel, 280
Peddie, Major, 223
Pereira, General, 53, 289, 295
Peronne, capture of, 10
Phillips, Mr. Percival, quoted, 279
Phillips, Sergeant, 291
Pilkem, 142, 143, 144, 156
Pinney, General, 46, 66, 193
Ploegstrate, 94
Plumer, General Sir Herbert, 2, 95, 96, 110, 115, 134, 138, 154, 155, 162, 179, 181, 187, 212, 237
Poelcapelle, 203, 204, 213, 216, 224
Polderhoek, 209, 210, 222, 228, 232, 298
Pollard, Lieutenant, V.C., 74, 75, 76

Polygon Wood, 188, 193, 196, 200, 208, 209
Pope, Lieutenant, 60
Prioleau, Colonel, 166
Pulteney, General Sir W., 238, 252

Radice, Colonel, 144
Rawlinson, General Sir Henry, 1, 2, 4, 8, 61, 114
Redmond, Major W., M.P., 103
Reed, General, 149
Regiments:
  Artillery—
  R.F.A., 13, 104, 274
  Honourable Artillery Company, 74, 221
  Cavalry—
  Royal Horse Guards, 47
  2nd Dragoon Guards, 252
  4th Dragoon Guards, 252
  2nd Dragoons, 263
  5th Dragoons, 263
  5th Lancers, 251
  10th Hussars, 47
  11th Hussars, 244, 263
  15th Hussars, 261
  19th Hussars, 262
  20th Hussars, 285
  Bedford Yeomanry, 263
  Essex Yeomanry, 47
  Fort Garry Horse, 246
  King Edward's Horse, 244
  Lucknow Cavalry Brigade, 10
  Northumberland Hussars, 276
  Umballa Brigade, 254
  Guards—
  Coldstream, 138, 139, 140, 215, 266, 284, 285
  Grenadier, 139, 140, 141, 264, 266, 284, 285, 286
  Irish, 138, 139, 140, 141, 215, 266, 267, 284
  Scots, 139, 140, 264, 266
  Welsh, 139, 285, 286
  Infantry—
  Argyll and Sutherland Highlanders, 31, 66, 67, 193, 198, 261
  Bedford, 26, 74, 75, 160, 161
  Berkshire, 12, 146, 147, 174, 250, 273, 293, 295
  Black Watch, 31, 92, 146, 147, 199
  Border, 15, 92, 100, 104, 113, 131, 208, 228, 279

INDEX

Regiments:
  Infantry—
  Buffs (East Kent), 79, 251, 275
  Cambridge, 146, 147, 199
  Cameron Highlanders, 159, 185
  Cameronians (Scottish Rifles), 35
  Cheshire, 14, 100, 106, 146, 147, 160, 161, 191, 225
  Connaught Rangers, 103, 170, 240
  Devon, 84, 92, 208, 209
  Dublin Fusiliers, 85, 168, 169, 240
  Duke of Cornwall's, 70, 83, 175, 209
  Durham Light Infantry, 82, 164, 175, 189, 247
  East Lancashire, 40, 85, 88, 203, 219
  East Surrey, 31, 83, 154, 251, 263, 264, 275
  East Yorkshire, 82, 209
  Essex, 34, 40, 50, 51, 77, 216, 224, 250, 273, 287, 291
  Gloucester, 12, 83, 174, 191, 204, 225
  Gordon Highlanders, 31, 32, 33, 88, 159, 208, 228
  Hampshire, 40, 50, 51, 85, 104, 189, 199, 203, 216, 241
  Highland Light Infantry, 12, 13, 15, 35, 131, 186, 194, 198, 263, 294
  Inniskilling Fusiliers, 102, 103, 168, 169, 170, 279
  King's Liverpool, 148, 164, 166, 185
  King's Own Royal Lancaster, 33, 40, 47, 148, 149, 184, 263, 264, 272
  King's Own Scottish Borderers, 35, 209
  King's Royal Rifles, 14, 29, 48, 77, 124, 125, 126, 127, 128, 129, 166, 181, 189, 190, 194, 210, 249, 250, 277, 285, 287, 293, 294
  Lancashire Fusiliers, 40, 81, 100, 131, 148, 160, 161, 177, 184, 219, 225, 249, 279
  Leicester, 116, 118, 154, 246
  Leinster, 55, 102, 103, 170
  Lincoln, 104, 105, 116, 118, 210, 223
  Liverpool, 26, 27, 32, 152, 183, 194, 198, 272

Regiments:
  Infantry—
  Liverpool Scottish, 272
  London Rifle Brigade, 80
  London Scottish, 28, 291
  London Irish, 296
  1st London, 27, 28, 78
  2nd London, 80, 183, 184, 291
  3rd London, 27
  4th London, 184
  6th London, 183, 296
  8th London, 183
  9th London (Queen Victoria Rifles), 27, 28, 80
  15th London (Civil Service), 296, 297
  — London (Queen's Westminsters), 80, 257, 291
  — London (Blackheath), 296
  — London (Poplar), 296
  — London (Post Office Rifles), 291
  — London (St. Pancras), 296
  Manchester, 12, 13, 27, 152, 153, 219, 228
  Middlesex, 27, 28, 31, 55, 66, 67, 78, 86, 88, 169, 193, 194, 204, 210, 249, 250, 261, 262, 276, 278, 279, 280, 291, 292
  Munster Fusiliers, 103, 104, 231, 240
  Norfolk, 77, 224, 246, 250, 274
  Northampton, 55, 124, 127, 129, 152, 154, 159, 273
  North Lancashire, 100, 125, 148, 160, 184
  North Staffordshire, 8, 118, 119, 154, 191
  Northumberland Fusiliers, 39, 49, 53, 89, 131, 189, 209, 224
  Oxford and Bucks, 29, 77, 166, 174, 250, 294
  Queen's (West Surrey), 31, 154, 161, 194, 198, 208, 228, 251, 276
  Rifle Brigade, 40, 48, 55, 77, 85, 109, 154, 166, 181, 189, 210, 216, 255, 277
  Royal Fusiliers, 29, 32, 46, 66, 74, 75, 109, 176, 189, 210, 249, 250, 274, 279, 293, 294, 295
  Royal Irish, 102, 241
  Royal Irish Fusiliers, 102, 103, 168, 169, 170, 171, 172, 241
  Royal Irish Rifles, 99, 100, 102, 104, 160, 161, 168, 169, 172

Regiments:
Infantry—
Royal Scots, 33, 78, 186
Royal Scots Fusiliers, 31, 152, 186
Royal West Kent, 190, 209, 228, 251
Seaforth Highlanders, 38, 39, 80, 81, 186, 203
Sherwood Foresters, 14, 70, 104, 105, 118, 119, 152, 159, 190, 225, 246
Shropshire, 33, 166, 175, 176
Somerset Light Infantry, 40, 80, 175, 203, 210
South Lancashire, 100, 113, 184, 185, 272, 273
South Staffordshire, 8, 104, 117, 208, 228, 291
South Wales Borderers, 106, 113, 143, 161, 231, 260, 279, 282
Suffolk, 32, 88, 198, 224, 250, 262, 263, 273
Sussex, 31, 55, 79, 125, 164, 193, 199, 250
Tyneside Scottish, 53
Warwick, 204, 221, 228
Welsh, 106, 142, 143, 191, 260, 261
Welsh Fusiliers, 31, 32, 66, 106, 141, 142, 143, 144, 197, 260
West Riding, 40, 81, 189, 244, 253, 254, 265
West Yorkshire, 32, 49, 82, 172, 189, 217, 256
Wiltshire, 100, 191
Worcester, 50, 51, 100, 161, 191, 194, 204, 214, 216
York and Lancaster, 82, 217, 244, 256
Yorkshire, 189, 261, 262
Yorkshire Light Infantry, 15, 166, 209, 217, 244

Royal Engineers, 47, 101, 104, 105, 141, 161, 216, 241, 284
Tunnelling Companies, 22, 241
Royal Naval Division, 53, 54, 70, 74, 226, 227, 298
1st Marines, 55, 74, 75
Overseas Forces—
Australians, 5, 10, 11, 14, 58, 59, 60, 61, 76, 90, 91, 92, 97, 98, 101, 127, 128, 156, 187, 188, 193, 194, 196, 197, 198, 205, 206, 220, 223, 227, 229

Regiments:
Overseas Forces—
New Zealanders, 97, 98, 99, 101, 114, 131, 132, 155, 156, 205, 211, 223, 224, 299
Canadians, 21, 38, 41, 42, 43, 54, 55, 73, 82, 83, 84, 116, 117, 121, 122, 123, 226, 227, 228, 229, 230, 231, 232
Newfoundland Regiment, 50, 215, 216, 248, 278, 282
South Africans, 37, 52, 53, 185, 186, 187
Reutel, 208, 209, 210, 221
Ritchie, General, 195
Ritchie, Captain, 141
Robertson, Colonel Forbes, V.C., 51, 280
Robinson, Captain, 291
Rœux, 48, 52, 65, 68, 72, 73, 80, 84, 85
Romilly, Colonel, 140
Russell, General Sir A., 98
Russia: revolution in, 17, 65; collapse of, before Central Powers, 132; effect of revolution in, on Allied offensive in the West, 235
Rutter, Lieutenant, 67

St. Eloi, 97
St. Julien, 145, 146, 147, 156, 158, 174, 182, 192, 195
St. Rohart, 76, 78, 79
Sanctuary Wood, 150, 152
Scarpe River, 31, 36, 37, 40, 50, 52, 68, 69, 72, 76, 78, 79, 84, 86
Selency, capture of guns at, 12-14
Sensée River, 66, 87
Serre, 6, 7
Sheepshanks, Colonel, 277
Shepherd, Private, V.C., 250
Shute, General, 106, 124, 131
Sinai Peninsula, progress in, 17
Slade, Captain, 164
Smith, Colonel, 27
Snow, General Sir T., 21, 25, 45, 65, 76, 238, 252, 269, 270
Soissons, 9, 10
Souchez River, 115, 121
Steenbeek, the, 143, 146, 147, 163, 166, 184, 189
Stone, Captain, 295
Stonebanks, Lieutenant, 176

INDEX

307

Strachan, Lieutenant Henry, V.C., 246
Strickland, General, 123, 124
Symon, Captain, 159

Taylor, Colonel, 144
Tollemache, Colonel, 129

Valentin, Lieutenant, 295
Vendhuille, 270, 298
Verdun, French victory at, 178
Villers-Guislain, 237, 272, 273, 275
Vimy Ridge, 21, 41-43, 54, 94, 134

Wallace, Lieutenant, V.C., 274
Wambach, Private, 129
Ward, Captain, 129
Ward, Lieutenant, 13, 14
Warden, Colonel, D.S.O., 263, 264
Watson, General, 41
Watts, General Sir H., 137, 145, 147, 149, 162, 167
Westhoek, 151, 159, 160, 161, 162
Wiart, Colonel Carton de, 85
Williams, General, 109
Wilson, President, 18
Woolcombe, General, 238, 288, 296
Woolley, Lieutenant, 190
Wytschaete, 94, 97, 103

Ypres, 57, 94, 95, 133, 134, 154, 162
Ypres, third battle of: British and German preparation before the battle detailed, 133 - 136; French co-operation, 134, 137, 156; advance of the Guards, 138-141; advance of the Welsh Division and capture of Pilkem village, 141-145; capture of St. Julien, 146, 147; advance of Fifty-fifth and Fifteenth Divisions, 147-150; of Second Army Corps, 150-155; first day's operations reviewed, 156-157; German counter-attacks, 158-159, 160-161; attack of Fourteenth Corps, 163-167; capture of Langemarck, 164; losses of the Irish Divisions, 168-172; work of the Field Artillery, 175; engagement of the Second Army, 179; September 20, 180-192; advance of the Fifty-fifth Division, 183-185; advance of the Ninth Division, 185-187; of the Australians, 187-188; German counter-attack, 192-195; advance renewed on September 26, 195-200; attack of October 4, 202-212; further British advance, 213-222; advance of Territorials, 218-220; H.A.C. at Reutel, 221; action of October 12, 222-224; action of October 26, 225; fine fighting by the Canadians, 226-231; capture of Paschendaale, 230; general results of the third battle of Ypres, 232-233
Yser River, fight of the King's Royal Rifles and the Northamptons at, 123-130

Zonnebeke, 169, 170, 172, 181, 202, 214

THE END

Printed in Great Britain by R. & R. CLARK, LIMITED, *Edinburgh.*